Who's got the power?
Transforming health systems
for women and children

Lead authors
Lynn P. Freedman
Ronald J. Waldman
Helen de Pinho
Meg E. Wirth
A. Mushtaque R. Chowdhury, Coordinator
Allan Rosenfield, Coordinator

UN Millennium Project
Task Force on Child Health and Maternal Health
2005

EARTHSCAN
London • Sterling, Va.

MillenniumProject

First published by Earthscan in the UK and USA in 2005

ISBN: 1-84407-224-X paperback

For a full list of publications please contact:

Earthscan
8–12 Camden High Street
London, NW1 0JH, UK
Tel: +44 (0)20 7387 8558
Fax: +44 (0)20 7387 8998
Email: earthinfo@earthscan.co.uk
Web: www.earthscan.co.uk
22883 Quicksilver Drive, Sterling, VA 20166-2012, USA

Earthscan is an imprint of James and James (Science Publishers) Ltd and publishes in association with the International Institute for Environment and Development

A catalogue record for this book is available from the British Library

Library of Congress Cataloging-in-Publication Data

A catalog record has been requested

This publication should be cited as: UN Millennium Project 2005. *Who's Got the Power? Transforming Health Systems for Women and Children.* Task Force on Child Health and Maternal Health.

Photos: Front cover Liba Taylor/Panos Pictures; back cover, top to bottom, Christopher Dowswell/UNDP, Pedro Cote/UNDP, Giacomo Pirozzi/Panos Pictures, Liba Taylor/Panos Pictures, Jørgen Schytte/UNDP, UN Photo Library, Giacomo Pirozzi/UNICEF, Curt Carnemark/World Bank, Pedro Cote/UNDP, Franck Charton/UNICEF, Paul Chesley/Getty Images, Ray Witlin/World Bank, Pete Turner/Getty Images.

This book was edited, designed, and produced by Communications Development Inc., Washington, D.C., and its UK design partner, Grundy & Northedge.

Printed on elemental chlorine-free paper

Foreword

The world has an unprecedented opportunity to improve the lives of billions of people by adopting practical approaches to meeting the Millennium Development Goals. At the request of the UN Secretary-General Kofi Annan, the UN Millennium Project has identified practical strategies to eradicate poverty by scaling up investments in infrastructure and human capital while promoting gender equality and environmental sustainability. These strategies are described in the UN Millennium Project's report *Investing in Development: A Practical Plan to Achieve the Millennium Development Goals,* which was coauthored by the coordinators of the UN Millennium Project task forces.

The task forces have identified the interventions and policy measures needed to achieve each of the Goals. In *Who's Got the Power: Transforming Health Systems for Women and Children*, the Task Force on Child Health and Maternal Health responds to the challenges posed by high rates of maternal mortality, continued child deaths due to preventable illnesses, enormous unmet need for sexual and reproductive health services, and weak and fragile health systems. In addition to identifying the technical interventions to address these problems, the report asserts that policymakers must act now to change the fundamental societal dynamics that currently prevent those most in need from accessing quality health care.

Who's Got the Power proposes bold and concrete steps that governments and international agencies can take to ensure that health sector interventions have significant effects on all aspects of development and poverty reduction.

This report has been prepared by a group of leading experts who contributed in their personal capacity and volunteered their time to this important task. I am very grateful for their thorough and skilled efforts and I am sure that the practical options for action in this report will make an important contribution to achieving the Millennium Development Goals. I strongly recommend this report to all who are interested in transforming health systems to save lives and promote development.

Jeffrey D. Sachs
New York
January 17, 2005

Contents

Boxes

Figures

Tables

Task force members

Task force coordinators
A. Mushtaque R. Chowdhury, Bangladesh Rural Advancement Committee (BRAC), Bangladesh

Allan Rosenfield, Mailman School of Public Health, Columbia University, United States

Senior task force advisors
Lynn P. Freedman, Mailman School of Public Health, Columbia University, United States

Ronald J. Waldman, Mailman School of Public Health, Columbia University, United States

Task force members
Carla AbouZahr, World Health Organization, Geneva

Robert Black, Johns Hopkins Bloomberg School of Public Health, United States

Flavia Bustreo, World Bank, United States

France Donnay, United Nations Population Fund, United States

Adrienne Germain, International Women's Health Coalition, United States

Lucy Gilson, University of Witwatersrand, South Africa

Angela Kamara, Regional Prevention of Maternal Mortality Network, Ghana

Betty Kirkwood, London School of Hygiene & Tropical Medicine, United Kingdom

Elizabeth Laura Lule, World Bank, United States

Vinod Paul, World Health Organization Collaborating Centre for Training and Research in Newborn Care, All India Institute of Medical Sciences, India

Robert Scherpbier, World Health Organization, Geneva

Steven Sinding, International Planned Parenthood Federation, United Kingdom

Francisco Songane, Ministry of Health, Mozambique

TK Sundari Ravindran, Sree Chitra Tirunal Institute for Medical Sciences and Technology, India

Cesar Victora, Universidade Federal de Pelotas, Brazil

Pascal Villeneuve, United Nations Children's Fund, United States

Task force associates

Rana E. Barar, Administrative Coordinator, Mailman School of Public Health, Columbia University, United States

Helen de Pinho, Policy Adviser, South Africa

Meg E. Wirth, Consultant, United States

Preface

What will it take to meet the Millennium Development Goals on child health and maternal health by 2015, including the targets of two-thirds reduction in under-five mortality, three-quarters reduction in maternal mortality ratios, and the proposed additional target of universal access to reproductive health services? This report reflects more than two years of discussions and meetings of an extraordinary group of experts in child health, maternal health, and health policy charged with responding to this question.

The task force agreed on several principles from the very start. First, although achieving the Goals depends on increasing access to a range of key technical interventions, simply identifying those interventions and calling for their broad deployment is not enough. Answering "what will it take?" requires wrestling with the dynamics of power that underlie the patterns of population health in the world today.

Second, those patterns reveal deep inequities in health status and access to health care both between and, equally important, within countries. Any strategy for meeting the quantitative targets must address inequity head-on.

Third, although child health and maternal health present very different challenges—indeed, often pull in different directions—they are also inextricably linked. The task force made a clear decision from the start that it would stay together as one task force and build linkages between the two fields. All task force members were convinced that the fundamental recommendation of the joint task force must be that widespread, equitable access to any of these interventions—whether primarily for children or for adults—requires a far stronger health system than currently exists in most poor countries. Moreover, only a profound shift in how the global health and development community thinks about and addresses health systems can have the impact necessary to meet the Goals.

This report seeks to capture the texture of the task force's discussions and major conclusions. It does not review the entire field of child or maternal health; it does not cover every important area of work or express every legitimate viewpoint on every issue. It most certainly does not offer a blueprint for all countries. Instead, it tries to offer a way forward, by posing the question that must be asked, answered, and confronted at every level in any serious strategy to change the state of child health, maternal health, and reproductive health in the world today, namely, "who's got the power?" How can the power to create change be marshaled to transform the structures, including the health systems, that shape the lives of women and children in the world today?

Acknowledgments

The coordination team of the task force extends its deepest thanks to the task force members, who contributed their insight, experience, and wisdom every step of the way. The members served on the task force in their personal capacities.

We are grateful to several colleagues for significant contributions to the report. Eugenia McGill, a task force consultant, wrote the first draft of chapter 6 and provided more detailed analysis in a commissioned paper. Task force member Vinod Paul gave several outstanding presentations on newborn health during task force meetings and wrote parts of the report on neonatal mortality. Giulia Baldi, of Columbia University's Center on Global Health and Economic Development, assisted with sections of the report on nutrition. We also benefited from a series of papers commissioned by the task force. The authors of all of these papers did outstanding work. The authors are Hannah Ashwood-Smith, Patsy Bailey, Deborah Balk, Gregory Booma, John Clements, Mick Creati, Candy Day, Enrique Delamonica, Ermin Erasmus, Walter Flores, Deborah Fry, Lucy Gilson, Wendy Holmes, Julia Kemp, Mandi Larsen, Samantha Lobis, Sunil Maheshwari, Clement Malau, Deborah Maine, Dileep Mavalankar, David McCoy, Eugenia McGill, Alberto Minujin, Chris Morgan, Susan Murray, Antoinette Ntuli, Valeria Oliveira-Cruz, Ashnie Padarath, George Pariyo, Bruce Parnell, Anne Paxton, Steve Pearson, Rajitha Perera, Ester Ratsma, Mike Rowson, Emma Sacks, Bev Snell, Freddie Ssengooba, Adam Storeygard, Mike Toole, Cathy Vaughan, and Meg Wirth.

We are also grateful to the many colleagues from around the world who provided comments and suggestions on the task force's background paper and interim report, on which this report builds. We received useful comments on drafts of this report from many quarters, including Zulficar Bhutta, Jack Bryant, Gary Darmstadt, Petra ten Hoope-Bender, and Joy Lawn, as well as collective comments from USAID and the World Bank. Three outside reviewers—Marge Berer, Di McIntyre, and Peter Uvin—carefully read and commented extensively on the draft. We are extremely grateful to all of them.

Our task force meetings in Bangladesh and South Africa were enlivened by the presentations and participation of colleagues from NGOs and various multilateral agencies, including Koasar Afsana, Yasmin Ali Haque, Ana-Pilar Betran, Genevieve Begkoyian, Jude Bueno de Mesquita, Marinus Hendrik Gotink, Marian Jacobs, Sunil Maheshwari, Elizabeth Mason, Zoe Matthews, Dileep Mavalankar, Antoinette Ntuli, Yogan Pillay, Ester Ratsma, Meera Shekar, and Wim van Lerberghe. We thank BRAC for hosting our meeting in Bangladesh and the Centre for Health Policy at the University of the Witwatersrand for hosting our meeting in Johannesburg.

The task force had the incredible good fortune to connect its work with several major global health research projects. The child health work drew on the findings of the Bellagio Study Group on Child Survival, the Child Health Epidemiology Research Group, and the Multi-Country Evaluation of Integrated Management of Childhood Illnesses (IMCI). Recent publications by these groups have been highly influential and made the job of summarizing the field infinitely easier. Members of the Global Equity Gauge Alliance (GEGA) prepared a series of commissioned papers and presented at the task force meeting in South Africa. The work of the Rights and Reforms Project, based at the Women's Health Project in South Africa, informed our deliberations on health systems and health financing. Close communication with the Joint Learning Initiative on Human Resources for Health provided important background for our thinking on the health workforce. The Maternal and Neonatal Health and Poverty project of the World Health Organization collaborated with us in jointly commissioning an important review of the literature on obstetric referral and participated in our South Africa meeting. The Special Rapporteur on the Right to Health, Paul Hunt, and his staff consulted on human rights issues and participated in our South Africa meeting as well.

We would also like to acknowledge the following colleagues for providing invaluable input to the report and assistance with tracking down data: Hilary Brown, Mariam Claeson, Mick Creati, Becky Dodd, Caren Grown, Davidson Gwatkin, Piya Hanvoravongchai, Kathy Herschderfer, Pamela Putney, G. N. V. Ramana, Della Sherratt, Joyce Thompson, and Jeanette Vega.

Our colleagues in the UN Millennium Project Secretariat, especially John McArthur, Margaret Kruk, and Stan Bernstein, provided input, support, and guidance throughout. The members of other task forces who joined with us in the cross–task force working groups on health systems and on sexual and reproductive health and rights have helped ensure that the issues that matter for maternal and child health ultimately matter for the entire UN Millennium Project as well.

At Columbia University, we thank our colleagues in the Averting Maternal Death and Disability project for commenting on drafts and providing background data. We also thank graduate research assistants Perry Brothers, Ann Drobnik, and Christal Stone for their administrative and research assistance over the three years of the project.

Finally, here's to our administrative coordinator, Rana Barar. We thank her for her unbelievable efficiency, unfailing good humor, and consistent dedication and support throughout this entire project.

Millennium Development Goals

Goal 1
Eradicate extreme poverty and hunger

Target 1.
Halve, between 1990 and 2015, the proportion of people whose income is less than $1 a day

Target 2.
Halve, between 1990 and 2015, the proportion of people who suffer from hunger

Goal 2
Achieve universal primary education

Target 3.
Ensure that, by 2015, children everywhere, boys and girls alike, will be able to complete a full course of primary schooling

Goal 3
Promote gender equality and empower women

Target 4.
Eliminate gender disparity in primary and secondary education, preferably by 2005, and in all levels of education no later than 2015

Goal 4
Reduce child mortality

Target 5.
Reduce by two-thirds, between 1990 and 2015, the under-five mortality rate

Goal 5
Improve maternal health

Target 6.
Reduce by three-quarters, between 1990 and 2015, the maternal mortality ratio

Goal 6
Combat HIV/AIDS, malaria, and other diseases

Target 7.
Have halted by 2015 and begun to reverse the spread of HIV/AIDS

Target 8.
Have halted by 2015 and begun to reverse the incidence of malaria and other major diseases

Goal 7

Ensure environmental sustainability

Target 9.
Integrate the principles of sustainable development into country policies and programs and reverse the loss of environmental resources

Target 10.
Halve, by 2015, the proportion of people without sustainable access to safe drinking water and basic sanitation

Target 11.
Have achieved by 2020 a significant improvement in the lives of at least 100 million slum dwellers

Goal 8

Develop a global partnership for development

Target 12.
Develop further an open, rule-based, predictable, nondiscriminatory trading and financial system (includes a commitment to good governance, development, and poverty reduction—both nationally and internationally)

Target 13.
Address the special needs of the Least Developed Countries (includes tariff- and quota-free access for Least Developed Countries' exports, enhanced program of debt relief for heavily indebted poor countries [HIPCs] and cancellation of official bilateral debt, and more generous official development assistance for countries committed to poverty reduction)

Target 14.
Address the special needs of landlocked developing countries and small island developing states (through the Program of Action for the Sustainable Development of Small Island Developing States and 22nd General Assembly provisions)

Target 15.
Deal comprehensively with the debt problems of developing countries through national and international measures in order to make debt sustainable in the long term

Target 16.
In cooperation with developing countries, develop and implement strategies for decent and productive work for youth

Target 17.
In cooperation with pharmaceutical companies, provide access to affordable essential drugs in developing countries

Target 18.
In cooperation with the private sector, make available the benefits of new technologies, especially information and communications technologies

Executive summary

What kind of world do we want to live in? The Millennium Declaration lays out a vision that links poverty reduction and development, human rights and democracy, protection of the environment, and peace and security. Like many proclamations before it, the Millennium Declaration is cast in soaring, inspirational language. Its goals are lofty. Its hopes are high. But are we serious? Does the global community, particularly those who hold power in countries both rich and poor, have the courage to make the decisions, to challenge the status quo, to guide the transformative change necessary to advance this vision? Will those whose lives and health depend on these actions have the space, the leverage, and the will to demand and ensure that they do?

The state of children's health and women's health in the world today can be described through data and statistics that catalogue death, disability, and suffering. On this score alone the picture is "staggering," to quote the World Bank, "dire," to quote USAID, "a human disaster," to quote the World Health Organization, a "health emergency," to quote the African Union (Konare 2004; USAID 2004; Wagstaff and Claeson 2004; WHO 2003g).

The technical interventions that could prevent or treat the vast majority of conditions that kill children and women of reproductive age and enable all people to protect and promote their health—and so, theoretically, enable all countries to meet the Millennium Development Goals—can be identified. On these points there is strong consensus among health experts: Effective health interventions exist. They are well known and well accepted. They are generally simple and low-tech. They are even cost-effective.

Yet vast swathes of the world's population do not benefit from them. For hundreds of millions of people, a huge proportion of whom live in Sub-Saharan Africa and South Asia, the health system that could and should make effective interventions available, accessible, and utilized is in crisis—a crisis ranging

The challenge posed by the Goals is deeply and fundamentally political

from serious dysfunction to total collapse. And behind the failure of health systems lies a deeper, structural crisis, symbolized by a development system that permits its own glowing rhetoric to convert the pressure for real change into a managerial program of technical adjustments.

The result is a terrible disconnect between the dominant development models and prescriptions and the brutal realities that people face in their daily lives. Mainstream development practice is effectively delinked from the broader economic and political forces that have generated a level of inequity, exclusion, divisiveness, and insecurity that will not be bottled up and stashed away. Too many bold attempts have been neutralized: the damage now lies exposed.

The chasm between what we know and what we do, between our ability to end poverty, despair, and destruction and our timid, often contradictory efforts to do so lies at the heart of the problem. The targets and indicators set by the Goals are framed in technical, results-oriented terms. But the response cannot be simply a technical one, for the challenge posed by the Goals is deeply and fundamentally political. It is about access to and the distribution of power and resources within and between countries; in the structures of global governance; and in the intimate spaces of families, households, and communities. Until we face up to the fundamental anchoring of health status, health systems, and health policy in these dynamics, our seriousness about achieving the Goals can be legitimately questioned.

Indeed, some have scoffed at the ambitious targets for child mortality and maternal health set by the Millennium Development Goals. But the Goals are attainable. There are inspiring examples of success. Huge reservoirs of skill and determination exist in every part of the world. The financial costs of meeting the maternal and child health Goals are dwarfed by what the world spends on preparing for and waging war. Indeed, they are dwarfed by the enormous sums already spent on interventions that do not reach those who need them—and by the terrible price being paid in human lives as a result.

The obstacles loom large as well. The impulse to continue business as usual gives way to talk about transcending business as usual. But talk is not action. Sometimes talk delays or deflates action, erects a wall of words that effectively blocks action. The Goals crack open a space in the wall. The task force hopes to help forge a pathway through that wall. But in the end, it is those who hold power and the people who demand their accountability who must take the first steps.

This report assesses progress on Goal 4 (on child mortality) and Goal 5 (on maternal health) and proposes best strategies for reaching them (table 1).

The report builds on a strong foundation of epidemiological data and analysis generated over the past several decades. This evidence base provides an increasingly refined picture of who dies or suffers poor health and why. It provides crucial information about the efficacy and safety of interventions to address those causes. It also generates insights about the effectiveness of different delivery systems for making interventions available, accessible, appropriate, and affordable.

Table 1	Goal	Targets	Indicators
Goals, targets, and indicators for child health and maternal health	Goal 4: Reduce child mortality	Reduce by two-thirds, between 1990 and 2015, the under-five mortality rate	Under-five mortality rate
			Infant mortality rate
			Proportion of 1-year-old children immunized against measles
	Goal 5: Improve maternal health	Reduce by three-quarters, between 1990 and 2015, the maternal mortality ratio	Maternal mortality ratio
			Proportion of births attended by skilled health personnel

This evidence base must be increased and strengthened. But epidemiological data and intervention-specific cost-effectiveness assessments cannot by themselves provide all the answers for achieving the maternal and child health Goals, because they capture only some dimensions of a highly textured problem. In addition to the epidemiology, therefore, this report puts forward a second line of analysis, which focuses on health systems and their unique role in reducing poverty and promoting democratic development. It demonstrates that functioning, responsive health systems are an essential prerequisite for addressing maternal and child health at scale and in a sustainable way—in short, for meeting the Millennium Development Goals.

To address health systems, the report draws on research from multiple disciplines, including epidemiology, economics and political economy, anthropology and the behavioral sciences, law, and policy analysis. Although the task force joins the call for increased health systems research to generate a deeper and stronger evidence base (*Lancet* 2004; Ministerial Summit on Health Research 2004), we explicitly recognize that policy responses to health systems do not just follow automatically from the data. Rather, policymakers face choices. And the choices they make must be fundamentally grounded in the values and principles that members of the global community have agreed should govern the world that we build together.

The report therefore takes its first principles—equity and human rights—from the Millennium Declaration and the long line of international declarations, binding treaties, and national commitments on which it is based. The values captured by these principles can be translated into specific steps, clear priorities, policy directions, and program choices, guided by the scientific evidence. The aim of this report is to set out the broad dimensions of the strategy that results.

A rights-based approach to the child health and maternal health Goals

"Women and children"—a tag line for vulnerability, an SOS for rescue, a trigger for pangs of guilt. Change must begin right there. The Millennium Development Goals are not a charity ball. The women and children who make up the statistics that drive the Goals are citizens of their countries and of the

The women
and children
who make up
the statistics
are citizens
with rights

world. They are the present and future workers in their economies, caregivers of their families, stewards of the environment, innovators of technology. They are human beings. They have rights—entitlements to the conditions, including access to healthcare, that will enable them to protect and promote their health; to participate meaningfully in the decisions that affect their lives; and to demand accountability from the people and institutions that have the duty to take steps to fulfill those rights.

What should those steps be? Indisputably, poor health is connected to broader social, economic, and environmental conditions, some of which must be addressed from outside the health sector. Meeting other Millennium Development Goals (MDGs), particularly the Goals on gender empowerment, education, water, hunger, and income poverty, can have a powerful effect on the health and survival of all people, including women and children. In some cases, the causation is direct (clean water directly reduces infection, for example). But in many other cases, the impact of factors outside the health sector is mediated through the health sector. For example, advances in women's equality and empowerment mean that women can more readily make the decision to access emergency care when they suffer obstetric complications or their children fall seriously ill.

Hence health sector interventions—ideally in synergy with other MDG strategies outside the health sector—are critical for achieving Goals 4 and 5. Health sector interventions can also have significant effects on many other aspects of development and poverty reduction.[1]

The proximate causes of poor health and mortality in children and in women of reproductive age are known

Approximately 10.8 million children under age five die each year, 4 million of them in their first month of life. While child mortality has steadily declined in the past two decades, progress on key indicators is now slowing, and in parts of Sub-Saharan Africa child mortality is on the rise. The great bulk of the mortality decline since the 1970s is attributable to reduction in deaths from diarrheal diseases and vaccine-preventable conditions in children under five. Other major killers of children, such as acute respiratory infection, have shown far less reduction and malaria mortality has been increasing, especially in Sub-Saharan Africa. Neonatal mortality has remained essentially unchanged. Therefore, as other causes of under-five mortality decline, neonatal mortality accounts for an increasing proportion of all childhood deaths. Malnutrition of children is a contributing factor in more than half of all child mortality, and malnutrition of mothers in a substantial proportion of neonatal mortality.

For maternal mortality—the death of women in pregnancy and childbirth—progress has been even more elusive. Despite 15 years of the global Safe Motherhood Initiative, overall levels of maternal mortality are believed to have remained unchanged, with the latest estimate of deaths standing at about 530,000 a year

Scaling up is not just a process of multiplication

(WHO, UNICEF, and UNFPA 2004). A handful of countries has experienced remarkable drops in the maternal mortality ratio (an indicator of the safety of childbirth and pregnancy)—an inspiring reminder that with the right policies and conditions in place, dramatic and rapid progress is possible. But in the great majority of high-mortality countries, where the great majority of maternal deaths occur, there has been little change. In some countries, where levels of HIV/AIDS and malaria are high and growing, the number of maternal deaths and the maternal mortality ratio are thought to have increased. And the half million maternal deaths are the tip of the iceberg: another 8 million women each year suffer complications from pregnancy and childbirth that result in lifelong health consequences.

Other aspects of maternal health present a mixed picture. While fertility has declined dramatically—from a total fertility rate of 5.0 births per woman in 1960 to 2.7 in 2001—an estimated 201 million women who wish to space or limit their childbearing are not using effective contraception that would enable them to do so. The result is about 70–80 million unintended pregnancies each year in developing countries alone (Singh and others 2003).

Meanwhile, violence continues to shatter the lives of women in every part of the globe. Sexually transmitted infections, including HIV/AIDS, ravage whole communities, with disastrous effects on families and societies. The 13 million "AIDS orphans" around the world—children who have lost one or both parents to AIDS—are testament to this fact.

Full access to and utilization of proven, effective interventions would avert two-thirds of child deaths and three-quarters of maternal deaths

The primary health interventions needed to address most of these conditions are known. The Bellagio Study Group on Child Survival estimated that with 99 percent coverage of proven effective interventions, 63 percent of child mortality would be averted (Jones and others 2003) (figure 1). The World Bank has estimated that if all women had access to the interventions for addressing complications of pregnancy and childbirth, especially emergency obstetric care, 74 percent of maternal deaths could be averted (Wagstaff and Claeson 2004) (figure 2). Moreover, universal access to sexual and reproductive health information and services would have far-reaching effects for both the maternal health and child health Goals and for virtually every other Goal, including those for HIV/AIDS, gender, education, environment, hunger, and income poverty.

If we know the causes of most death and disability and we have the interventions to prevent or treat those causes, then why have the problems of maternal health and child health been so intractable? It is simple enough to call for massive scaling up of these interventions, but scaling up is not just a process of multiplication, of more providers, more drugs, more facilities in more places. Scaling up—ensuring that healthcare is accessible to and used by all those

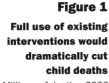

Figure 1

Full use of existing interventions would dramatically cut child deaths

Millions of deaths, 2000

Source: Adapted from Jones and others 2003; neonatal deaths based on Save the Children 2001.

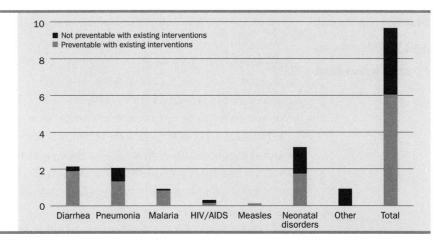

Figure 2

Full use of existing services would dramatically reduce maternal deaths

Share of deaths averted, 2000 (%)

Source: Wagstaff and Claeson 2004.

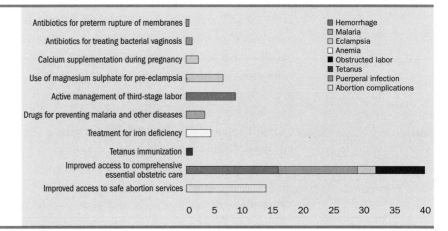

who need it—also means tackling the social, economic, and political contexts in which people live and in which health institutions are embedded. Both dimensions—concrete operational issues and wider, contextual issues—need sustained attention and investment.

Scaling up has technical dimensions, including priority-setting and sequencing of interventions

The task force recommends that highest priority be given to strengthening the primary healthcare system, from community-based interventions to the first referral-level facility at which emergency obstetric care is available. This implies a focus on the district level where, in many countries, critical planning, budgeting, and implementation decisions are made. There is no single blueprint for how a health system at this level should be organized. In the fields of maternal, child, and reproductive health, multiple scenarios have proven successful. Based on these experiences and on a large body of scientific data, the task force suggests basic principles and guidelines that countries should consider in developing detailed plans for meeting the Goals.

Countries must make hard choices about setting priorities

Strategies for tackling maternal and neonatal mortality should focus on delivery and the immediate postpartum period

The ideal scenario is this: as part of an integrated primary healthcare system, every birth, whether it takes place at home or in a facility, is attended by a skilled birth attendant, backed up by facilities that can provide emergency obstetric care and essential newborn care and by a functioning referral system that ensures timely access to the appropriate level of services in case of a life-threatening complication. On the way to that ideal, countries must make hard choices about setting priorities. One challenge is to determine whether there are immediate interim steps that can address some significant proportion of mortality while simultaneously strengthening the foundations of the health system so that ultimately the optimal level of care is provided for every woman and every newborn.

The most appropriate interim steps for addressing newborn care may well be different from the most appropriate interim steps for addressing maternal mortality. For newborns a substantial proportion of life-threatening conditions can be addressed within the community, by healthcare workers with only a few months of training.

But healthcare providers with this level of skill will not be able to effectively address obstetric complications experienced by the woman giving birth. These are the complications that kill women—and often their babies as well. Such emergencies must be handled by skilled professionals with the supplies, equipment, and healthcare teams that are available only in health facilities that provide emergency obstetric care.

A number of interventions, such as malaria prophylaxis and active management of third-stage labor, can have some impact on maternal mortality by preventing complications. These interventions certainly should be provided as part of routine antenatal and delivery care, and research to improve their safety and effectiveness—research on uniject oxytocin or misoprostol, for example—should be encouraged. Complications of unsafe abortion, which now account for some 13 percent of maternal deaths globally, could also be prevented through access to contraception and safe abortion services.

However, most obstetric complications occur unexpectedly around the time of delivery in women with no known risk factors, striking about 15 percent of all pregnant women. Therefore, to meet the MDG target of reducing the maternal morality ratio by 75 percent by 2015, it is critical for countries now to put priority focus on ensuring that women who experience life-threatening complications can and do access the emergency obstetric care that can save their lives. This necessarily means tackling the facility-based health system and its interaction with the communities and individuals it serves. Both supply-side factors (the availability of high-quality services) and demand-side factors (the barriers to appropriate utilization) are relevant, but initiatives to address them in any given geographic area must be carefully sequenced. A rights-based approach will pay particular attention to the link between supply and demand, establishing constructive accountability mechanisms that involve the community to ensure consistent 24-hour-a-day, 7-day-a-week functioning, equitable access, and high-quality, responsive care.

Strategies for reducing the under-five mortality rate begin in the community

For children, much can be accomplished without the involvement of the health system. Improved water supplies and sanitation and cleaner sources of energy to reduce indoor air pollution could significantly reduce the incidence of some of the more common diseases of childhood. Exclusive breastfeeding for the first six months and appropriate complementary feeding could prevent almost 20 percent of childhood deaths in the 42 countries where 90 percent of those deaths occur (Jones and others 2003). Teaching mothers and other primary caretakers how to recognize the early signs of potentially fatal illnesses and where to seek care for them is also essential.

Bringing appropriate curative care into the community would help overcome low utilization rates of health facilities. New policies allowing closer-to-client services, such as the use of antibiotics by community-level healthcare workers, recently recommended by the WHO and the United Nations Children's Fund (UNICEF), would be welcome. Development of new and more heat-stable vaccines and new antibiotics and other drugs that can be given in shorter and easier-to-administer courses would also be welcome.

But peripheral workers will always need close supervision and support from higher level health professionals, and both they and mothers will need to be able to access well staffed and supplied facilities for outpatient care. First-level referral hospitals are indispensable for treating severe illnesses. In other words, further reductions in child mortality must rely heavily on an accessible and competent health system that is actively involved through the entire range of primary healthcare services. Recent evaluations of the Integrated Management of Childhood Illness (IMCI) strategy supported by the WHO and UNICEF and implemented widely throughout the world have indicated that good results are obtained only when health systems are strong.

Full access to sexual and reproductive health information and services is critical to the health of women and children

A comprehensive district health system is critical for ensuring full access to sexual and reproductive health information and services which, together with good nutrition, form the foundation of good health for women and for children. It includes access to contraception, since control over the number and spacing of children can have a profound impact on the health and well-being of both women and their children. It also includes safe abortion services, as well as information and services for preventing and treating sexually transmitted infections, including HIV/AIDS. Indeed, for HIV/AIDS interventions to be maximally effective they should be integrated into sexual and reproductive health services, since this is where most women access healthcare.

Adolescents deserve special attention with services tailored to meet their needs, including the differing needs of married and unmarried adolescents. As the largest cohort—1 billion strong—ever to make the transition from childhood to adulthood, today's adolescents are a key to meeting the Goals in a long-term, sustainable way.

Changes in human resource policies are necessary to deliver these interventions at scale

One enormous barrier to providing these interventions is the lack of adequately trained providers deployed at the appropriate levels of the health system and geographic locations—a problem intensified in recent years by massive migration of health professionals from poor countries to rich countries (the so-called "brain drain") and by HIV/AIDS, which has decimated the health workforce in some high-prevalence countries.

To address the crisis in human resources, policymakers should take several key steps:

- Revise laws and practices to enable mid-level providers, such as midwives, surgical technicians, and general medical practitioners, to perform procedures they can be trained to do safely and effectively but that now are restricted to specialist physicians. These procedures include all basic emergency obstetric care functions, as well as anesthesia and even cesarean section.
- Enable community health workers to perform key child and newborn health and reproductive health interventions within the community, with supportive supervision from the health system.
- Substantially increase salaries and improve career paths and working conditions of health providers.

Simply identifying these kinds of technological interventions that must be available at scale to meet the Goals gets us only marginally closer to the kind of functioning health system that is needed to deliver them. The wider context in which health services are delivered and accessed must also be addressed.

Scaling up toward universal access and full utilization requires tackling social, economic, and political conditions

Social, economic and political conditions present complex environments that resist formulaic solutions, particularly when imposed from outside and above. But too often recognition of this fact spells paralysis or, even worse, new rounds of technical solutions designed to dodge the issues altogether.

This report focuses on three kinds of interconnected challenges that can provide meaningful entry points for addressing the broader context and are

**A trickle-down
approach to
addressing
disparities
will not work**

themselves high-priority issues essential to MDG strategies: health inequity and the experience of poverty, health systems as social institutions that are greater than the sum of the medical interventions they deliver, and international aid levels and the development policies and processes through which the levels are determined and the aid distributed.

Trickle-down approaches to health disparities are not good enough; inequities must be explicitly addressed

The disparity between rich and poor countries in maternal mortality is dramatic. In some parts of Sub-Saharan Africa women have a 1 in 6 chance of dying in childbirth, while in parts of North America and Europe, lifetime risk is as low as 1 in 8,700 and maternal mortality has virtually disappeared as a public health problem (WHO, UNICEF, and UNFPA 2001).

Although the disparities in child mortality are less dramatic, nearly all child deaths occur in low- and middle-income countries, 75 percent in Sub-Saharan Africa and South Asia alone. For both maternal and child health, Sub-Saharan Africa (with the highest mortality rates) and South Asia (with the largest number of deaths) form the two epicenters of the crisis.

Less well documented, and far less understood, are the massive disparities that occur within high-mortality countries. Differences in health are not random; a growing body of research demonstrates that the disparities are systematic and track underlying hierarchies of social disadvantage. The magnitude of inequities varies from country to country and across different health conditions and health interventions. Disparities by wealth, geographic area, and gender have been most widely documented, but health disparities often follow other lines of social disadvantage as well, including race and ethnicity, urban or rural location, and linguistic or religious divisions.

To some extent the disparity in health status is due to disparities in living and working conditions that fall outside the health sector. But it is critical to recognize that social and economic disadvantages also directly influence access to and utilization of healthcare, as well as the patterns of health spending. While the health system could and should function as a safety net, providing care to those who need it most, too often the reverse is true: socially excluded groups do not have access to badly needed care, despite their higher burden of disease, and when they are able to access care, it often involves catastrophic costs that deepen their impoverishment.

The implication for MDG strategies is clear: a trickle-down approach to addressing disparities will not work. The fact that a particular health intervention is used to prevent or treat a disease that is more prevalent among the poor does not mean that the poor will be the ones who benefit from increased spending on that intervention. In fact, without specific attention, just the opposite is likely to happen. For strategies to meet the Goals, it is not only the poor and marginalized, but inequity—the gap itself—that must be explicitly addressed.

"Pro-poor" strategies must deal meaningfully with the roots of inequity

Countries—including health authorities at the local and even the facility level—must document and understand disparities in health status and the utilization of healthcare. Although there is enormous room for new work and innovation in health equity research, a wealth of information is now buried in the data generated by current health information systems (Wirth and others 2004). Progress in closing the equity gap can and should be monitored as an intrinsic part of the MDG initiative. The task force therefore recommends that the maternal health and child health targets be modified so that they are equity sensitive. These same monitoring processes can also feed directly into human rights monitoring at the international and national levels, since nondiscrimination is a crosscutting norm codified in human rights law.

A far more complex question is exactly what kinds of interventions will best address inequity. The answer will be context specific, and the process by which the answer is formulated—ideally, a process that includes the marginalized in a meaningful way—will be intrinsic to the solution. The overriding recommendation of the task force is that so-called "pro-poor" strategies should not deal only with the symptoms; they must deal meaningfully with the roots of inequity. Much writing in the international health field in recent years has referred to "pro-poor" interventions, sometimes with little thought about whether such interventions are necessarily "pro-equity" or even "anti-poverty." Sometimes interventions do need to be carefully "targeted" to geographic areas or even populations that are disadvantaged. But if the more basic sources of inequity within the structure of the health system are not acknowledged and addressed, the danger is a targeted intervention that stigmatizes or a superficial equity initiative that breeds little more than cynicism. "Pro-poor" interventions deployed around a deeply inequitable core structure are insufficient.

Equitable, well functioning health systems play a central role in poverty reduction, democratic development, and the fulfillment of human rights

The very structure and functioning of the health system must be considered. One objective of the health system is, of course, to ensure equitable access to the technical interventions necessary to promote health and treat disease. But development planners and government authorities have often failed to grasp the extent to which abusive, marginalizing, or exclusionary treatment by the health system has come to define the experience of being poor. Moreover, they have often failed to grasp that the converse is also true: the health system as a core social institution, part of the fabric of social and civic life, has enormous potential to contribute to democratic development.

Health claims—claims of entitlement to healthcare and enabling conditions—are assets of citizenship. Their effective assertion and vindication through the operation of the health system helps build a human rights culture and a stronger, more democratic society.

Market-based health reforms fail to reach the poor

A fundamental shift in the approach to health systems is needed

Our ability to meet the Millennium Development Goals turns on our ability to think differently and act differently about health systems. The status quo is unacceptable, in multiple respects:

- The fragile and fragmented health systems that now exist are unable to ensure availability, access, and utilization of key health interventions in sufficient volume and quality to meet the Goals.
- The costs individuals incur in managing (or failing to manage) their health are often catastrophic, thus deepening poverty.
- As core social institutions, dysfunctional and abusive health systems intensify exclusion, voicelessness, and inequity while simultaneously defaulting on their potential—and obligation—to fulfill individuals' rights and contribute to the building of equitable, democratic societies.

The approach put forward in this report responds to the dominant policy packages that have been promoted for health sector reform over the past two decades and to the realities that have resulted on the ground. These prescriptions for reform have been based on the fundamental conviction that healthcare is best delivered to populations through competitive markets. To create such markets, the dominant approach converts healthcare into a marketable commodity, that is, into a product or service to be bought and sold; encourages the development of a competition-driven private sector to deliver health services on a for-profit basis (and in practice also encourages private, nonprofit providers, such as nongovernmental organizations and church-owned facilities); and tries to expand the choices available to healthcare consumers, who are assumed to make optimal decisions for themselves in seeking healthcare.

This basic approach to the health sector, championed largely by donors, has been part of a broader strategy for poorly performing public sector institutions—a strategy that is ideologically opposed to a strong state presence. The strategy minimizes the role and, in practice, the legitimacy of the state.

Even the most ardent health sector reformers, however, recognize that market-based reforms based on the commodification of healthcare will end up failing to reach the poor, who simply do not have sufficient cash or other assets to purchase the care they need. They also recognize that such "market failure" means that a segment of the population will continue to suffer poor health, which, especially in the case of infectious disease such as HIV/AIDS and severe acute respiratory syndrome (SARS), has clear "externalities"—that is, effects on the broader society beyond the poor health of the individuals who are unable to purchase healthcare. Thus even strongly market-based health reforms see a role for public sector services. In this model, the central role of the public sector is to "fill the gap" by providing a minimum level of essential services—often formulated as an "essential services package"—for the poor. Government also acts as the "steward" of the system, setting policies, law, and regulations, even if it does not deliver services directly.

**Health systems
are core social
institutions**

Health sector reforms were expected to increase both efficiency (through markets) and equity (through the broader reach of an invigorated private sector for those who could pay and a "residual" public sector for those who could not). That was the theory. The reality has been far different and, of course, rather varied as well. But, quite systematically, these reforms have been experienced as deeply unequalizing. Moreover, the theoretical neatness of discrete public and private sectors, each with its own role, pertains almost nowhere. People rich and poor face a pluralistic market with a wide and chaotic array of services of wildly varying quality that in virtually all cases require outlays of cash to access, even in the public sector where fee exemption schemes are in place.

The overall weakening of the state has left it unable to perform the regulatory and governance functions on which a market-based system depends (in many cases it was not strong enough to perform these functions well in the first place). That failure and the chaos and inequity that result intensify the problem: they further delegitimize the state in the eyes of both the people who make up the health system and the people who look to it for managing health and disease—quite often for matters of life and death. Confronting this reality, this report puts forward the outlines of a different approach to health systems (table 2).

The conventional and the proposed approaches are not mutually exclusive. Indeed, many elements of the conventional approach, such as burden of disease assessments, user preferences, or even market operations, are also important elements of the task force approach. But the task force advocates a basic shift in perspective and mindset. That shift begins with the need to understand the nature and functioning of the health system differently, in effect to change the primary unit of analysis from specific diseases to health systems as core social institutions.

The proposed approach also adopts a different view of the role of the state. It does not propose a particular model for state involvement in service delivery, recognizing that there are many different routes to and providers of excellent

Table 2

**Task force approach
to health systems**

Item	Conventional approach	Task force approach
Primary unit of analysis	Specific diseases or health conditions, with focus on individual risk factors	Health system as core social institution
Driving rationale in structuring the health system	Commercialization and creation of markets, seeking financial sustainability and efficiency through the private sector	Inclusion and equity, through cross-subsidization and redistribution across the system
Patients/users	Consumers with preferences	Citizens with entitlements and rights
Role of state	Gap-filler where market failure occurs	Duty-bearer obligated to ensure redistribution and social solidarity rather than segmentation that legitimates exclusion and inequity
Equity strategy	Pro-poor targeting	Structural change to promote inclusion

healthcare. But it does propose a different understanding of state responsibility and obligation in relation to health and a different understanding of the role of health systems in the overall project of democratic development. Among other things, the approach places increased importance on equity, seeing it as a central objective of health policy. This means taking seriously the need for redistribution within the health system.

To do that, the report puts forward three principles to guide context-specific policymaking and offers supporting rationales and specific possible policy interventions that derive from each. These principles are:

- Strengthening the legitimacy of the state.
- Preventing excessive segmentation by enhancing norms of collaboration to improve services in both public and private sectors.
- Strengthening the voice and power of the poor and marginalized to assert claims.

Health spending must increase dramatically if the Goals are to be met

Current levels of expenditure are simply not enough to effect the changes necessary to meet the Goals. In the poorest countries of Sub-Saharan Africa, health expenditures are in the range of $1–$10 per capita, with a substantial proportion coming out of the pockets of users. In many cases the costs of healthcare are catastrophic, pushing already poor people deeper into poverty. In 2001 the Commission on Macroeconomics and Health determined that a basic package of primary healthcare would cost about $34 per capita per year (Commission on Macroeconomics and Health 2001). It is the obligation of national governments and the international community to ensure that such amounts are available and spent to improve and safeguard health.

Development practices must create a policy environment that ensures appropriate policies, expenditures, and accountability for implementation

Many of the steps needed to meet the child health and maternal health Goals can begin immediately, at the national, district, and local levels. For example, inequity can start to be tackled immediately by initiating the local documentation and problem-solving processes. Failures in the provision of emergency obstetric care can often be fixed by focusing attention on the problem and making changes in facility-based management or logistical systems that do not require massive infusions of new money.

But the kind of transformational change required to meet the Goals at the national level will also entail serious revisions in the policy environment, including the processes and practices by which aid is determined and distributed. Far too often, the best laid plans of the health sector are quashed or neutralized when put through the wringer of financing and planning mechanisms that operate at the national and international levels. Finance and planning ministries and the officials of international financial institutions with

Accountability should lie at the heart of the MDG initiative

whom they negotiate need to have a profoundly different appreciation of the importance of health and health systems for economic growth, poverty reduction, and the building of democratic societies.

The UN Millennium Project calls for poverty reduction strategies that are based on the Millennium Development Goals. In the area of health, this requires more than a list of statistics of poor maternal and child health and a statement of determination to address them. It entails making hard decisions about priorities, examining the underlying health system, and ensuring that implementation, monitoring, and accountability processes are in place.

Accountability should lie at the heart of the MDG initiative. In the end, poverty reduction and the strategies to make it happen will require meaningful participation by those whose lives and health depend on it and serious, determined, courageous action from those who have the power to initiate, sustain, and guarantee change.

Goals 4 and 5 are attainable—but not without extraordinary effort

The principal recommendations of the task force for achieving the Goals are as follows:

Health systems. Health systems, particularly at the district level, must be strengthened and prioritized in strategies for reaching the child health and maternal health Goals.
- Health systems are key to sustainable, equitable delivery of technical interventions.
- Health systems should be understood as core social institutions indispensable for reducing poverty and for advancing democratic development and human rights.
- To increase equity, policies should strengthen the legitimacy of well governed states, prevent excessive segmentation of the health system, and enhance the power of the poor and marginalized to make claims for care.

Financing. Strengthening health systems will require considerable additional funding.
- Bilateral donors and international financial institutions should substantially increase aid.
- Countries should increase allocations to the health sector.
- User fees for basic health services should be abolished.

Human resources. The health workforce must be developed according to the goals of the health system, with the rights and livelihoods of the workers addressed.
- Any health workforce plan should include plans for building a cadre of skilled birth attendants.

- "Scope of profession" regulations and practices must be changed to empower mid-level providers to perform life-saving procedures safely and effectively.

Sexual and reproductive health and rights. Sexual and reproductive health and rights are essential to meeting all the Millennium Development Goals, including those on child health and maternal health.
- Universal access to reproductive health services should be ensured.
- HIV/AIDS initiatives should be integrated with sexual and reproductive health and rights programs.
- Adolescents must receive explicit attention with services that are sensitive to their increased vulnerabilities and designed to meet their needs.
- In circumstances where abortion is not against the law, abortion services should be safe. In all cases, women should have access to quality services for the management of complications arising from abortion.
- Governments and other relevant actors should review and revise laws, regulations, and practices, including those on abortion, that jeopardize women's health.

Child mortality. Child health interventions should be scaled up to 100 percent coverage.
- Child health interventions should be increasingly offered within the community, backed up by the facility-based health system.
- Child nutrition should get added attention.
- Interventions to prevent neonatal deaths should get increased investment.

Maternal mortality. Maternal mortality strategies should focus on building a functioning primary healthcare system from first-referral facilities to the community level.
- Emergency obstetric care must be accessible for all women who experience complications.
- Skilled birth attendants, whether based in facilities or in communities, should be the backbone of the system.
- Strategies to ensure skilled attendants at all deliveries must be premised on integrating them into a functioning district health system that supplies, supports, and supervises them adequately.

Global mechanisms. Poverty reduction strategy processes and funding mechanisms should support and promote actions that strengthen equitable access to quality healthcare and not undermine them.
- Global institutions should commit to long-term investments.
- Restrictions on funding of salaries and recurrent costs should be removed.

- Donor funding should be aligned with national health programs.
- Health stakeholders should participate fully in policy development and funding plans.

Information systems. Information systems are an essential element in building equitable health systems.
- Indicators of health system functioning must be developed and integrated into policy and budget cycles.
- Health information systems must provide appropriate, accurate and timely information to inform management and policy decisions.
- Countries must take steps to strengthen vital registration systems.

Targets and indicators. All targets should be framed in equity-sensitive terms.
- Universal access to reproductive health services should be added as a target to Goal 5.
- All targets should have an appropriate set of indicators as shown in table 3, where new indicators and changes to the targets appear in italics.

Table 3	Goal	Targets	Indicators
Proposed targets and indicators for the child health and maternal health Goals *Note:* Proposed modifications appear in italics.	Goal 4: Reduce child mortality	Reduce by two-thirds, between 1990 and 2015, the under-five mortality rate, *ensuring faster progress among the poor and other marginalized groups*	Under-five mortality rate Infant mortality rate Proportion of 1-year-old children immunized against measles *Neonatal mortality rate* *Prevalence of underweight children under 5 (see Goal 1 indicator)*
	Goal 5: Improve maternal health	Reduce by three-quarters, between 1990 and 2015, the maternal mortality ratio, *ensuring faster progress among the poor and other marginalized groups* *Universal access to reproductive health services by 2015 through the primary health-care system, ensuring faster progress among the poor and other marginalized groups*	Maternal mortality ratio Proportion of births attended by skilled health personnel *Coverage of emergency obstetric care* *Proportion of desire for family planning satisfied* *Adolescent fertility rate* *Contraceptive prevalence rate* *HIV prevalence among 15- to 24-year-old pregnant women (see Goal 6 indicator)*

Chapter 1

Introduction

The new millennium requires new thinking about the relationship between health and development. It is not simply the turn of a calendar page that beckons us to new thinking. It is the growing conviction that, notwithstanding enormous gains in many critical areas of health over the past 50 years, the old strategies are no longer sufficient. Indeed, to a large degree, they are failing.

In many parts of the world declines in mortality have slowed or stagnated; in others they have reversed, leaving billions suffering from avoidable mortality and morbidity. Inequalities in health status and in access to healthcare are wide and deep—and they are growing. Such inequalities are linked to deep inequities—profound injustices that ultimately feed the corrosive insecurity that now plagues all societies, rich and poor alike. Conventional strategies have done little to stem these tides. They may even have contributed to them.

The old strategies are failing in another sense as well: they no longer describe reality. The field suffers from a terrible disconnect between the dominant models and the prescriptions that flow from them on the one hand and the reality that people are coping with on the other. This is a warning sign. We need to rethink. The Millennium Development Goals and the UN Millennium Project provide a strategic setting in which to do just that.

Health interventions already exist to prevent or treat the vast majority of conditions that kill children and women of reproductive age and to enable all people to protect and promote their health. Thus, the challenge in meeting Goals 4 and 5 (see the list of Goals on pages xvi–xvii) is not to discover new medical technology but to tackle the problems of implementation, of ensuring access to these interventions by means that simultaneously promote the fundamental aims of development. That challenge is social, economic, cultural, and unavoidably political, in the sense that it relates to the distribution of power and resources within and between countries.

**Health is vital
to meeting all
of the Goals**

Power comes in many guises. Among them is the power to set the terms of the debate, to structure the patterns of thought and language, the fundamental taken-for-granted assumptions that shape our approaches to problems and solutions. If the current situation is indeed untenable, if the dominant categories no longer address the dominant problems, then these terms must be challenged and opened to new debate and directions.

The targets and indicators set by the Millennium Development Goals are framed in technical, results-oriented terms. But the response must go beyond these technical terms to address access to and distribution of power and resources within and between countries, in the structures of global governance, and in the intimate spaces of families, households, and communities. Unless we face up to the fundamental anchoring of health status, health systems, and health policy in these dynamics, our seriousness about achieving the Goals can legitimately be questioned.

Facing up to these dynamics means more than simply describing the connections among them, although that is a critical step. It requires a conscious decision to develop and pursue strategies that are honest in their efforts to confront and transform these realities of power and resource distribution while simultaneously being pragmatic about how these very dynamics so often blunt implementation of the best laid plans.

Here, where elegant theory and pristine logic meet the messy, complex reality that operates on the ground, lies the second fundamental challenge: ideology—any ideology—must not blind us to the serious operational problems that confront the health sector and to the urgent need for evidence-based actions to tackle them. Nor should our critique of current trends blind us to the important lessons that can be drawn from the truly dramatic examples of success that dot the health and development landscape. The goal of this report is to analyze problems in order to frame workable solutions to push toward as actionable an agenda as our positioning responsibly allows.

Health is vital to meeting all of the Goals. Most accounts of the relationships between health and development and between health and poverty reduction give two explanations. First, health is an intrinsic good, valuable in and of itself, and thus an important goal of development. As Amartya Sen has put it, good health enables each person to "lead the kind of life he or she has reason to value" (Sen 2001). The right to health codified in the Universal Declaration of Human Rights and in binding treaties is based on a related proposition: health is part of the very essence of what it is to be human.

Second, at the national level, health is a precondition for economic growth. Economic growth, in turn, is necessary to pull countries out of poverty traps, including the vicious circle of disease and deprivation that characterizes them (UN Millennium Project 2005a). At the individual level, serious health conditions can push already poor people even deeper into poverty when disabling illness prevents workers from earning income or the out-of-pocket cost of

Neglect, abuse, and exclusion from the health system are part of being poor

obtaining healthcare has catastrophic impact. In India, for example, 25 percent of people who went into the hospital above the poverty line came out below it (Wagstaff and Claeson 2004).

There is a third way that health and healthcare relate to poverty and development. Poverty is not just an individual state of being, it is relational. It concerns interaction with structures of power. Poverty—especially the experience of poverty—is characterized by exclusion, marginalization, voicelessness, and humiliation. This experience can contribute to or result from income poverty, and it can contribute to poor health (Krieger 2001). But even for those not catastrophically ill and those above the income poverty line the experience of exclusion, abuse, and voicelessness is a kind of poverty and must be understood unequivocally as a failure of development (Narayan 2000; Kern and Ritzen 2001).

This conception of poverty relates directly to the way we think about and address health. The health system is a core social institution, not simply a mechanical structure for delivering technical interventions the way a post office delivers letters. Health systems function at the interface between people and the structures that shape their broader society. Neglect, abuse, and exclusion from the health system are part of the very experience of being poor (Mackintosh 2001). Conversely, claims to health—claims of entitlement—are assets of citizens in a democratic society. Health actions, the choices and means that enable individuals and communities to control their health, to participate as agents, not victims, in shaping their own life circumstances are not only important for individual capabilities and the enjoyment of individual rights, they are also among the essential freedoms that shape democracy and development.

Qualitative research has demonstrated this over and over again. It is the multidimensional experience of poverty that matters to people who are poor. Although these observations about the relational nature of poverty are well documented in the literature and viscerally understood by those who work directly with the poor, current practice is remarkably thin when it comes to working through the implications for policies and programs. In response to the finding of "voicelessness" and "exclusion" come the solutions of "community participation" and, more recently, "accountability." These are certainly important tools of good development practice, but until they are grounded in deeper systemic change, the risk is that they will breed little more than cynicism.

This disconnect between the textured experience of poverty and the thinness of policy responses to it hints at a larger set of questions about why well intentioned plans for the health sector so often fail—indeed, why the solutions favored by the development community so often become the problem that the next generation of solutions must address (Pritchett and Woolcock 2004). Some would simply call this progress. But a recent analysis of "solutions" in social sectors in which key public services are both highly discretionary and transaction-intensive—services such as curative healthcare—finds a common

Identifying the common structure of failed solutions is an important step in devising best strategies

structure to the repeated failure (Pritchett and Woolcock 2004). Identifying and understanding that common structure are important preliminary steps in devising best strategies to achieve the Goals.

Starting with attempts by postcolonial states in poor countries to meet the needs of their people with a needs/supply/civil service model, Pritchett and Woolcock contend that the common structure of failed solutions is found in a kind of "bureaucratic high modernism" (Scott 1998), a push to find simple, measurable, replicable, standardized, top-down solutions—solutions that attempt to replicate the end points of successful social sectors in high-income countries without going through the often contentious, painstaking, and lengthy social and political processes that preceded such successes.

Three more examples help deepen the analysis of the common structure of failure:

During the 1990s the World Bank and other donors and international agencies promoted health sector reforms explicitly designed to address the manifest inequities of failing health systems. Why were the policies intended to address inequity so widely experienced as unequalizing? How can this repeated "redistributive failure" be explained (Mackintosh and Tibandebage 2004)?

Poverty Reduction Strategy Papers, a primary tool in current aid regimes, were proposed as a response to the perception that donors, especially international financial institutions, had emphasized economic growth without paying adequate attention to poverty reduction and had imposed new policies without ensuring country ownership. Development of a Poverty Reduction Strategy Paper was supposed to begin with a participatory poverty assessment, intended to give voice to the poor, and then proceed with deliberations involving civil society, intended to provide ownership to citizens and national governments.

But Poverty Reduction Strategy Papers have been widely criticized—even by internal evaluations of the World Bank (World Bank Operations Evaluation Department 2004) and International Monetary Fund (IMF Independent Evaluation Office 2004)—for ignoring the very processes they initiated, as outside consultants generate standardized strategies that conform to the policies of international financial institutions. Ironically, a process explicitly designed to give voice to the poor solicits but then ignores their views, confirming and reinforcing their marginalization.

It is indisputable that low-income countries need additional investment in order to make serious progress. There is an absolute scarcity of domestically generated resources. Yet studies document countless instances of failure of aid to reach precisely the services that need it most.

These examples suggest several connected dimensions to the common structure of failure.

First, context matters. The drive for technocratic, managerial fixes fails because of its inability to acknowledge that effectiveness in highly discretionary, transaction-intensive services, such as the aspects of healthcare in which

Context matters, values matter, process matters, and acknowledging responsibility matters

failure has been most acute, truly cannot be one size fits all. Until initiatives genuinely draw on context-specific knowledge and local capacity, health initiatives will not succeed at scale.

Second, values matter. When problems that are deeply political, that involve the distribution of power and resources, are systematically converted into managerial problems addressed by technical adjustments that avoid the heart of the problem, the result cannot be success. Standard health sector reform attempts at promoting equity are deployed around the edges of a system whose structure is profoundly inequitable. Until the structure is addressed, the solutions will not work. This does not necessarily mean that a massive, immediate overhaul is necessary. It does mean that values must play an important role in setting the direction of change, even if change is managed and gradual.

Third, process matters. Conventional views of policymaking as a linear, top-down process of agenda-setting, policy design, and implementation miss the many forces from the ground up that have the power to sabotage or neutralize such plans. They also ignore the fundamental rights of people to have a say in their societies. Superficial attempts to engage so-called stakeholders will be experienced as just that.

Fourth, acknowledging responsibility matters. To truly achieve the substance of the Goals, both sides in the Millennium Development compact—rich countries and poor countries—will have to look long and hard at how their actions block progress and at the constraints faced by those sitting across the table. This is not an excuse for the status quo. It is the first step in changing the structure of international development politics that fail hundreds of millions of citizens of the world today.

In the health sector many of these problems cluster around health systems. The central argument of this report is that dramatic, meaningful, sustainable progress toward both the spirit and the quantitative targets of the Millennium Development Goals requires a shift in perspective and mindset. This new perspective must pay close attention to systemic problems and to the problems of health systems anchored in their socioeconomic and political contexts. It must recognize the multiple ways in which health and health systems relate to poverty (table 1.1).

The conventional approach and the task force approach are not mutually exclusive. The task force approach does not claim that burden of disease assessments are useless, that market forces are irrelevant to healthcare, or that citizens with rights are not also consumers with preferences. Rather, this report sketches the framework of basic principles that the task force believes must inform—not dictate—policy, as decisionmakers at each level consider the changes necessary to meet the Goals in their specific contexts.

The goal of this report is not to propose and argue for the theoretically ideal health system. Instead, it describes the realities on the ground and in the international community in order to try to find actionable, principled ways to

Table 1.1

Task force approach to health systems

Item	Conventional approach	Task force approach
Primary unit of analysis	Specific diseases or health conditions, with focus on individual risk factors	Health system as core social institution
Driving rationale in structuring the health system	Commercialization and creation of markets, seeking financial sustainability and efficiency through the private sector	Inclusion and equity, through cross-subsidization and redistribution across the system
Patients/users	Consumers with preferences	Citizens with entitlements and rights
Role of state	Gap-filler where market failure occurs	Duty-bearer obligated to ensure redistribution and social solidarity rather than segmentation that legitimates exclusion and inequity
Equity strategy	Pro-poor targeting	Structural change to promote inclusion

move forward. The dream of an ideal inspires and guides, and it is politically potent. It helps us defy business as usual and to think and act more boldly. But debates over ideals must not be allowed to derail concrete actions to address the actual conditions that each society faces.

The task force advocates substantial new investment in health sectors in order to meet the Goals, which cannot be met on annual per capita health expenditures of $5–$10 or less. But even massive new aid poured into the same old strategies will not lead to success. The Millennium Development Goals must be more than a high-stakes negotiation over the bottom line of official development assistance.

Creative, effective solutions that positively transform societies and their health ultimately grow from processes that take place within those societies. In both child health and maternal health, powerful stories of success tell us that change is possible, that the Goals need not be pie in the sky, and that leaders of change speak many languages. But we are also keenly aware that global forces both constrain and facilitate the ability of local and national actors to think and act boldly. The global community, and the wealthy nations that strongly influence it, are not rescuers of poor countries or poor communities in distress; nor are they solely responsible for all of the world's problems. But they are complicit in having created the conditions that define the dismal state of health today and they must therefore be part of the solution. Their complicity lies not just in the economic and political realm. In the health arena the global community, including multilateral and bilateral agencies, does critical work in setting technical norms and standards, generating and evaluating scientific evidence, forging consensus strategies, and facilitating or frustrating implementation on the ground. Transformative change must also be on their organizational agendas.

The 2015 target date for achieving the Millennium Development Goals should spur countries and the global community to action, to take immediate concrete steps. But the fundamental transformations discussed here need to be part of dynamic, ongoing processes of revitalizing—sometimes recreating and rebuilding—health systems as part of broader social change. That requires new vision about where we are going and how we get there, a realization that 2015 is a stop along the way, not the final destination.

Chapter 2

Analytical context

This chapter provides a brief overview of the current picture of child health and maternal health, introducing the multiple perspectives that are developed in the rest of the report. It also introduces the analytic lens of health equity and links it to human rights and the multifaceted practice developing under the rubric of rights-based approaches. These perspectives provide support for the underlying premise of this report: that analysis of health conditions and interventions, as well as strategic choices of policies and programs, must be firmly rooted in their social, economic, and political contexts. Context is not only cross-sectional. Just as the choices made today have serious consequences for future conditions and decisions, so the current situation must be understood in historical context.

As an important backdrop to the chapters that follow, this chapter raises some crucial questions about the role of different kinds of evidence in the health field. The focus is on the quintessential challenge for the UN Millennium Project, namely, scale. What evidence helps us move from proof of efficacy of specific interventions (often in experimental settings) to the implementation of health sector policies and programs that meet the needs of entire populations?

Global health from three perspectives

The current global health picture can be described in a variety of ways, particularly for low- and middle-income countries, where more than 98 percent of both maternal and child deaths take place. These include an epidemiological approach, which describes health status; a structural approach, which focuses on health systems; and a power-mapping approach, which charts patterns of decisionmaking. Each yields a different, vital perspective on the problem. Each tends to structure thinking about solutions in a different way. Together these approaches lay the foundation for the task force's recommendations.

"Business as
usual" will not
be enough to
reach the Goals

*Epidemiological evidence reveals that progress is slowing—and even
being reversed*

The most conventional way to characterize the global health picture is to
describe health and disease. The picture that emerges is a grim one.

About 10.8 million children under the age of five die each year (Black,
Morris, and Bryce 2003). While child mortality has steadily declined in the
past two decades, progress on key indicators is now slowing, and in parts of
Sub-Saharan Africa child mortality is on the rise. The great bulk of the mortality decline since the 1970s is attributable to reductions in deaths from diarrheal diseases and vaccine-preventable conditions in children under five. Other
major killers of children, such as acute respiratory infection, have shown far
less reduction, and malaria mortality has been increasing, especially in Sub-
Saharan Africa.

The rate of neonatal mortality has remained essentially unchanged. As
a result, neonatal mortality now accounts for an increasing proportion of all
childhood deaths. Yet interventions and strategies for reducing neonatal mortality have remained largely unaddressed and unimplemented. This report pays
particular attention to this problem and suggests that a new indicator, the neonatal mortality rate, be added to the measurement of Goal 4 (see chapter 5).

Malnutrition of children is a contributing factor in more than half of all
child mortality, and malnutrition of mothers contributes to a substantial proportion of neonatal mortality. For this reason, this report pays close attention
to the nutrition aspects of Goal 1.

Although some bright spots exist, sluggish progress overall makes clear that
"business as usual" will not be enough to reach the health Goals. According
to a World Bank study conducted in 2003, only 16 percent of countries (with
only 22 percent of the developing world's population) are on track to meet
the child mortality target, and not a single country in Sub-Saharan Africa is
among them. Most developing countries are on track to meet the somewhat
less ambitious indicator on reducing the prevalence of underweight children.
But just 17 percent of countries in Sub-Saharan Africa are on track for doing
so (Wagstaff and Claeson 2004).

National trends mask deep disparities within countries. On average the
poorest fifth of the population saw child mortality falling half as fast as the
general population. This means the gap between rich and poor is widening
(Wagstaff and Claeson 2004). A paper commissioned by this task force to
analyze data from Demographic and Health Surveys and Multiple Indicator
Cluster Surveys reveals that wealth is only one axis of inequality (Wirth and
others 2004). Ethnic, linguistic, and other divisions are equally or more significant markers of gaps in child mortality in many countries. For some countries,
particularly in South Asia, gender matters immensely: girls lag behind boys
on many indicators, including the under-five mortality rate and utilization of
healthcare services (Bhan and others 2005; Fikree and Pasha 2004).

The half million maternal deaths are the tip of the iceberg

For maternal mortality, progress has been even more elusive. Despite 15 years of the Safe Motherhood Initiative, overall levels of maternal mortality are believed to have remained unchanged, with the latest estimate of deaths standing at about 530,000 a year (WHO, UNICEF, and UNFPA 2004). And as with child mortality, the burden of maternal death falls disproportionately on the poor (Graham and others 2004). A handful of countries have experienced remarkable drops in maternal mortality ratio, and the Middle East and North Africa region appears to be on track for meeting the maternal mortality target (Wagstaff and Claeson 2004). But the only other region even close to being on track is Latin America and the Caribbean. In the great majority of high-mortality countries, where the great majority of maternal deaths occur, there has been little change. Indeed, in some countries in which levels of HIV/AIDS and malaria are high and growing, the number of maternal deaths as well as the maternal mortality ratio are believed to have increased (McIntyre 2003). Moreover, the half million maternal deaths are the tip of the iceberg: every year another 8 million women suffer complications from pregnancy and child-birth that result in lifelong health consequences, including obstetric fistulae (WHO 2003c).

Other aspects of maternal health present a mixed picture. While globally fertility has declined dramatically—from 5.0 births per woman in 1960 to 2.7 in 2001—an estimated 201 million women who wish to space or limit their childbearing are not using effective contraception that would enable them to do so.[1] The result is about 70–80 million unintended pregnancies each year in developing countries alone (Singh and others 2003).

Meanwhile, violence continues to shatter the lives of women in every part of the globe (Heise, Ellsberg, and Gottemoeller 1999). And sexually transmitted infections, including HIV/AIDS, ravage whole communities, with disastrous effects on families and societies. The 13 million children in the world who have lost one or both parents to AIDS are testament to this fact (UNICEF 2003a).

The Goals for child health and maternal health are constructed in epidemiological terms (see Goals on pages xvi–xvii). Chapter 3 examines the epidemiological picture more closely and discusses the interventions that can address the primary proximate causes of poor child health and maternal health.

Poorly functioning health systems are a primary obstacle to meeting the Goals

Epidemiological data form the skeleton of the picture of health status. But people's actual experience of health and disease—and, critically, of poverty itself—is inseparable from their experience interacting with health systems. In poor, high-mortality countries, those systems are in profound crisis. A second way to characterize the global health picture is thus to examine the state of healthcare in poor countries. Indicators of the crisis that has overtaken health systems across developing countries include the following:

The problems of
health systems
have become a
primary obstacle
to meeting
the Goals

- Users routinely describe abusive and humiliating treatment by health providers.
- Health providers routinely describe dehumanizing and demoralizing working conditions, including public sector salary levels that have plunged well below a living wage.
- Huge gaps in the staffing of front-line facilities make reliable, good-quality services virtually unattainable. Many clinics stand empty; others are dangerously overcrowded.
- Ministries of health at all levels are grossly unprepared to manage the crises they face, a situation often exacerbated by rapid decentralization and a proliferation of uncoordinated, donor-driven initiatives.
- The lack of basic drugs and equipment cripples facilities' ability to function, damages the system's reputation, raises out-of-pocket costs to patients, and fuels a spiral of distrust and alienation.

The result in many countries is a mass exit from the public health system into a chaotic, unregulated, wildly diverse, and sometimes dangerous private sector (Standing and Bloom 2002) and catastrophic costs, formal and informal. These costs are borne disproportionately by the poor, leading one commentator to coin the term "iatrogenic poverty" (Meessen and others 2003).

The problems of health systems have become a primary obstacle to meeting the Goals. Chapter 4 examines health systems, not simply as mechanisms for delivering medical interventions but as core social institutions—a role that makes their improved functioning a vital element of poverty reduction strategies.

Identifying who has the power to change health is a key step in formulating strategies

The conception of health systems as core social institutions moves the analysis beyond a simplistic view of healthcare as a technical, biomedical fix to a recognition that both health and healthcare are deeply embedded in broader webs of social and economic forces. A third way to approach the global health picture is through power-mapping. Who makes the decisions that shape health and healthcare in poor countries, and what is the context that shapes their decisions?

At the country level, national policies obviously matter greatly. But priority must also be given to the critical decisionmaking that happens at the district level, where integrated primary health systems are needed to effectively deliver child, maternal, and reproductive health interventions. Facilities—both governmental and nongovernmental—are critical to the district health system. But so are community-based primary care activities, often linked to those facilities, especially when they truly empower the communities they serve.[2]

Chapter 6 examines the effect of international aid mechanisms—Poverty Reduction Strategy Papers and associated resource allocation tools, public

A rights-based approach should ask hard questions about who has the power

expenditure reviews, and medium-term expenditure frameworks—on countries' ability to meet the Goals. It also raises questions about the dynamics of power between the people and communities whose health is at stake and the wider social structures—including the health system—responsible for addressing it. Invoking notions of "participation" and "accountability" is almost de rigueur in the health literature. A rights-based approach should go beyond the formal mechanisms through which such notions are implemented to ask hard questions about who actually has or shares the power to effectuate change.

First principles: equity and human rights

If health is central to poverty reduction, then issues of equity must be central to health. In recent years, researchers, donors, and activists have taken up the call for health equity, which has become an increasingly sophisticated lens through which to document and understand disparities in health. Its power to generate or guide change could be substantially increased in many settings by connecting to the principles and evolving practices derived from human rights. These concepts are introduced here and used throughout the report to demonstrate what difference they make in actual strategic choices, policy directions, and program design and implementation—in short, for strategies for reaching the Goals.

Health equity

Our concern with disparities in health status and in access to healthcare reflects not simply a concern with the statistical range that exists across ungrouped individuals in a population. Rather our primary concern is with the relationship that inequality has to the socially defined hierarchies that exist in every society (Braveman, Starfield, and Geiger 2001). The report adopts the operational definition proposed by Braveman and Gruskin (2003, p. 254): "Equity in health is the absence of systematic disparities in health (or in major social determinants of health, including access to healthcare) between groups with different levels of underlying social advantage/disadvantage." Health equity is therefore an expression of social justice.

The coincidence of multiple inequities in health and the multifaceted nature of poverty make for a very complex field. People living at the margins of society suffer numerous and overlapping inequities—in health, voice, agency, living conditions. Often their poverty and ill health keep them perpetually trapped. Just as an intervention might spare a child from malaria only to leave her to die a year later of measles, a policy change in the health sector might be successful in eliminating one source of inequity (for example, financial barriers to care) only to have another emerge or persist (for example, gender bias). Among the poor, gender inequities further increase women's vulnerability (Sen, Iyer, and George 2002). And among poor women, those of a particular ethnicity or religion may face additional stigma or marginalization.

Public spending in the health sector disproportionately benefits the wealthier

The idea that poverty, social exclusion, and marginalization underlie disease has deep historical roots, and has been articulated by influential health movements, such as the social medicine movement in Latin America (Tajer 2003) and the sexual and reproductive health and rights movement globally (Correa 1994). Theories of social epidemiology recognize social conditions and exclusion as fundamental causes of ill health. One of the ways these fundamental social causes translate into disparities in physical health conditions is by influencing access to the resources necessary to prevent and treat illness (Link and Phelan 1995). This often plays out in differential access to health interventions or exclusion from the health system.

Utilization is a somewhat more complex concept, since it potentially implicates not only availability and accessibility of services but also the decision-making dynamics of users themselves. But here, too, disparities are rampant. For key maternal and child health interventions, utilization data reveal wide disparities between the lowest and highest wealth quintiles, with attendance of births by skilled health personnel—an indicator for the maternal health Goal—displaying the widest gap (figure 2.1). These are aggregate data for developing and transitional countries as a whole, but in many countries, the disparities in utilization are far wider.

Another important dimension of health equity analysis is detected through benefit-incidence studies, which measure the extent to which different segments of the population benefit from public spending (Castro-Leal and others 2000). These studies generally find that public spending in the health sector disproportionately benefits the wealthier, although the extent of the disparity varies across healthcare services and countries (Gwatkin, Bhuiya, and Victora 2004).

Much work on health equity has focused on "sounding the alarm," pointing to widening gaps in health status between population groups. Joining with many in the health equity field, the task force maintains that it is critical to

Figure 2.1

Use of health services by lowest and highest wealth quintiles in developing and transitional countries

Coverage (%)

Source: Gwatkin, Bhuiya, and Victora 2004.

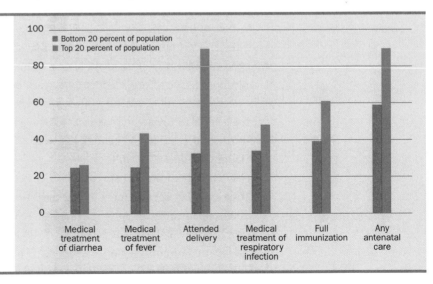

The health equity literature is surprisingly silent on rights

go beyond the mapping of disparities to pointed inquiries into determining "who and what is responsible for population patterns of health, disease, and well-being, as manifested in present, past, and changing social inequalities in health" (Krieger 2001, p. 668). As health equity research increasingly looks upstream, documenting the roots of health disparities in wider social, economic, and political conditions as they have developed over time, its potential synergy with rights-based approaches to health becomes clear (Krieger and Gruskin 2001).

Human rights and rights-based approaches to health

With a few exceptions, the health equity literature is surprisingly silent on rights. More often, health researchers who effectively expose and document disparities have used concepts of fairness, based on need, to work toward recommendations for policy change (Daniels and others 2000). Sometimes health equity is framed as a moral issue. Sometimes it is framed as an economic issue, premised on the fact that a healthy labor force is necessary for economic growth and that disparities raise concerns about "externalities" or "market failure." There is little talk of entitlement or claims—and even less of violation.

Often the outcome of health equity and of rights-based analyses has been a search for so-called "pro-poor" interventions, with little attention paid to the roots of inequity or the social dynamics that reinforce it (Vega and Irwin 2004). Although "pro-poor" is rarely defined, it often refers simply to an intervention that, in theory or demonstrated fact, is used more by the poor than the wealthy (Wagstaff and Claeson 2004). Yet such "pro-poor" interventions are not necessarily pro-equity or anti-marginalization. Narrowly focused but well conceived targeted interventions are sometimes powerful short-term steps that are essential parts of a broader equity-based strategy (see chapter 4). But policies that segregate and "target" the poor can deepen and institutionalize inequality by increasing their marginalization.

Moreover, even when "pro-poor" interventions effectively combat poverty, they are generally discussed in the health literature as interventions floating free from any structure of entitlement or accountability. There is no sense that the state is obligated to provide such interventions or that the law should guarantee them. There is no sense that citizens in a country have any recourse when access is denied. This despite the fact that virtually all countries in the world have ratified at least one human rights treaty that legally commits them to addressing such disparities in health.

To effectively move from a research-oriented approach of health equity to an action-oriented agenda for meeting the Millennium Development Goals as true development goals, we need human rights. Human rights provides a normative framework that has generated exceptionally wide consensus in the international community—not least in its invocation as a central theme of the Millennium Declaration. The norms include both outcomes (obligation of

Human rights offers a set of norms and values that have special resonance when turned to women's and children's health

results, such as the highest attainable standard of health) and processes (obligation of means, such as participation and maximum use of available resources). Equally important, human rights offers a set of values: individual human dignity, nondiscrimination, and social justice. These values have special resonance when turned to the shameful statistics of women's and children's health.

In addition, human rights provides a language that has multiple uses beyond its analytic role. It is a tool for advocacy and mobilization: deployed in a consciously political struggle, it "crystallizes the moral imagination" (Uvin 2004, p. 134) and the commitment and action that imagination inspires.

At another level, the language and categories of human rights act as a counterweight to the hegemony of economics in development practice today. This is not a minor point. The tendency to convert every issue into a technical, measurable, cost-able, managerial problem both preserves the balance of power in particular expert groups and, by sidestepping the true issues at stake, undercuts many development projects (Pritchett and Woolcock 2004; Scott 1998; Uvin 2004). For the UN Millennium Project, no less than for health policymakers, economic analysis needs to be complemented by politics of principles and values. There is no avoiding it: there is no such thing as a value-free or objectively scientific perspective on the recommended solutions. The status quo implies acceptance of the values that currently drive health and health systems, even if those values are not often acknowledged or made explicit.

If the current state of global health is unacceptable, if the status quo needs to be transformed, then consciously identifying and addressing the values that operate in health-related decisionmaking in households, communities, districts, countries, and throughout the world—and the relationship of those values to the distribution of power and resources—will be an essential part of the transformative process. Health equity analysis reveals one panel of a picture that is unacceptable from any point of view—moral, economic, legal—and uses scientific methods to probe its origins. Human rights is ultimately about identifying the workings of power that keep these unacceptable situations as they are and then using a different vision of human well-being and a growing set of rights-based practices to demand, implement, and ensure the rearrangements of power necessary for change.

We should not be naïve, however. Human rights often comes with baggage. Some suspicion of human rights talk grows from its cynical use by those who hold power in countries both rich and poor. Too often the invocation of human rights is mere rhetorical repackaging of the same old policies or a justification for aid conditionalities that, because of their selective and inconsistent application, can seem like little more than a raw exercise of political and economic power (Uvin 2004). Other attacks on human rights challenge its claim of universality, arguing that rights are "Western" and hence inauthentic and illegitimate for non-Western societies. Such a charge is profoundly cynical and manipulative when lobbed by regimes with checkered, sometimes appalling

Virtually every country has endorsed at least some human rights treaties

human rights records against their own citizens, including human rights advocates who bravely stand for justice in their own societies.

In fact, virtually every country in the world has endorsed at least some human rights documents. But we must be clear: The standing of human rights treaties as international law binding on governments does not vitiate the need to build—not assume—cultural legitimacy for human rights principles (An-Na'im 1992). The health field can be especially fertile ground for that process.

Finally, it is fair to say that within the field of international health, human rights are far too often invoked as a substitute for the crucial work of evidence-based health interventions and policy development. But, as this report seeks to show, that need not be the case.

Implementing human rights in health

The approach to human rights used in this report and recommended by the task force begins by making a basic distinction between two concepts:

1. Human rights as formal law, including the international human rights system of treaties and reporting mechanisms (treaty bodies, special rapporteurs, and working groups) and domestic courts.
2. Rights-based approaches in development practices, in which principles and values derived from human rights are incorporated into policy and program design and implementation (whether or not the term "human rights" is used).

This distinction underscores the difference between doing human rights work on health and doing health work that uses human rights as one of its guiding principles. The distinction relates to methodologies.

Mainstream human rights organizations have pioneered a methodology that focuses on violations of applicable human rights law, using a "name and shame" or "expose and denounce" technique that is particularly effective for civil and political rights violations, such as torture and unfair trials, and sometimes for rights related to health as well. But human rights should not be conflated with this traditional methodology. The complexity and diversity of human rights problems requires a much more varied and nuanced set of human rights tools and human rights practices. Health is a good example.

The formal human rights system has taken major steps in recent years to clarify the right to health and demonstrate its applicability to specific problems. The Economic and Social Committee's General Comment 14 on the right to health and the appointment of a special rapporteur on the right to health are two important milestones. These processes need to be supported and strengthened, as they are crucial to the building of international consensus on the meaning and application of the norms.

But when it comes to healthcare workers, health activists, and health policymakers facing concrete problems on the ground, human rights initiatives fixated

The right to health is often misunderstood as the right to be healthy

on and bound by chapter and verse of human rights treaties often miss the mark. In the provocative words of Peter Uvin, such legal formalism "is about as useful to on-the-ground change as knowing the lyrics to 'We Are the World' is to ending hunger" (Uvin 2004, p. 140). We can do much more. Rights-based approaches that build human rights principles and practices into the larger, multifaceted, and multidisciplinary endeavor of health development work and of health advocacy and activism are a central element in the strategies proposed here. Indeed, the Special Rapporteur on the Right to Health has now joined the call for this expansion of methodologies (Special Rapporteur on the Right to Health 2004).

The right to health is often misunderstood as the right to be healthy. Given the multiple determinants of health, including genetics, this would make little sense as a legal standard. No one can guarantee good health. Rather, the right to health encompasses both freedoms, such as the right to be free from torture or to have control over one's reproductive capacity, and entitlements, such as access to healthcare or to the social and environmental conditions that make good health possible (UN CESCR 2000).

Key human rights principles include the following:

- *Entitlement and obligation.* Human rights law relates primarily—but not exclusively—to the relationship between citizens and states. With globalization, this aspect of the law has been evolving in crucial ways relating to nonstate actors (corporations, individuals, and other groups) and the growing recognition that a state can have duties outside its own borders, particularly when it is complicit in creating an extraterritorial situation that contributes to deprivations of human rights (International Council on Human Rights Policy and EGI 2003; Special Rapporteur on the Right to Health 2004). But even beyond formal law, relationships of entitlement and obligation arise throughout healthcare systems.

- *Accountability.* The concept of "constructive accountability" is used here to make clear that human rights work is not only or always about identifying violations, finding blame, and imposing punishment (Freedman 2003). Fulfillment of the right to health will mean building responsive, equitable health systems. Positive relationships of accountability—including transparency and answerability (Brinkerhoff 2004)—will be an important dynamic in making such systems function (World Bank 2003b). When properly grounded in a broader social and political framework, these ideas, together with the more conventional understanding of accountability as including mechanisms that provide recourse for violations suffered, become key parts of a rights-based approach.

- *Claims.* Principles of obligation, entitlement, and accountability translate into claims for healthcare and the social conditions critical for good health. Health claims are valuable assets that people use to wage their own battles against poverty and to exercise their citizenship rights. It is the obligation of the state to acknowledge and create the conditions for

Obligation, entitlement, and accountability translate into claims for healthcare

the effective assertion of health claims, in the broadest sense (not just through a legal malpractice system). This is a critical principle in the approach to health systems presented in this report.

- *Participation, voice.* The involvement of people in the decisions that affect their fundamental rights is an essential principle of rights-based practices. Such involvement is often promoted for instrumental reasons, because it has been shown to lead to programs with better outcomes. But participation or involvement is also the opposite of exclusion or marginalization: it has value in its own right as part of the process by which people become effective agents in their lives and their societies.

- *Respect, protection, and fulfillment.* The obligation of duty-bearers is to respect (not to violate), to protect (prevent others from violating), and to fulfill (take steps to ensure positive enjoyment of) rights. The adoption of a rights-based approach to health must not be permitted to divert attention from the steps needed to address the nitty-gritty—but not trivial—problems of functioning healthcare systems. Human rights is indeed about political action, but allowing ideological debate to derail real action on operational issues is itself a statement about the value we place on truly meeting the needs—and the rights—of the poor and the marginalized.

- *Progressive realization.* It is one thing for a state or any other responsible actor to acknowledge a right—by ratifying a treaty, for example—and quite another for it to take action to ensure that that right is enjoyed. The right to health will not be fulfilled through legal formalism, by the stroke of a pen. It takes time, money, commitment—and action. The principle of progressive realization articulated in human rights treaties requires states to take all appropriate steps to realize the right in question "to the maximum extent of available resources."

This report uses the principle of progressive realization to highlight three critical issues:

- *Action must be concrete, deliberate, and targeted.* All states, no matter how poor, can take certain immediate, concrete measures to advance the right to health (UN CESCR 2000).

- *Budget allocations are relevant.* Allocations of budget and official development assistance are relevant to human rights. Discretionary, harmful cuts to the health budget arguably violate this right.

- *Some interventions must take priority over others.* Not all interventions are equally important for ensuring enjoyment of a right. When fundamental rights are at stake, particularly when the historical context points to a legacy of neglect, some interventions must take priority over others. This principle has been invoked in the HIV/AIDS field (Minister of Health v. Treatment Action Campaign 2002). Chapter 3 shows how it applies to maternal mortality.

The right to
health takes
time, money,
commitment
—and action

The health systems crisis in historical context

At independence most countries in Asia and Africa found themselves confronting the legacy of a colonial health system that had focused almost exclusively on urban, tertiary hospitals. Traditional providers of different kinds, unconnected to the state, were the major sources of healthcare outside the family. Newly independent states advanced a new vision of healthcare as part of the nationalist ideals that had inspired the struggles for independence (Mackintosh 2001). Into societies often marked by deep inequalities (by wealth, gender, and sometimes race and ethnicity), governments advanced a strategy that would extend basic curative and preventive services through a network of health posts or health centers in "a highly organized, supervised, and regulated publicly financed service which would cover the entire population" (Bloom and Standing 2001, p. 8).

In this scenario, households and communities would provide basic social support and voluntary labor for public health, while the state would provide specialist knowledge, drugs, and other supplies, through an extensive infrastructure of basic health posts and centers (Bloom and others 2000). To meet the daunting challenge of staffing such a system, most countries planned to train massive numbers of "medical assistants" or "health assistants" to work as government employees at the most basic level of the local health infrastructure. In addition, they planned to train "community health workers," typically volunteers, who were expected to lead public health campaigns and provide simple preventive and curative care in their own communities. These cadres of workers were generally people with little formal education, who were given a limited amount of training. A strong supervision system in which doctors and nurses would provide regular monitoring and back-up to health assistants and community health workers was therefore an essential element of this vision.

During the 1960s and 1970s, many countries invested heavily in training and deploying community-based healthcare workers, including to underserved rural areas. The boldest, and most successful, application of this kind of system was the "barefoot doctors" program in China, which became an inspiration for international public health policymakers. In countries such as Bangladesh, these workers are crucial to strategies such as "doorstep" family planning services designed to circumvent gender-based barriers to utilization, for example *purdah* restrictions that prevent women from leaving their homes to access family planning facilities on their own (Schuler, Hashemi, and Jenkins 1995; Simmons and others 1988).

BRAC (formerly known as the Bangladesh Rural Advancement Committee), a large NGO, has been training female community health workers since the 1970s. The program grew out of frustrations with existing public and private healthcare system and experience with male paramedics. As of 2003, it had trained nearly 30,000 community health workers in as many villages (box 2.1).

Primary healthcare

From this basic vision of an appropriate health system that responds to the needs of the entire population grew the concept of primary healthcare, formally articulated at the Alma Ata conference in 1978. Although primary healthcare is now often equated only with community-based, low-tech healthcare, the Alma Ata declaration very clearly recognized the importance of a facility-based health system with a strong referral network, of which outreach into communities was an integral part. As the director general of the WHO, Hafdan Mahler, said in 1981, "A health system based on primary care cannot, and I repeat, cannot be realized, cannot be developed, cannot function, and simply cannot exist without a network of hospitals" (Van Lerberghe, de Bethune, and De Brouwere 1997, p. 801).

Primary healthcare was not just a blueprint for organizing a public health system. It was a fundamental approach to health itself based on the notion that services should be delivered as close to the community as possible, in a system that the country could afford, in an integrated manner, with the participation of the community. Health was understood in its full social and economic dimensions, and healthcare was understood as an essential part of what good governance should mean. These were optimistic times: the commitment to primary healthcare and to "Health for All by the Year 2000" developed hand

Box 2.1

BRAC trains village women as volunteer community health workers

Source: Chowdhury and others 1997; Watts 2004.

Community health workers trained by BRAC are married, middle-age women eager to work for their communities. Only a few have any schooling. They are members of BRAC–organized village organizations, groups of poor women designed to advance their social and economic well-being. Village organization members select one of their own to be trained as the community health worker for their area. These workers receive no salary from BRAC, but they supplement their income through opportunities created and facilitated by BRAC. With small loans from BRAC, they set up revolving funds for drugs, which they sell at a small mark-up. They also sell selected health products, such as contraceptives, iodized salt, oral rehydration salts, soap, safe delivery kits, sanitary napkins, sanitary latrines, and vegetable seeds, at a profit. BRAC also provides them with small loans to undertake other income-enhancing enterprises.

Community health workers receive four weeks of initial training, supplemented by one-day refresher sessions every month. They are trained to treat common illnesses, such as diarrhea, dysentery, the common cold, scabies, anemia, gastric ulcers, and worm infestation. A subset of these workers has also been trained to provide directly observed therapy, short course (DOTS) for tuberculosis and to treat acute respiratory illnesses, particularly pneumonia (Chowdhury and others 1997).

Each community health worker is assigned about 300 households, which she visits once a month. During household visits, she provides health education and treats illnesses. She also uses this opportunity to sell health products. When she encounters an illness she is not trained to manage, she refers the patient to government health centers or to BRAC facilities. While BRAC doctors and other trained health paraprofessionals provide professional supervision, the community health worker is accountable to her village organization and the community she serves.

**Primary
healthcare
understands
health in its
full social
and economic
dimensions**

in hand with the vision of a new international economic order that promised poor countries not only prosperity but also control over their own destiny.

Neither the optimism nor the international commitment lasted long. Some recent commentators attribute the nearly immediate reversal of primary healthcare policies to the idea that the West did not want to put priority-setting responsibilities in the hands of the developing countries (Hall and Taylor 2003). At the time, however, the main rationale for abandoning Alma Ata was affordability, as the debt crisis of the 1980s descended on many of the poorest countries of the world. Some argued that if primary healthcare was too ambitious and too expensive for immediate implementation in countries mired in debt, then a targeted approach aimed at a few of the disease conditions responsible for the highest number of deaths and for which relatively inexpensive, safe, and effective interventions already existed could be a way to have an impact on health in the short term (Walsh and Warren 1979). Much debate ensued, but this selective approach eventually won the day in the international health policy arena. Its rationale became the basis for UNICEF's Child Survival and Development Revolution, launched in 1982. The strategy was to push for massive coverage of a few key interventions that would address the most important causes of child mortality and morbidity. Known by the acronym GOBI and then GOBI-FFF, these interventions were growth monitoring, oral rehydration, breastfeeding, immunization, and then also food supplementation, family planning, and female education.

Several of these interventions have had very substantial effects on child mortality. Oral rehydration therapy has been credited with bringing about dramatic declines in diarrhea-related deaths. Immunization has had a major impact as well. But its fate is, in many ways, emblematic of the dilemmas raised by selective approaches delivered through vertical systems. The Expanded Programme on Immunization, which garnered substantial donor support in the 1980s and 1990s, using a dedicated delivery system, achieved high coverage and had a measurable impact on vaccine-preventable diseases. But even when vaccination programs attained their highest levels of performance, the overall functioning of health systems remained weak. Today, as some donors and implementing agencies withdraw from vaccination programs and turn their resources and attention to new priority diseases, such as HIV/AIDS, coverage has ceased to increase and, in some areas, is slipping.

With hindsight the effect of selective primary healthcare was particularly problematic for maternal mortality. The shift toward community-level, low-cost interventions translated into a push toward training traditional birth attendants as the primary strategy for providing safer delivery care—a strategy that eventually proved largely ineffective in reducing maternal mortality (Campbell 2001), as discussed in chapter 3. While many in the international health field shifted their attention to the community level, the budgets of many countries remained skewed toward urban tertiary hospitals. Squeezed out and

**Structural
adjustment
programs
slashed
spending in the
health sector**

neglected were the crucial first-referral facilities, mostly health centers and district hospitals, on which reduction of maternal mortality so heavily depends (Van Lerberghe, de Bethune, and De Brouwere 1997).

As vertical programs were being deployed in the 1970s and 1980s, often quite separately from the basic health infrastructure, that infrastructure was coming unhinged. Mired in debt, many countries had little choice but to adopt stabilization and structural adjustment programs promoted by the IMF and World Bank requiring them to slash spending in all social sectors, including health. The effect of drastic cutbacks in health sector spending was magnified by the overall impoverishment and dislocation associated with economic crisis and with the policies pressed by the Bretton Woods institutions and adopted by national governments to address that crisis. In some parts of Sub-Saharan Africa, for example, not only was the health system in a state of collapse (Simms, Rowson, and Peattie 2001), "the economic context was experienced locally as a crisis of extended family support systems, a crisis to which social sectors were unable to respond" (Mackintosh 2001, p. 179).

The marketization of healthcare

By the early 1990s health systems were in serious disarray, particularly in Sub-Saharan Africa and parts of Asia. In some quarters of the international health policy world, primary healthcare conjured up not images of self-reliant communities engaged with committed healthcare workers and professionals in locally relevant health structures but images of empty clinics, lacking staff, drugs, and equipment, and a public system riddled with corruption, abuse, and waste (Filmer, Hammer, and Pritchett 2000).

By the 1990s the World Bank had become the leading funder of health sectors, and its view of the problems and prescriptions for solutions dominated the field. The highly influential *World Development Report 1993: Investing in Health* (World Bank 1993) introduced new priority-setting techniques for public spending and ushered in a new orthodoxy in health policy. Drawing on the neoliberal ideology that framed policies of the international financial institutions in other sectors, the core of the new orthodoxy was the view that the private sector could most efficiently meet most healthcare needs and should be allowed—indeed, actively encouraged—to do so. The public sector would be assigned the task of "gap-filling" to correct "market failures." It would provide a set of cost-effective services determined on the basis of burden of disease measures, which would become an "essential service package" offered to the poorest through public sector facilities.

The consequence of this approach was the marketization of healthcare. In every part of the health system (whether nominally public or nominally private), healthcare—professional services, drugs, transport, basic access, and decent, humane treatment—came to be bought and sold. "The marketisation of public services has become so ubiquitous in some countries that parts of

The marketization of public services has become ubiquitous

the health system are more appropriately understood as government-subsidized private services than as a publicly funded service with minor problems with corruption" (Bloom and Standing 2001, p. 9). Health policy, still grounded in an idealized model of public-private sectors, was becoming dangerously disconnected from the reality on the ground.

Bloom and Standing have argued persuasively that instead of premising policy discussions (or prescriptions) on the increasingly insupportable view of discrete public and private health sectors, the situation in many—perhaps most—poor countries can be more accurately described as pluralistic and more appropriately divided into "organized" and "unorganized" categories. The choice that people confront is not between a private health system that charges for a broad menu of high-quality services and a public health system that offers essential services at no or low cost. Instead, all users, rich and poor alike, are confronted with a bewildering array of sources for healthcare, from medicine peddlers to traditional healers to highly trained specialist physicians to civil servants setting up private practices of wildly uneven quality. Indeed, in some places the community health workers who had been given minimal training with the expectation that they would be the backbone of a public health service working under the careful, supportive supervision of health professionals, actually now represent a substantial portion of private sector providers. As Bloom and Standing point out, the weakening of government supervision systems is "an important factor contributing to the de facto marketisation of health services" (Bloom and Standing 2001, p. 9).

For community health workers and other health providers faced with woefully inadequate salaries, the selling of services and even the pilfering of drugs and supplies is sometimes the only way to survive (Ferrinho and others 2004; Van Lerberghe and others 2002). Studies examining workers' survival strategies in the face of health sector reforms help make the link between structural policies and the individual behavior that is often addressed simply as widespread corruption (Kyaddondo and Whyte 2003). (Coping mechanisms and their implications are addressed in chapter 4.)

The marketization of healthcare and the mushrooming of unorganized markets alongside collapsing organized ones have profound ramifications for health equity. Unorganized markets "do their greatest harm to the poor. They suffer the greatest information asymmetries and are much more likely to be at the purchasing end of shoddy or dangerous goods and services" (Standing and Bloom 2002, p. 7).

In societies in which inequality is deeply entrenched, the marketization of healthcare implicitly, but powerfully, legitimizes exclusion (Mackintosh and Tibandebage 2004). Any approach to rebuilding health systems—essential for meeting all of the health Goals—must confront this fact (see chapter 4).

The disintegration of the public health system—or, indeed, the failure ever to reach a functioning point from which it could disintegrate—is a core factor

The
marketization
of healthcare
implicitly, but
powerfully,
legitimizes
exclusion

in the grim failure of many countries to address maternal mortality. Neither the obstetric complications that kill women in pregnancy and childbirth nor the consequences of severe pneumonia or cerebral malaria that kill children can be managed outside of a functioning health system. Even when families are willing to pay—willing to incur truly catastrophic costs (Borghi and others 2003)—women with life-threatening complications need professional, skilled healthcare and the drugs and equipment on which it depends in order to survive.

Population and family planning: a parallel evolution

Slow progress on reducing maternal mortality in most countries—and rapid progress in others—can also be understood from the perspective of a second narrative sketching the evolution of reproductive health policy and its implications for health systems. Historically, family planning programs have been justified and shaped by three different rationales, receiving different weights at different times and places: demography (reducing population growth), health (initially of children but also of women), and human rights (of women and men) (Seltzer 2002). The feminist-defined right of women to control fertility and family size has also had an impact across these policy rationales and in services themselves (Dixon-Mueller 1993).

Does it matter for health system functioning which rationale is the force behind a contraceptive program? Evidence from the family planning field suggests that it does.

In the 1950s and 1960s, censuses conducted in newly independent nations revealed rapid population growth. Some policymakers believed that the ability to provide (publicly funded) social services and generate savings for the investment necessary for economic development would be imperiled if declines in mortality were not accompanied by declines in fertility. International donors, influenced in part by geopolitical concerns, offered support to family planning services in an effort to hasten the demographic transition. The earliest policy and program developments were in South Asia.

Driven primarily by demographic concerns, these early family planning programs were constructed as vertical programs, with their own infrastructure of facilities, staff, logistics, and supplies. In countries such as India, where political energy was intensely focused on family planning as a primary tool of "population control," the distortions to the health system were enormous (Visaria, Jejeebhoy, and Merrick 1999). The fate of auxiliary nurse midwives in the Indian system is a good example. Initially intended as community-based midwives who would provide skilled care for deliveries, auxiliary nurse midwives were de facto converted into family planning workers when they were held to numerical targets for bringing in "contraceptive acceptors" and monitored and held accountable for only this aspect of their job (Mavalankar 1997). While in some cases family planning enhanced the value of auxiliary nurse midwives within their communities, to a certain degree all other aspects

Where was the M in MCH?

of women's health were accorded less importance. Moreover, the reliance on targets, on incentives and disincentives, and on the promotion of sterilization as the only method of contraception created a potentially coercive situation for patients, sowing distrust in the government system as a whole.

In some countries, particularly in Sub-Saharan Africa, health rationales dominated family planning programs and policy (Seltzer 2002). In these settings population growth was rapid, as traditional birth-spacing practices were eroding and motivation for limiting fertility was weak. Governments were concerned primarily with children's health; donors recommended and funded family planning as a child survival strategy. Strong evidence does support the important link between family planning and improved child health and survival (National Research Council Committee on Population Commission on Behavioral and Social Sciences and Education 1989). Maternal and child health (MCH) and family planning programs were the mode of service delivery adopted in many countries (Stewart, Stecklov, and Adewuyi 1999). It was not until the influential 1985 *Lancet* article subtitled "Where Is the M in MCH?" that the international health community recognized what was missing: programs that viewed maternal health primarily as a means to improve the health of children were failing to address the health system capacities necessary to avert the death of mothers (Rosenfield and Maine 1985). Indeed, international actors shared responsibility for the skewing of services. Even programs for improving delivery practices, a concern for many donors in the 1950s and 1960s, were crowded out in the 1970s and 1980s, as the WHO, USAID, and UNICEF turned the bulk of their attention to family planning and child health (Campbell 2001).

Several countries adopted broader approaches. In Malaysia and Sri Lanka family planning services developed in conjunction with an expanding primary healthcare system (including development of a cadre of professional midwives linked to and supported by that system) and a complementary set of policies and services advancing girls' education and women's status more generally. The impact on both fertility and maternal mortality, and even on child mortality, has been dramatic. Once modern contraceptive methods were introduced in these countries' primary healthcare systems, in the 1960s and 1970s, total fertility and maternal mortality fell to quite low levels. As a World Bank study explains, "it can be expected that when a health system provides credible and attractive basic services in key areas of women's health (that is, maternal healthcare and contraceptive care), those services will reinforce each other. Maternal mortality and fertility declines are thus interwoven through increased uptake of both services" (Pathmanathan and others 2003, p. 52).

Human rights rationales for family planning first appeared in international documents in the late 1960s (Seltzer 2002). Although the earliest statements justified the right to decide on the number and spacing of children by its importance for population stabilization and child health (Freedman and Isaacs 1993), with the entering into force of the Convention on the Elimination of All Forms

Maternal mortality and fertility declines are interwoven

of Discrimination against Women (CEDAW) in 1981, the "right to decide freely and responsibly on the number and spacing of their children and to have access to information, education and means to enable them to exercise these rights" (Article 16.1) was codified in formal law as a woman's human right (UN 1979). Indeed, evidence from social science research confirms the position put forward by women's health and rights advocates that, from the perspective of women themselves, contraceptive services are an essential tool in their struggle not only to protect their own health and that of their children but also to participate as full citizens in their societies (Correa 1994; Petchesky and Judd 1998).

From this perspective, it mattered very much how contraceptive services were organized and delivered (Freedman 1995). If "health system functioning" is understood to include the experience of users interacting with that system—and not simply the technical capacity to deliver contraceptives—then a human rights rationale for family planning introduced a range of issues, from technical questions about contraceptive safety to policy questions about who should have a voice in decisions affecting health systems and services (Maine and others 1994). The rights-based, user-centered perspective was an important factor in the policy dialogue and programmatic recommendations that, during the 1980s, increasingly came to see informed choice and access to information, technically competent providers, and a range of contraceptive methods offered in a context of respectful interpersonal relations and an appropriate constellation of services as the key features of good quality of care (Bruce 1990).

By the 1990s a growing body of evidence had confirmed the importance of contraceptive services for health, for human rights, and for reduction in population growth as well. Simultaneously, a substantial research effort was devoted to the question of how best to deliver such services. That research, developed over several decades, overwhelmingly demonstrates that the mere supply of contraceptives is not sufficient to ensure that even women who want to limit or space births can or will use them. Utilization depends on many variables, including factors outside the formal health system, such as gender and age dynamics within households, economic survival strategies, and education. But utilization also depends on the very nature of the services themselves: the quality of care has been shown to have a significant impact on the level of contraceptive use (Koenig, Hossain, and Whittaker 1997; Samara, Buckner, and Tsui 1996; Seltzer 2002).

Quality of care, in turn, requires a functioning health system that can, for example, appropriately integrate an expanded range of contraceptive methods (Diaz and others 1999) or address the problems facing providers so that they can better address client needs (Shelton 2001). A particularly important question relates to the integration of family planning services with the broad set of services necessary to address a range of women's reproductive health concerns, such as reproductive tract infections, HIV/AIDS and other sexually transmitted infections, cervical cancer, antenatal and delivery care, and gender-based violence (Berer 2003b).

Quality of care requires a functioning health system

The ferment within the family planning field reflected larger changes taking place in the post–Cold War world, including the growing recognition that women, as full citizens in their communities and countries, are essential to the development process and that sexual and reproductive health and rights are fundamental to the ability of both women and men to exercise citizenship. At the international policy level, the expanded dialogue on rights, the roles of women, participation, and development culminated in the consensus of the Programme of Action of the International Conference on Population and Development (ICPD) held in Cairo in 1994. That consensus amounted to a paradigm shift that consolidated new thinking that had been emerging in the international health community in response to both new evidence and the growing voices of civil society movements. The ICPD paradigm shift was captured in the concept of reproductive health endorsed by the 179 countries that signed the conference declaration (box 2.2).

Reproductive health entails both an approach to health generally and a set of healthcare services aimed at improving the reproductive and sexual health status of all people (WHO 1999). As an approach, reproductive health actually shares much with the original notion of primary healthcare articulated at Alma Ata in 1978. Reproductive health is understood broadly, linking biomedical to social, economic, and political dimensions, and conceptualized as an essential part of development and a fundamental human right. Translating the commitment to human rights into reproductive health policies and programs means paying new attention to individual dignity and autonomy; to the right to make decisions free from coercion, violence, and discrimination; and to broader systemic questions of equal access and social justice (Copelon and Petchesky 1995; Helzner 2002).

This brief account has exposed the perennial tension that exists between strategies, such as primary healthcare and reproductive health, committed to the development of integrated health systems as part of equitable development on the one hand and vertical programs, such as immunization or contraceptive delivery, often supported by outside donors looking for short-term impact on discrete health outcomes, on the other. But the deterioration of healthcare systems has rendered this dichotomy almost moot. Whether due to vertical programs that draw off the resources of fragile health systems, to the impact of macroeconomic conditions and policies, to poor management, or simply to blind neglect, it is now indisputable that health systems are in deep trouble. With the resurgence of tuberculosis and malaria and the devastating rise of HIV/AIDS, this stark fact is once again laid bare. There is serious question about whether tuberculosis or HIV/AIDS can be effectively managed without strengthening health systems more generally (Buve, Kalibala, and McIntyre 2003; Mahendradhata and others 2003).

As the world swings toward addressing HIV/AIDS with a new seriousness of purpose, a new page in the narrative of global health policy is being written. The

Box 2.2
The UN International Conference on Population and Development definitions of reproductive health and reproductive rights

Source: UN 1994.

The Programme for Action of the UN International Conference on Population and Development defines both reproductive health and reproductive rights:

Reproductive health is a state of complete physical, mental and social well-being and not merely the absence of disease or infirmity, in all matters relating to the reproductive system and to its functions and processes. Reproductive health therefore implies that people are able to have a satisfying and safe sex life and that they have the capability to reproduce and the freedom to decide if, when and how often to do so. Implicit in this last condition are the right of men and women to be informed and to have access to safe, effective, affordable and acceptable methods of family planning of their choice, as well as other methods of their choice for regulation of fertility which are not against the law, and the right of access to appropriate healthcare services that will enable women to go safely through pregnancy and childbirth and provide couples with the best chance of having a healthy infant. In line with the above definition of reproductive health, reproductive healthcare is defined as the constellation of methods, techniques and services that contribute to reproductive health and well-being through preventing and solving reproductive health problems. It also includes sexual health, the purpose of which is the enhancement of life and personal relations, and not merely counseling and care related to reproduction and sexually transmitted diseases (paragraph 7.2).

Bearing in mind the above definition, reproductive rights embrace certain human rights that are already recognized in national laws, international human rights documents and other consensus documents. These rights rest on the recognition of the basic right of all couples and individuals to decide freely and responsibly the number, spacing and timing of their children and to have the information and means to do so, and the right to attain the highest standard of sexual and reproductive health. It also includes their right to make decisions concerning reproduction free of discrimination, coercion and violence, as expressed in human rights documents. In the exercise of this right, they should take into account the needs of their living and future children and their responsibilities towards the community. The promotion of the responsible exercise of these rights for all people should be the fundamental basis for government- and community-supported policies and programmes in the area of reproductive health, including family planning. As part of their commitment, full attention should be given to the promotion of mutually respectful and equitable gender relations and particularly to meeting the educational and service needs of adolescents to enable them to deal in a positive and responsible way with their sexuality (paragraph 7.3).

question is whether the Millennium Development Goals, and the strategies they inspire, will enable that page to be written well, to have lasting effect on all aspects of health and on the critical role that health systems will play in strengthening—or tearing apart—the fabric of society in poor countries around the globe.

Evidence and the challenge of scaling up

The central argument of this report is that dramatic, meaningful, sustainable progress toward improving child, maternal, and reproductive health requires a shift in perspective and mindset. The argument builds on the crucial distinction

Health systems are complex structures into which new interventions cannot simply be wedged

between an evidence-based understanding of the medical, behavioral, or public health interventions that will successfully address the primary causes of child health and maternal mortality and morbidity and an evidence-based understanding of and approach to the social, political, economic, and institutional structures that will enable societies—locally, nationally, globally—to ensure that all people have access to those interventions (Bryce and others 2003).

These are two dramatically different exercises. In recent decades much work in the public health field has focused on the first, on identifying the primary causes of poor health, including their prevalence and distribution, and developing an evidence-based understanding of the interventions that will work to addresses those causes. There is broad consensus on the methodology for evaluating evidence of the efficacy of interventions. The randomized controlled trial is widely accepted as the "gold standard," though many other techniques are used to produce valuable evidence that is considered in setting health policy. That evidence base has then been extended through economic analysis of cost-effectiveness, as typified by the World Bank's burden of disease work and the priority-setting techniques articulated in *World Development Report 1993* (World Bank 1993). Building on the concept of disability-adjusted life years (DALYs), the evidence of cost-effectiveness is used to arrive at "best buys" and the "essential service packages" that have been promoted by major international donors over the past decade.

The transition from efficacy of interventions to effectiveness of delivery strategies is where we so often lose our way. If efficacy is "proven" by techniques such as the randomized controlled trial, which screens out the noise of confounding variables, then the techniques to assess the effectiveness of delivery strategies and to set priorities for health sector policy must do just the opposite. They must take into account—they must even grow out of—precisely the messy, contradictory, dissonant noises of real life. In this sense, "delivery strategy" is a misleading term, implying a one-way flow, almost as a postal service organizes to deliver a letter. In fact, health systems and the health sector need to be approached as a dynamic, complex structure into which new interventions cannot simply be wedged. Over and over again, international strategies built on disease epidemiology simply assume that the societal structures to "deliver" those strategies exist and function. And over and over again, such strategies fail to have the expected impact. In subsequent evaluations the obstacles are identified—but the epidemiology alone yields no new strategies for surmounting them, only new strategies for avoiding them.

This will no longer work. We need to grapple with the true systemic obstacles to scaling up and to access, utilization, and equity—and so to dramatic improvements in maternal, child, and reproductive health. The ultimate solutions will include the infrastructure and resource requirements to deliver priority interventions, but that cannot be the starting point of the analysis of scaling up. Instead, a second line of inquiry, analysis, and evidence-building needs to

Inquiry, analysis, and evidence-building need to include the social and political dimensions of health

be opened up—one that begins, not ends, with the social and political dimensions of health and healthcare as they are experienced by the people whose lives make up the grim statistics that are the focus of the Goals.

That analytic and evidentiary problem is distinct from the equally important exercise of identifying social, economic, and other environmental (non-physiological) determinants of health and disease. Identifying such determinants—and understanding the mechanisms through which they influence biological status and mortality and morbidity levels—provides a more accurate and refined picture of the importance of interventions outside the health sector. For example, virtually all of the health conditions identified in the Millennium Development Goals correlate with income poverty. But the solution to good health is not simply reducing poverty—full stop. Understanding the causal link is key.

For some health conditions, such as the mortality of children under five, improvements in the basic living environment—water, sanitation, nutrition— that can come with economic growth will have a powerful effect, because of the huge influence that malnutrition and infectious disease have on children's health in the postneonatal period (Black, Morris, and Bryce 2003). For other health problems, however, such as maternal mortality, improvements in living conditions will, by themselves, make very little difference, because the correlation between poverty reduction and maternal mortality reduction works through the impact that economic growth can have on the health system (Wagstaff 2002). Improved living conditions do not substantially change the chance that a woman will experience a life-threatening obstetric complication during pregnancy or childbirth, but access to a health system that can treat such complications will save women's lives and dramatically lower maternal mortality (Lule and others 2003; Maine 1991). For other aspects of maternal health, such as preventing sexually transmitted infections, poverty reduction can have a significant impact when it facilitates access to education, control over income, and a supportive legal system. Poverty reduction affects HIV/AIDS risk status in part through its effect on women's empowerment (Matinga and McConville 2002).

These multisectoral analyses are, of course, critical for improving health and must be part of overall MDG-based strategies. But the focus of this report is on the core challenge for health sector strategies. That challenge is typically characterized as one of "scaling up." In the health literature, "scaling up" is undertheorized and underconceptualized. Often the tacit assumption is that scaling up is largely a matter of doing the same things that have been proven in small-scale demonstration projects but extending them to wider geographic areas and larger, more diverse populations. The obstacles to scaling up are identified as insufficient capacity and resources: not enough money, not enough human resources, not enough managerial skills, not enough information, not enough political will.

Scaling up must be approached systematically

While all of these deficiencies do indeed exist and must certainly be addressed, the aim of this report is to begin to identify and approach the problems systemically (Potter and Brough 2004). This means building a far stronger base of understanding of the complex functioning of the health system (broadly defined) in social and political life. With that foundation, the deficiencies in resources can be addressed in a context that can make strategies more pertinent and effective.

Chapter 3

Health status and key interventions

Understanding key technical interventions for improving maternal health and child health and recognizing how these interventions relate to one another is a prerequisite for making strategic choices about health sector policy and programs. This chapter lays out disease-specific causes of mortality and morbidity, presents estimates (where possible) of the prevalence or the burden of disease associated with those conditions, and describes the primary interventions to address each.

Connecting maternal health and child health

Although child health and maternal health interventions are examined in separate subsections, as lived experience and as a matter of biology they are sometimes—but not always—closely related. The chapter uses a lifecycle approach and the concept of sexual and reproductive health and rights to explicate these relationships. The lifecycle framework is useful for understanding connections over time, as health events at one stage influence health at a later stage across the life span and influence the next generation through the life cycle. The sexual and reproductive health and rights framework is useful because it grounds us in the all-important social, cultural, and political contexts of health. In particular, it reminds us that none of the health interventions considered here "falls like manna from heaven" (Wagstaff and Claeson 2004). Not only must the health system be organized to ensure its availability, but—barring coercion—each woman must make an active decision to use it for herself or her children. That decision will be made from within the tighter or looser web of constraints that bind her specific lived reality (Petchesky and Judd 1998; Shepard 2000).

A sequence of interactions and events frames the experience of sexual and reproductive health over the lifespan (figure 3.1).[1] The conceptual map shown in figure 3.1 is two-dimensional, but as its authors note, the map could also

Figure 3.1

Conceptual map of sexual and reproductive health

Source: Adapted from Cottingham and Myntti 2002. Reprinted with permission from MIT Press.

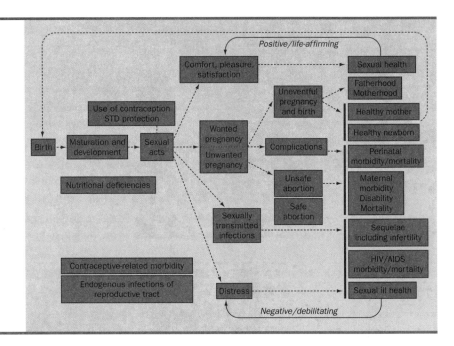

be imagined in layers (Cottingham and Myntti 2002). The base layer is the framework depicted in figure 3.1, including processes (such as maturation), events (such as pregnancy), and outcomes (such as pleasure or distress, health or disease)—simply moving through the stages of life. Superimposed on this base could be a layer of social and institutional arrangements that influence the way in which the different stages are experienced. These social and institutional arrangements include intimate and family relationships; community institutions, such as schools, religious institutions, the media, and the market; preventive and curative healthcare services; and governmental institutions, including the laws and policies they are responsible for implementing.

Such social and institutional arrangements influence the way events depicted in the map are experienced, because these arrangements function as the repositories of power and resources that individuals draw on to protect their health and prevent or treat disease (Link and Phelan 1995). These resources include not simply economic resources but also such nonmonetary assets as social networks, prestige, education, information, and legal claims. For example, a woman who, because of access to resources such as education, legal claims to gender equality, and strong social networks, has been able to obtain formal employment and achieve financial independence is likely to have greater power to negotiate the conditions of intimate relationships, including use of contraception, and to have the resources to obtain the contraceptive that best meets her needs. The constellation of power and resources—the assets— that this woman accesses through multiple social and institutional arrangements thus influences her experience of the box in figure 3.1 labeled "use of contraception/STD protection" and the subsequent sexual and reproductive

Women's agency is positively correlated with women's health and children's health

health stages in the map (sexual acts, wanted/unwanted pregnancy, comfort/pleasure/satisfaction, and so on).

These assets are not evenly distributed in any society. Gender, class, race, and ethnicity are intersecting social hierarchies that often act as a grid of inequality through which an individual's experience of the social and institutional arrangements is filtered. Imagined this way, the map helps conceptualize the mechanisms by which inequality in access to power and resources ultimately affects health.

The map also clarifies the critical relationship between sexuality and reproduction, making the important point that many aspects of sexuality are separate from reproduction and have consequences—both positive and negative—for physical and mental health independent of pregnancy and childbearing (Miller 2000). This point becomes critical for developing effective interventions, including strategies for preventing the transmission of HIV. It is also a crucial point in understanding some of the controversy that has sometimes blocked health interventions.

Sexuality and reproduction—both separately and together—are at the core of the intimate, economic, and institutional relationships that characterize both women's oppression and their potential for determining the course of their own lives, that is, for their agency. As the UN Millennium Project Task Force on Education and Gender Equality elaborates in its report, agency is a basic component of gender equality, itself a Goal. As assessed through various indicators of women's status and empowerment (such as control over income and education), agency is in turn positively correlated with aspects of women's health (Lule and others 2003; Barnett and Stein 1998) and children's health (Hobcraft 1993; Wagstaff and Claeson 2004). Thus agency becomes a core principle of sexual and reproductive health, best expressed in the legal concept of sexual and reproductive rights (see box 2.2).

Figure 3.1 refers to both men and women and to both fatherhood and motherhood. The health literature rarely connects the health of children to the health or even the actions of their fathers, apart from genetics.[2] In societies gripped by epidemics of sexually transmitted infections, including HIV/AIDS, this is a dangerous omission. Although newborns contract HIV from their mothers, virtually all HIV-positive pregnant women contracted HIV from the men with whom they have sexual relationships. The sexual and reproductive health of men, and men's actions, can therefore have a significant effect on the health of both women and their children.

Child health

Important gains were made in child survival during the second half of the twentieth century (Freedman and others 2003). Globally, the under-five mortality rate (the number of deaths per 1,000 live births per year) declined from 159.3 in 1955–59 to 70.4 in 1995–99 (Ahmad, Lopez, and Inoue 2000). The decline

In parts of the
world, progress
in reducing
child mortality
has stalled

was most rapid during the 1970s and 1980s. Although the rate of decline slowed during the 1990s, child mortality still fell about 15 percent during that decade. This was an impressive achievement given the events that affected international public health development programs toward the end of the twentieth century—economic stagnation, increasing political instability and conflict, growing resistance to antimalarial drugs, and the relentless spread of the HIV/AIDS pandemic, to name a few. Overall the number of children under the age of five who die in the world each year fell from about 13 million in 1980 to an estimated 10.8 million by the end of the century (Black, Morris, and Bryce 2003).

Despite these gains, more recent trends suggest that there is serious reason to be concerned. The rate of mortality decline seems to have slowed considerably. Part of the decline reflects the fact that very low rates have already been achieved in Europe, the Americas, the Western Pacific, and the Eastern Mediterranean (to use the geographical divisions of the WHO). But the decline also reflects failure to make progress in Sub-Saharan Africa and Southeast Asia. In fact, in a few countries, notably those in southern Africa, where AIDS is taking its greatest toll, child mortality rates have stagnated and even begun to increase.

In 2003 a major review of child mortality was undertaken that addressed disease-specific causes of death and the potential of available public health interventions to prevent them. From a series of articles published in *The Lancet* and in a number of meetings held to discuss the findings and recommendations, six themes emerged:

- A small number of diseases and underlying biological factors are responsible for the large majority of childhood deaths.
- The Goal for reducing child mortality cannot be met without a major effort to reduce newborn deaths—those that occur during the first four weeks of life.
- Existing interventions, if implemented through efficient and effective strategies (in a way that reaches those who need to be reached), could prevent a substantial proportion of existing mortality.
- Child mortality is distributed in an extremely uneven manner. Not only between regions and countries but also within countries, socioeconomic inequities, to a large degree, determine which children live and which ones die.
- Existing interventions can be implemented most effectively in countries where health systems work best.
- Child health programs in developing countries are grossly underfunded; major new investments will be needed in order to achieve the Goal.

Geographical distribution and causes of death

Some 10.8 million children are estimated to die before the age of five every year (Black, Morris, and Bryce 2003). Forty-one percent of these deaths occur

A few diseases are responsible for the majority of childhood deaths

in Sub-Saharan Africa, and 34 percent occur in South Asia. Just six countries account for half of all childhood deaths (table 3.1), and 90 percent of deaths occur in 42 countries.

Five diseases—diarrhea, pneumonia, malaria, measles, and AIDS—are responsible for an estimated 56 percent of deaths in children under five (table 3.2). In addition, about one-third of all deaths occur during the first month of life and have conventionally been grouped together as "neonatal deaths." These have been attributed to a small number of biological conditions: complications of prematurity (27 percent), sepsis and pneumonia (26 percent), birth asphyxia (23 percent), and tetanus (7 percent) (Lawn and others 2005). These neonatal deaths have been relatively neglected in programs aimed at reducing child mortality and, for this reason, they are a special focus of this report.

The impact of these causes of death varies significantly across regions. For example, while deaths from AIDS are not likely to have an appreciable impact on child mortality rates in settings in which HIV prevalence is low, pediatric AIDS is much more important in parts of Sub-Saharan Africa, where prevalence is high (Mahy 2003). The authors of the *Lancet* series grouped the 42 countries that account for 90 percent of annual childhood deaths into five distinct epidemiological profiles, based on the proportion of deaths due to each of the most common causes of child mortality (Black, Morris, and Bryce 2003). In two of these groups, AIDS accounted for more than 10 percent of all under-five mortality; in the smallest group, AIDS was the leading disease-specific cause of death, accounting for 23 percent of under-five deaths. Although the

Table 3.1

Six countries with highest number of annual deaths of children under age five
Thousands

Source: Black, Morris, and Bryce 2003.

Country	Deaths per year
India	2,402
Nigeria	834
China	784
Pakistan	565
Democratic Republic of Congo	484
Ethiopia	472
Total of six countries	5,541
Global annual deaths	10,800

Table 3.2

Causes of deaths of children under age five
Percent

Note: Figures are based on data from the 42 countries that account for 90 percent of all deaths.

Source: Adapted from Black, Morris, and Bryce 2003.

Disease or condition	Share of under-five deaths
Neonatal	33
Diarrhea	22
Pneumonia	21
Malaria	9
Measles	1
AIDS	3
Other	9

Deaths from injuries are becoming proportionally more important

countries in this group account for only 1.1 million childhood deaths a year, a small proportion of the global total, for them the AIDS problem has substantial programmatic implications. Many children in these countries are living with AIDS, and many uninfected children have been orphaned by AIDS and may be at greater risk of morbidity and mortality due to their social circumstances. Interventions for the prevention and treatment of pediatric AIDS, a chronic condition, or for the care and support of AIDS orphans and other vulnerable children may be expensive and complicated to implement; providing such care risks drawing resources from other, more common, more easily treatable conditions. But no matter how difficult it may be, for these countries AIDS control is clearly a priority of the highest order. Outside of this relatively small number of countries in Sub-Saharan Africa, however, the contribution of AIDS to under-five mortality is small and will probably remain so (Bellagio Study Group on Child Survival 2003).

In Asia the situation is different. There, mortality from traditional infectious diseases has been substantially reduced. Neonatal causes have emerged as the leading cause of infant mortality, accounting for almost 60 percent of all deaths in the first year of life, according to a series of surveys recently conducted under the auspices of the Alliance for Safe Children and UNICEF (2004).[3] The same surveys reported that injuries are a leading cause of death in 1- to 4-year-old children in Asia, causing more than 40 percent of mortality, equal to the proportion caused by all of the common infectious diseases combined. Among children under five, drowning is by far the leading cause of death, representing more than 60 percent of all injury deaths. Drowning is also the leading cause of injury deaths among 5- to 9-year-olds, with road traffic accidents and intentional injuries increasingly important in the later childhood years.

Deaths from injuries are becoming proportionally more important as other causes of death are being reduced. If substantial progress toward the Goal of reducing child mortality is made in Africa, through the control of common infectious diseases, injuries could emerge as a leading cause of death there as well.

And yet, few programs have been directed at preventing injuries. Surveillance data on injury are difficult, if not impossible, to obtain in the absence of surveys such as those conducted by the Alliance for Safe Children and UNICEF. Most health information reporting is from health facilities, whereas most injury deaths occur in the community. Because vital registration systems are weak in most developing countries, and sample sizes for most nationally representative surveys—such as the Demographic and Health Surveys and Multiple Indicator Cluster Surveys—are too small to reveal a comprehensive epidemiology of childhood mortality, deaths due to injury fall below the radar screen. As the importance of deaths from injury grows, and as the deadline for achieving the Goals approaches, behavioral change and other interventions aimed at preventing these deaths will need to be further developed, communicated, and implemented.

**Low birthweight
also remains
a significant
public health
problem**

Describing the causes of childhood deaths is not as simple as table 3.2 suggests. At least two issues complicate attempts to attribute deaths to a single cause. For one thing, two or more potentially fatal infectious diseases of childhood can occur simultaneously, particularly if they are associated with shared risk factors. Unsanitary environmental conditions in the home, for example, can contribute to the incidence of both diarrhea and pneumonia. When these occur together, and the child dies, assigning the death to one or the other cause is difficult.

Second, although not listed specifically as a cause of death, undernutrition (low weight-for-age) contributes greatly to child mortality. Mildly underweight children under age five are twice as likely as their nourished peers to die; moderately underweight children are five times as likely to die, and severely undernourished children are eight times as likely to do so (Pelletier, Frongillo, and Habicht 1993). Overall, 52.5 percent of all postneonatal childhood deaths are associated with undernutrition: 60.7 percent of diarrhea deaths, 57.3 percent of malaria deaths, 52.3 percent of pneumonia deaths, and 44.8 percent of measles. Ensuring the adequate nutrition of children under five could prevent more than 2.5 million deaths from these diseases (Caulfield and others 2004).

Low birthweight (less than 2,500 grams) also remains a significant public health problem in many parts of the world. Shrimpton (2003) estimates that low birthweight is a feature of 25 percent of all births in South Asia, 12 percent in Latin America, and 10 percent in Africa. These are probably gross underestimates, since the data come mostly from hospital deliveries in urban areas. But the importance of low birthweight is clear: an increase of 100 grams in mean birthweight has been associated with a 30–50 percent reduction in neonatal mortality (Shrimpton 2003).

Focus on nutrition

Early childhood malnutrition is strongly influenced by fetal growth, and low birthweight is strongly determined by maternal influences. In fact, it has been suggested that more than half of low birthweight is attributable to maternal nutritional factors (Ramakrishnan 2004). These factors are not ones that can be affected by improved care during pregnancy, however. A clear distinction must be made between women's health and maternal health. A principal emphasis of this report, and that of the Task Force on Education and Gender Equality, is that attention to women's health throughout the life cycle, and not only during pregnancy, childbirth, and lactation, is essential in order to achieve several of the Goals, particularly the child health Goal.

In addition to undernutrition, specific micronutrient deficiencies have been shown to play a major role in child mortality. Several reviews of vitamin A supplementation trials have shown that such programs can reduce mortality among children between 6 months and 5 years by 20–50 percent (Beaton and others 1993; Ramakrishnan and Martorell 1998).

The importance of adequate nutrition cannot be over-emphasized

Zinc deficiency is becoming increasingly recognized as an important contributor to child mortality. Zinc supplementation may reduce the incidence of diarrhea by 18 percent and pneumonia by 41 percent; used therapeutically for diarrhea, it shortens the duration and probability of recurrence in the several months following the illness (Walker and Black 2004). The impact of zinc supplementation on malaria incidence is less conclusive. The *Lancet* series reports that zinc given as a preventive intervention can reduce child mortality by 4 percent and that an additional 4 percent of mortality can be averted by making it an essential component of the treatment of diarrhea (Jones and others 2003).

Maternal iron deficiency and its associated anemia is another important risk factor for low birthweight (its role in maternal mortality is discussed below). In malaria-endemic areas, *P. falciparum* infection is the principal cause of anemia during pregnancy and may be responsible for an estimated 8–14 percent of all low-birthweight babies, and 3–8 percent of all infant deaths (Roll Back Malaria 2004).

In short, the importance of adequate nutrition, including micronutrients, throughout the life cycle cannot be overemphasized.

Focus on neonatal mortality

Most of the reduction in child mortality during the 1990s occurred in older children, who had already survived the neonatal period. Because this was not accompanied by an appreciable reduction of neonatal deaths, these began to account for a higher proportion of total under-five mortality. Indeed, by 2000, 37 percent of the 10.8 million deaths in children under the age of five occurred during the neonatal period (WHO forthcoming). A 50 percent reduction in neonatal mortality between 2000 and 2015 is essential if Goal 4 is to be achieved (Healthy Newborn Partnership 2004).

Of the approximately 4 million neonatal deaths each year, 99 percent occur in low- and middle-income countries (Lawn and others 2005). While nearly 40 percent of all neonatal deaths occur in South Asia, the highest rates of neonatal mortality, exceeding 45 per 1,000 live births per year, are found largely in Sub-Saharan Africa, where nearly 30 percent of all neonatal deaths take place.

Enormous disparities exist between rich and poor countries. A mother in West Africa, for instance, is 30 times as likely as a mother in Western Europe to lose her newborn in the first month of life (Save the Children 2001). Within countries poor families are more likely to suffer the loss of newborns: the neonatal mortality rate among the poorest 20 percent of the population in Ghana and India, for instance, is almost twice that of the richest 20 percent, and in Bolivia the two figures differ by a factor of more than five (Healthy Newborn Partnership 2004).

Also associated with high neonatal mortality are the low levels of education, nutrition, and health of women. Poor access to health services plays an important role. Gender bias in some parts of the world may also result in compromised care-seeking for newborn girls (Dadhich and Paul 2004).

Systemic infections account for about one-fourth of neonatal deaths

Despite the huge number of deaths, the health of newborn babies has been relatively neglected by the global public health community, for several reasons (Lawn and others 2004). Most neonatal deaths are unseen and undocumented. In rich countries childbirth is accompanied by a fanfare, but in many poorer countries childbirth is accompanied by apprehension for the mother and baby, who may remain hidden at home, in confinement. Local traditions frequently dictate that the baby remain unnamed for one to six weeks, reflecting a sense of fatalism and cultural acceptance of high mortality in the earliest stages of life.

Yet interventions capable of saving newborn lives and strategies for their implementation exist, even for poor, rural areas. There is a misconception that newborn survival interventions can be delivered only through high-tech, high-cost, intensive care services. In the United Kingdom, the fall in neonatal mortality rate from more than 30 deaths per 1,000 live births in 1940 to 10 in 1979 coincided with the introduction of free antenatal care, improved care during childbirth, and the increased availability of antibiotics (Lawn and others 2004).

Some developing countries have improved neonatal health by investing in primary care. In Sri Lanka the neonatal mortality rate declined to 22 deaths per 1,000 live births by 1980, before the first neonatal intensive care unit was established (Paul and Singh 2004). Utilization of antenatal care services is nearly universal in Sri Lanka, and 86 percent of births occur at government hospitals, where services are free and attended by a cadre of skilled hospital midwives. The southern Indian state of Kerala has achieved a neonatal mortality rate of 10 deaths per 1,000 live births per year, far below the national average of 44, with hardly any specialized newborn care units (Dadhich and Paul 2004).

Systemic infections, usually pneumonia, septicemia, diarrhea, or tetanus, account for 36 percent of neonatal deaths worldwide (table 3.3). Prematurity and birth asphyxia each account for about a quarter of neonatal deaths, and these causes dominate during the first week of life, when almost 75 percent of all neonatal deaths occur. Low birthweight is the most important underlying risk factor, associated with 60–80 percent of all deaths during the neonatal period. Low birthweight is due to preterm birth, to growth restriction in utero, or both (Kramer 1987). A preterm baby has a much higher risk of death than a baby born at term with growth restriction. Preterm birth is both a direct cause of death and a major underlying cause of death, especially death from neonatal infections. But many of these deaths can be prevented with closer attention to basic elements of care, including warmth, feeding, and early treatment (Daga and others 1988; Aleman and others 1998; Datta 1985).

Interventions to reduce child mortality rates

Knowing the causes of death of children under five allows interventions to be developed that reduce the incidence of potentially fatal diseases or treat those conditions when they occur. Of course, child mortality can also be reduced by increased economic growth and, by extension, improved social and economic

Table 3.3	Direct cause	Share of deaths
Causes of neonatal mortality *Percent*	Preterm birth	27
	Sepsis, pneumonia	26
	Asphyxia	23
Source: Lawn and others 2005.	Congenital malformations	7
	Tetanus	7
	Diarrhea	3
	Other (jaundice, bleeding)	7

circumstances of families and households. Interventions that are implemented outside the health sector, such as improvements in the quantity and quality of water or improved environmental conditions, also play a role. Nevertheless, it is widely believed that the development and implementation of a relatively small number of safe and effective disease-specific interventions explain much of the dramatic decline in child mortality rates during the last quarter of the twentieth century. The discussion of interventions in this report is therefore restricted to those that have traditionally been implemented through the health sector in developing countries.

The second article in the *Lancet* series lists 23 interventions (15 preventive and 8 curative) that are most likely to have an impact on child mortality (Jones and others 2003). Based on estimated mortality in 2000 and assuming universal (100 percent) coverage with these interventions, the *Lancet* authors estimated the number of childhood deaths that could be prevented (table 3.4).

Taking into account the fact that several interventions can contribute to the saving of a single life, the *Lancet* authors estimate that of the 10 million deaths in the 42 countries in which 90 percent of the world's childhood deaths occurred in 2000, 6 million could have been prevented.

A few points are of special note. Several interventions, if fully implemented, could reduce child mortality by at least 5 percent. These include breastfeeding,[4] oral rehydration therapy, use of insecticide-treated bednets, appropriate weaning and use of complementary foods, use of antibiotics for the treatment of antenatal sepsis and childhood pneumonias, and zinc supplementation.

Many of the interventions that are of proven effectiveness can be implemented at the household and community levels and depend largely on the behaviors of mothers and families; the role of health facilities and healthcare professionals is supportive, not essential. More emphasis is needed on what can be accomplished within communities, but the facility side of health systems also needs to be strengthened. The treatment of life-threatening illnesses, including pneumonia and severe malaria, not to mention emergency obstetric care (addressed fully in other sections of this report), depends on competent healthcare professionals being present in fully equipped health facilities on a permanent basis.[5]

Current coverage with many of the most essential interventions, including those that are of proven effectiveness, is quite low, ranging from 1 percent

Intervention	Deaths (thousands)	Preventable proportion of all deaths (percent)
Preventive interventions		
Breastfeeding	1,301	13
Insecticide-treated materials	691	7
Complementary feeding	587	6
Zinc supplementation	459	5
Clean delivery	411	4
Hib vaccine	403	4
Water, sanitation, and hygiene	326	3
Antenatal steroids	264	3
Newborn temperature management	227	2
Vitamin A supplementation	225	2
Tetanus toxoid	161	2
Nevirapine and appropriate feeding	150	2
Antibiotics for premature rupture of membranes	133	1
Measles vaccine	103	1
Intermittent presumptive treatment of malaria during pregnancy	22	<1
Treatment interventions		
Oral rehydration therapy	1,477	15
Antibiotics for neonatal sepsis	583	6
Antibiotics for pneumonia	577	6
Antimalarials	467	5
Zinc supplementation	394	4
Newborn resuscitation	359	4
Antibiotics for dysentery	310	3
Vitamin A	8	<1

Table 3.4

Estimated number of preventable deaths of children under age five

In the 42 countries that account for 90 percent of child mortality, assuming 100 percent coverage

Note: Interventions include only those for which the *Lancet* authors determined that there is at least limited evidence of an effect.

Source: Jones and others 2003.

for the intermittent presumptive treatment of malaria during pregnancy to 68 percent for measles vaccine. Only breastfeeding, with a mean estimated coverage of 90 percent, approaches full coverage—although the prevalence of exclusive breastfeeding (recommended for the first six months of life, and on the basis of which the potential impact of breastfeeding was calculated) is considerably lower (UNICEF 2003c). And even in this case, culture and tradition, not interventions carried out within the health sector, are probably most responsible for high coverage rates.

Global health policies today prioritize a number of interventions that are directed at diseases that are not responsible for most childhood deaths. Emphasis on the prevention of mother-to-child transmission of AIDS, for example, (which currently accounts for only 3 percent of global deaths, most of them in a relatively small number of countries in Africa) may divert resources from increasing coverage with oral rehydration therapy or antibiotics for pneumonia.

About two-thirds of current child mortality could be reduced in a short period

But the point is not that some important intervention programs should be sacrificed for the sake of others. Shifting scant resources around within a very small envelope will, in the end, accomplish nothing: forcing proponents of child survival interventions to compete with those of maternal mortality reduction or pitting advocates of expanded vaccination programs against those calling for increased access to treatment for common childhood illnesses is a no-win strategy. Instead, the resources must be made available that would allow for all high-priority child intervention programs to be fully implemented.

Jones and others (2003) note that their estimates of lives saved are conservative, since they include only interventions for which cause-specific mortality prevention data are available. Their report does not analyze the potential impact of birth spacing, for example, which may reduce child mortality by almost 20 percent in India and by more than 10 percent in Nigeria (the two countries with the highest number of deaths of children under five). In addition, new interventions are on the horizon. A rotavirus vaccine, a vaccine to prevent pneumococcal pneumonia, and a malaria vaccine are in various advanced stages of development and could make substantial contributions to reducing mortality before 2015.[6]

This brief review suggests that about two-thirds of current child mortality could be reduced in a relatively short period of time if existing interventions were scaled up to the point that they were made available to and utilized by 100 percent of the population in developing countries. This is, of course, a very big if. This reduction cannot be realized if the international child health community continues to go about its business as usual. The Goal for child health is within reach, but only if the kind of bold and assertive changes called for in this report are implemented without delay.

Interventions for reducing neonatal mortality

Recent and ongoing work has resulted in the identification of a number of evidence-based interventions that can prevent neonatal deaths (Bhutta and others 2005; Darmstadt and others 2005). Interventions to prevent neonatal deaths can be divided into three groups: a universal package, which should be available in all settings; situational interventions, for use in areas with particular epidemiological characteristics, such as a high prevalence of malaria; and additional interventions, which could be implemented where stronger health systems capable of supporting them exist (table 3.5).

Predictions based on the recent application of the Marginal Budgeting for Bottlenecks tool developed by the World Bank and UNICEF in five Sub-Saharan countries and in five states in India indicate that, if taken to scale, existing neonatal survival interventions could prevent 60 percent of neonatal deaths in South Asia and 70 percent of neonatal deaths in Sub-Saharan Africa, where baseline neonatal mortality rates are higher. In the *Lancet* series, Jones and others (2003) and Lawn and others (2004) estimated a potential global reduction

Table 3.5		Interventions		
Evidence-based priority interventions for improving neonatal survival				**Additional interventions** *(where the healthcare system has additional capacity and the neonatal mortality rate is lower, for example, transition countries)*
PIH: pregnancy induced hypertension.	**Timing of intervention**	**Interventions for universal coverage** *(priority interventions for high-mortality settings)*	**Situational interventions** *(where specific conditions are prevalent)*	
a. HIV infection is not a cause of neonatal deaths, but the antenatal and postnatal periods are critical entry points for prevention of mother-to-child transmission interventions. *Source:* Darmstadt and others 2005.	Antenatal	• Antenatal care package • Tetanus toxoid immunization • Detection and management of PIH/eclampsia • Birth and emergency preparedness • Syphilis screening and treatment • Breastfeeding promotion	• Malaria presumptive intermittent therapy • Prevention of mother-to-child transmission of HIV[a]	• Peri-conceptual folate supplementation • Detection and treatment of asymptomatic bacteriuria • Antibiotics for preterm premature rupture of membranes • Antenatal cortico-steroids for preterm delivery
	Intrapartum	• Clean delivery practices • Newborn resuscitation • Skilled obstetric care • Comprehensive emergency obstetric care		
	Postnatal	• Essential care package • Hygienic cord and skin care • Hypothermia prevention and management • Breastfeeding promotion (immediate, exclusive) • Extra care of low-birthweight infants (extra attention to warmth, hygiene, feeding) • Community case management for pneumonia • Emergency management for sepsis and very low birthweight	• Prevention of mother-to-child transmission of HIV[a]	

Why do 10.8 million children die each year?

of up to 55 percent of neonatal deaths, but the package of interventions on which that work was based did not include important interventions aimed at maintaining the health of mothers, including emergency obstetric care.

The new estimates show that universal (99 percent) coverage of these interventions could avert 41–72 percent of global neonatal deaths (Darmstadt and others 2005). Assuming that the recent gains in survival rates of older children are maintained, reductions of neonatal deaths of these magnitudes in Asia and Africa would ensure achievement of the Goal.

Inequities in child health

If child mortality is due to a limited number of known causes, and if interventions for preventing or treating those causes are currently available, why do 10.8 million children die each year? A 2004 World Bank report found that none of 47 countries in Sub-Saharan Africa was "on track" to reduce child mortality by two-thirds by 2015 (Wagstaff and Claaeson 2004).

Poverty clearly influences survival rates. The poorer people are, the more likely their children will die in childhood. In fact, globally, there is a twenty-fold difference in child mortality between rich and poor (table 3.6). This influence of wealth on child survival is evident in countries throughout the world (figure 3.2).

Table 3.6

Under-five mortality rates, by country income level
Deaths per 1,000 live births per year
Source: UNICEF 2004.

Income level	Under-five mortality rate
Industrialized countries	7
Developing countries	88
Poorest countries	120

Figure 3.2

Under-five mortality rates by socioeconomic status in selected developing countries, 1978–96
Deaths per 1,000 live births

Source: Wagstaff and others 2003.

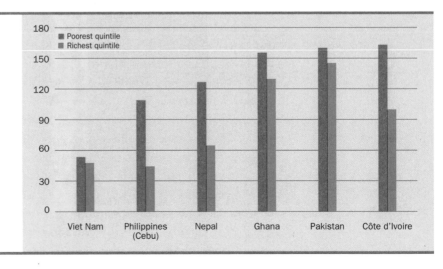

Specific measures need to be taken to ensure that the poor are not left behind

Children of poor families living in unhealthy environments are more likely to become ill due to increased exposure to health risks, including higher levels of undernutrition. They also have greatly limited access to care. In rural Nigeria, for example, children from the lowest socioeconomic quintile of the population need to travel seven times as far as children from the highest quintile to reach the nearest health facility. Similar disparities are found in Bolivia, the Dominican Republic, India, and other countries (World Bank 2003b).

Even among poor people living in the same area, income-based inequities exist. In a recent study of sick children in rural Tanzania, where the likelihood of children falling ill was the same, care-seeking behaviors differed markedly. Caregivers of children in the highest economic quintile were more knowledgeable about the potential danger of their children's illness and were four times as likely to bring sick children to a primary care facility. Children from these households were therefore much more likely to receive antimalarials or antibiotics (Schellenberg and others 2003).

The *Lancet* series on child survival suggests several potential approaches to improving equity in order to reduce child mortality (Victora and others 2003):

- Improve knowledge and change care-seeking behavior of poor mothers.
- Improve access to water and sanitation for poor families.
- Empower poor women (through microcredit schemes, for example).
- Make healthcare more affordable for the poor.
- Make health facilities more accessible to the poor.
- Provide an adequate number of trained health workers in poor communities.
- Make health facilities more inviting.
- Match health expenditures to the needs of the poor.

The *Lancet* authors note that there are essentially two strategies available for redressing inequities in child health. One is to target the poor, identifying poor households and providing them directly with cash, goods, or services; or redistributing health services to geographic areas within which a high proportion of poor households live. The second is to improve the health status of the poor by seeking universal coverage of health services. If everyone is offered better access, and if essential health interventions reach the entire population, both rich and poor benefit. The risk of the second approach is that, because it is easier to reach the better-off with improved services, programs may run out of steam before benefiting the poor. Allowing this to happen would increase, not decrease, the equity gap. Specific measures need to be taken to ensure that the poor are not left behind if universal coverage targets are not met. One measure is to incorporate equity-specific indicators into programs, as proposed in chapter 5. Holding national and local health authorities accountable for reducing the equity gap by making improvements in health status of the poor a criterion

**A profound
understanding of
the relationship
between the
community
and the health
system is
important**

for evaluating the success or failure of their programs could be an important intervention in and of itself.

This section of the report has briefly reviewed the major disease-specific causes of mortality in children and the interventions aimed at reducing their impact. Yet, throughout the report, we contend that the political, social, and economic dimensions of maternal and child health have been even more neglected than the biological. Increasing the ability of the poor to access health services to the same degree as the wealthier can provide a major impetus toward achieving the Goal for child health. In fact, if the under-five mortality rate in developing countries could be lowered just to that already prevailing among the richest 20 percent of the population of those countries, the global child mortality rate could be reduced by as much as 40 percent (Victora and others 2003). This reduction is similar to what would be achieved from full-scale implementation of the four most effective interventions listed in table 3.5.

Home- and community-based interventions are critical to reducing child mortality

A profound understanding of the relationship between the community and the health system is important for ensuring access to health services and coverage of children, especially poor children, with existing safe and effective interventions. Although these are frequently considered to be separate entities, the best-functioning health systems are those that are fully integrated within the community.

A useful depiction of the relationship between the household and the health system for child health is presented in figure 3.3. The dotted horizontal line separates actions that need to take place in the home from those that need to take place outside the home in order for child mortality to be reduced. The dotted vertical line separates things that are done to prevent illness from actions that are needed to treat a sick child. For example, preventive interventions that can be implemented by mothers alone include breastfeeding, improved complementary feeding, and the use of insecticide-treated materials, such as bednets. Actions that require the more active participation of the facility-based health system or its extension include vaccination, improved water supply, and improved management of newborns.

For all potentially fatal conditions, mothers and other caregivers must learn to recognize the signs of severe illness and know when to take prompt action. For some common childhood conditions, such as diarrhea, mothers can administer oral rehydration fluids and continue feeding at home, or community health workers can make the diagnosis and provide treatment, as is now recommended for pneumonia management. Appropriate management of the child at home, without recourse to facility-based care at any time during the illness, can result in reduced mortality (Aguilar and others 1988).

Similarly, most of the neonatal survival interventions in the universal and situational packages presented above can be delivered through either family-oriented approaches or population-oriented outreach services that even a

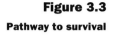

Figure 3.3

Pathway to survival

Source: Waldman and others 1996.

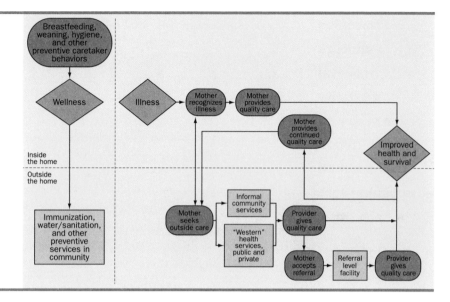

country with a relatively weak health system can deliver. Together communities, families, and community health workers can avert millions of newborn deaths in the next few years, even as individual-oriented services requiring skilled professionals and a well functioning health system are strengthened and made available in even more remote areas.

Studies in South Asia have shown convincingly that community-based approaches to newborn health can work extremely well. In different studies community-based health workers without midwifery skills succeeded in reducing neonatal mortality by 25–62 percent (Pratinidhi and others 1986; Datta and others 1987; Daga and others 1992; Bang and others 1999).

The key strategic factor common to these studies was the presence of community health workers who visited homes to ensure multiple contacts with the babies, mothers, and families, starting at or soon after birth. A randomized controlled trial in rural Nepal achieved a 30 percent decline in neonatal mortality rate by using a participatory intervention with women's groups, demonstrating the power of community education and participation to change unhealthy behaviors (Manandhar and others 2004). Importantly, in all of these studies, the measured impact was not only on key behaviors but also on birth outcomes, and substantial improvements were achieved within only a few years of program implementation.

Although the emphasis on prevention and home care is appropriate, it does not substitute, in any way, for the need for accessible health facilities, both outpatient and primary referral hospitals. Mothers will frequently want to, and will often have to, seek care outside the home.

In addition, there are important differences between strategies aimed at reducing child deaths and those aimed at reducing deaths associated with pregnancy. This report has highlighted those differences, stressing the importance

Strategies to address neonatal mortality and maternal mortality are linked but do not substitute for each other

of skilled attendants, emergency obstetric care, and an intact referral system for reducing maternal mortality. Interventions that take place in the home or are provided by community health workers (or traditional birth attendants) play little or no role in reducing maternal deaths.

It is therefore essential to understand that although neonatal and child survival strategies can and should be linked to strategies to address maternal mortality, they should never be allowed to substitute for them. A health system capable of attaining both Goal 4 and Goal 5 must be able to deliver appropriate, high-quality services at each of the household, community, outpatient facility, and referral hospital levels.

Improving care-seeking behaviors is clearly a critical function of the health system. Both knowing when to seek care for potentially fatal childhood illnesses and knowing where to go are important. Mothers have a wide variety of choices once they make the decision to seek care outside the home. In addition to the marketplace, where they can purchase drugs without consulting professional advice, they can, and often do, seek first recourse from traditional healers ("informal community services" in figure 3.3). If "modern" or "Western" care is sought, mothers can choose between private sector and public sector providers. In many, even most, cases, mothers will seek care from multiple sources. Unfortunately, in other cases mothers are prevented from seeking care for their children, as care-seeking decisions are made by husbands, other relatives, or others in the community. In either case, mortality will be reduced only if care of appropriate quality is available and utilized correctly. Training of first-level healthcare workers is clearly necessary, but it is hardly sufficient to reduce childhood mortality.

Whichever provider the mother consults, another choice quickly becomes apparent. The provider can decide that he or she is competent to deal with the illness or decide that referral to a more sophisticated, better equipped facility is required. For many of the more severe cases of illness, the ones that are most likely to result in death, children should be referred. Attention must be paid to strengthening the referral level of the system, especially the district hospital. However, in many cases the mother may not comply with the recommendation of referral. Distance, cost, and competing priorities may determine whether she can and does follow medical advice (English and others 2004; Peterson and others 2004).

In most cases, after consultation with a facility-based healthcare worker, responsibility for the care of the child reverts to the mother. Compliance with professional advice again becomes a critical issue. Completing a course of prescribed antibiotics or antimalarials, maintaining an adequate state of hydration until diarrhea subsides, continuing to breastfeed, and other home-based actions all contribute to whether or not a child survives any episode of illness.

The most common strategy for implementing the interventions known to substantially reduce child mortality is the Integrated Management of

Linking facility-based IMCI to community-level IMCI is critical

Childhood Illnesses (IMCI) strategy, promoted principally by the WHO and UNICEF. IMCI was initially developed as a facility-based initiative to encourage health professionals to diagnose and treat correctly or to refer to an appropriate level of the health system children presenting with the clinical signs of pneumonia, diarrhea, malaria, measles, and malnutrition, as well as to check a child's vaccination and nutritional status. IMCI eventually added nonclinical components as well. Later the program emphasized strengthening the health system to support IMCI activities, especially in the areas of drug supply, monitoring, and supervision. A third, community-level component promotes a number of key household behaviors that prevent illness or reduce the likelihood of complications (box 3.1).

The interventions presented above for reducing neonatal mortality can easily be incorporated into an enriched version of the IMCI strategy. The WHO has recently prepared a generic neonatal IMCI algorithm, and several countries have already included neonatal care in their national adaptations of IMCI. Linking the primarily facility-based IMCI approach to the community-level IMCI strategies—shown to be crucial to reducing neonatal mortality rate—is critical, as most babies in developing countries are born, fall sick, and die at home.

India's version of IMCI (named Integrated Management of Neonatal and Childhood Illness, IMNCI) has attempted to do exactly that (Bang and others 1999). It mandates multiple home visits during the baby's first week of life by healthcare workers who deliver the essential care package. Of course, this is only one possible approach among many, and rigorous evaluations of all efforts to better mobilize communities for improving both neonatal and child health outcomes will be required before the best possible approaches can be described and adapted to local settings.

In fact, recent evaluations of the IMCI strategy, conducted in several countries, provided useful insights into the constraints that limit its successful implementation and the conditions necessary for it to have a major impact (Schellenberg and others 2004; el Arifeen and others 2004). The main constraints to successful implementation were lack of health system support for IMCI (poor supervision, low utilization of government facilities, lack of management support at national or district level, lack of drugs or supplies at implementing facilities, high staff turnover, and other factors) and insufficient implementation of community-based IMCI interventions. The community-based component of IMCI was found to be less successful than the other components. Added emphasis will need to be placed on this aspect of the strategy over the next few years, and new approaches to mobilizing communities and households will need to be developed, tested, and evaluated.

As part of the IMCI evaluations, 12 countries were visited by the research team, 5 of which were selected for in-depth study. In these countries IMCI training of healthcare workers was shown to have improved the quality of care

Box 3.1

Twelve simple family practices can prevent illness or reduce the likelihood of complications

Source: www.who.int/ child-adolescent-health/ PREVENTION/12_key.htm.

Communities need to be strengthened and families supported to provide the necessary care to improve child survival, growth, and development. The evidence suggests that 12 simple family practices can prevent illness or reduce the likelihood of complications:

- Breastfeed infants exclusively for at least six months. (HIV-positive mothers require counseling about alternatives to breastfeeding.)
- Starting at about six months, feed children freshly prepared energy- and nutrient-rich complementary foods, while continuing to breastfeed up to two years or longer.
- Ensure that children receive adequate amounts of micronutrients (particularly vitamin A and iron), either in their diet or through supplementation.
- Dispose of feces, including children's feces, safely, and wash hands after defecation, before preparing meals, and before feeding children.
- Take children as scheduled to complete a full course of immunizations (BCG, DPT, OPV, and measles) before their first birthday.
- Protect children in malaria-endemic areas, by ensuring that they sleep under insecticide-treated bednets.
- Promote mental and social development by responding to a child's needs for care, through talking, playing, and providing a stimulating environment.
- Continue to feed and offer more fluids, including breast milk, to children when they are sick.
- Give sick children appropriate home treatment for infections.
- Recognize when sick children need treatment outside the home and seek care from appropriate providers.
- Follow the health worker's advice about treatment, follow-up, and referral.
- Ensure that every pregnant woman has adequate antenatal, delivery, and postpartum care. This includes having at least four antenatal visits with an appropriate healthcare provider and receiving the recommended doses of tetanus vaccination. The mother also needs support from her family and community in seeking care at the time of delivery and during the postpartum and lactation period.

To provide this care, families need knowledge, skills, motivation, and support. They need to know what to do in specific circumstances and as the child grows and develops. They need skills to provide appropriate care and to solve problems. They need to be motivated to try and to sustain new practices. They need social and material support from the community. Finally, families need support from the health system, in the form of accessible clinics and responsive services, and healthcare workers able to give effective advice, drugs and more complex treatments when necessary.

at facilities. Although three of the countries experienced serious constraints to implementation, in the other two there was good evidence that the IMCI strategy had had an impact. In Tanzania, IMCI was implemented in two districts where health systems had been strengthened, and utilization rates of government facilities were high. IMCI was associated with a 13 percent reduction in under-five mortality over a two-year period, and stunting (low height-for-age) was reduced significantly (Schellenberg and others 2004). In Bangladesh all three components of IMCI are being implemented. Early results show that the utilization of government facilities—generally low throughout South Asia—has improved substantially as a result of its availability (el Arifeen and others 2004).

Interventions that target households, communities, first-line facilities, and district-level hospitals are all necessary

IMCI is not the only way to ensure that the most important interventions for reducing child mortality are implemented. All countries must adapt the WHO/UNICEF generic protocols. Policies regarding drug treatment, job descriptions for different categories of health personnel, fee scales, and many other variables must be carefully considered. What is most important is that the relationship between households, communities, and the facility-based health system be clearly understood and that interventions specific to and adapted to each level be made accessible to all.

In summary, a limited number of nondisease determinants make important contributions to health (see figure 3.3). Mothers (or other caregivers) need to know how to recognize the signs of serious illness, how to treat an illness at home, and where to seek care when care outside the home is required, and they need to understand the importance of complying with prescription advice and counseling. But good decisionmaking along these pathways is not a function of knowledge alone. Before deciding to seek care outside the home, for example, a mother will take into consideration physical access to health services, the cost of those services, their quality, and the reception she will receive.

Health workers need appropriate knowledge and skills in order to be able to provide high-quality care to children. In addition, they need to be properly motivated. They need a clear understanding of norms and standards of care, upgraded skills in order to be able to provide the best care in accordance with national child health policies, constructive oversight by supervisors and community members, incentives in the form of career advancement, and, of course, adequate financial compensation.

We contend that although the epidemiology of childhood diseases in developing countries has been reasonably well described, and that although the medical and public health interventions to deal with the most common fatal diseases of childhood exist, much more attention needs to be paid to the nonbiological aspects of healthcare if the Millennium Development Goal is to be achieved. Appropriate preventive and care-seeking behavior by mothers is essential. Opportunities to provide treatment outside of health facilities, while well accepted for diarrhea, need to be explored further for pneumonia and malaria. And the ability of primary care facilities and referral hospitals to make a greater contribution to the health of the communities they serve must be significantly improved.

Adolescent health

Adolescents represent a new generation of 1 billion, the largest generation in history to make the transition from childhood to adulthood. This new cohort presents a tremendous opportunity. As the Committee on the Rights of the Child notes, "the dynamic transition period to adulthood is also generally a period of positive changes, prompted by the significant capacity of adolescents to learn rapidly, to experience new and diverse situations, to develop and use critical thinking, to familiarize themselves with freedom, to be creative and to socialize" (UN CRC 2003). Despite the importance of adolescents, their reproductive and sexual health needs have long been ignored and their views silenced by decisionmakers who influence health and education policy and programs (Dehne and Riedner 2001; Bruce and Clark 2003).

For both biological and social reasons, adolescents, particularly adolescent girls, are a vulnerable group. In many areas of the world, especially South Asia and West, East, and Central Africa, a large percentage of girls are already married by their mid- to late teenage years and have given birth at least once by the age of 18. Early marriage reduces girls' educational opportunities; starts them on a path toward early childbearing, with its resultant health risks (including mortality); and often locks them into highly unequal relationships with much older men (Mathur, Greene, and Malhotra 2003). Adolescents, particularly those living in highly dependent, precarious circumstances—for example, in intense poverty, in refugee settings, or as orphans—are subject to high rates of abuse, including sexual abuse (UNICEF and UNAIDS 2002; McGinn 2000; UNHCR and Save the Children-UK 2002; Luke and Kurz 2002).

In many countries in Africa, being young and female means having a substantially higher risk of HIV/AIDS. In some settings, women ages 15–24 are 2.5 times as likely as their male counterparts to be infected with HIV; in Zambia and Zimbabwe, women account for 80 percent of all 15- to 24-year-olds with HIV/AIDS (UN Global Coalition on Women and AIDS 2004).

Increased risk of HIV infection among young women stems, in part, from situations in which adolescent girls, with very little negotiating power to either refuse sex or insist upon condom use, are having sex with older boys and men who are themselves at higher risk of HIV infection because of their age (UN Global Coalition on Women and AIDS 2004; Luke and Kurz 2002; Berer 2003a; Dowsett 2003; Machel 2001; Frasca 2003).

Adolescent boys and young men are also at elevated risk of HIV infection and must be part of strategies to stem the epidemic (Dowsett 2003; Berer 2003a). Countries attending the International Conference on Population Development +5 (ICPD+5) recognized this and set a specific target for halving the prevalence of HIV in men and women ages 14–25 by 2010 in countries most affected (UN 1999b). The MDG on HIV includes an indicator for reducing HIV/AIDS among pregnant women ages 15–24.

HIV is not the only reproductive health issue for adolescents. Fifteen million girls between 15 and 19 give birth every year, and another 5 million adolescent pregnancies end in abortion (Pillsbury, Maynard-Tucker, and Nguyen 2000). The risk of dying from pregnancy-related causes is twice as high for women ages 15–19 than for women in their twenties, making pregnancy the leading cause of death for girls ages 15–19 in the developing world (UNFPA 2003a). Reproductive and maternal morbidity also take an enormous toll on adolescents.

Strategies for unmarried adolescents are not reaching married adolescents

The obstacles facing married and unmarried adolescent girls and young women differ. In many cultures married adolescents are seen as poised between childhood and adulthood. They are likely to be engaging in more unprotected sex and more frequent sex with their partners than their unmarried counterparts. They may also be more isolated, out of school or away from their family support structures and familiar social networks, with healthcare decisions dictated by husbands and mothers-in-law (Bruce and Clark 2003; Barua and Kurz 2001). In contrast, in many cultures unmarried adolescents are viewed as children, and their reproductive health needs and sexuality are overlooked (Dehne and Riedner 2001). Increasingly, attention is being paid to the different policies and programs that must be developed to reach married and unmarried girls and women. Strategies for unmarried adolescents, such as youth centers and peer education, are not reaching married adolescents, and messages on HIV/AIDS prevention tailored to unmarried adults are inappropriate for married adolescents (Bruce and Clark 2003; Barua and Kurz 2001).

In short, a complex set of social, cultural, and economic forces shapes and constrains the social worlds in which adolescents struggle to make choices. Younger women are more likely to lack accurate information about reproductive health, family planning, and sexually transmitted infections, including HIV/AIDS. As a result, married and unmarried adolescents often engage in sexual activity in ways that place them at risk. They lack the knowledge and the access to health services or family planning that would help them protect themselves from sexually transmitted infections and unplanned pregnancies. Even when girls are aware of modern methods of birth control, they often lack knowledge or skill in using contraception. As a result, they experience contraceptive failure more often than adults do (Alan Guttmacher Institute 1998; Malhotra and Mehra 1999). Adolescents are also more likely to resort to unsafe and self-induced abortion and to postpone abortion until later in pregnancy (Friedman 1994). Of unsafe abortions among adolescents in the developing world, 40 percent occur in Sub-Saharan Africa (Shah and Aahmane forthcoming).

Younger women are also less likely to recognize complications during pregnancy (Miller and others 2003). And, in some settings, even when adolescents deliver their babies in health facilities, they suffer higher rates of mortality than older women (Kwast, Rochart, and Kidane-Mariam 1986).

Adolescent childbearing affects infants and children as well. Babies born to adolescent mothers are at increased risk of stillbirth and perinatal mortality (Miller and others 2003). In both developed and developing countries, adolescents are at greater risk of preterm delivery (the most significant cause of infant mortality in the developed world) and of having low-birthweight infants, including very low-birthweight infants (WHO 2003a; Scholl, Hediger, and Belsky 1994). Very young adolescents (under 15) are at even greater risk of having a low-birthweight baby. The higher mortality rates of children born to mothers younger than 20 persist through the age of 5 (Malhotra and Mehra

Special efforts
must be made
to reach very
young first-
time mothers

1999). Special efforts must be made to reach very young first-time mothers through the health system. Health services for adolescents must be tailored to address their unique needs and circumstances (Alan Guttmacher Institute 1998; UNFPA 2002b; UN CRC 2003).

Sexual and reproductive health

The burden of sexual and reproductive health conditions can be expressed in absolute numbers: 60–80 million infertile couples; 120–201 million couples with unmet need for contraception; 4 million newborn deaths; 8 million life-threatening maternal morbidities; 529,000 maternal deaths, including 68,000 from unsafe abortion—the list goes on. The aim of disability-adjusted life years (DALYs) as a measure of the burden of disease is to put these and other health conditions into a unit that will allow comparison across different health conditions and will enable cost-effectiveness comparisons for priority setting. Notwithstanding serious flaws that bias downward the burden of disease calculations for sexual and reproductive health (Hanson 2002), DALYs can give a general sense of the scale of sexual and reproductive health conditions and their overall importance in relation to other disease conditions.

According to the most recent calculations by the WHO, sexual and reproductive health conditions account for a substantial portion of the global burden of disease: 17.8 percent of all DALYs lost. But for women in their reproductive years (15–44), the burden of sexual and reproductive health conditions is far higher than any other category of illness, a full 31.8 percent of DALYs lost, of which sexually transmitted infections, including HIV, account for 16 percent. Maternal health conditions (death and disability resulting from pregnancy and childbirth) account for 12.4 percent. For women in Sub-Saharan Africa, the burden of sexual and reproductive health conditions is particularly alarming (figure 3.4).

The burden of sexual and reproductive health conditions worsened in the past decade, mainly due to the rise of HIV/AIDS (figure 3.5). But, as figure 3.5 demonstrates, virtually no improvement occurred during the 1990s in other areas of sexual and reproductive health.

Unwanted and mistimed pregnancies

Unwanted pregnancies contribute directly to the level of maternal mortality. Put simply, if a woman does not get pregnant, she will not die in pregnancy or childbirth. Therefore increasing access to methods to control fertility can have a significant impact on the number of maternal deaths, by reducing the number of times that a woman runs the risk that a fatal obstetric complication will occur. It has been estimated that if unmet need for contraception were filled and women had only the number of pregnancies at the intervals they wanted, maternal mortality would drop 20–35 percent (Maine 1991; Daulaire and others 2002).

However, family planning will not change the maternal mortality ratio (the MDG indicator). The maternal mortality ratio is a measure of the risk

Figure 3.4

Disability-adjusted life years lost among women of childbearing age, 2001

Share of DALYs lost by women ages 15–44 (%)

a. Includes sexually transmitted infections other than HIV/AIDS; iron deficiency anemia for women of reproductive age; breast, ovarian, cervical, and uterine cancer; and genitourinary diseases, excluding nephritis and nephrosis.

Source: WHO 2004b.

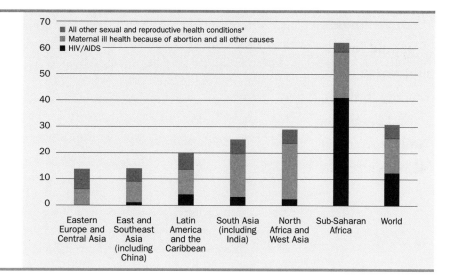

Figure 3.5

Disability-adjusted life years lost by women of childbearing age due to sexual and reproductive health conditions, 1990 and 2001

DALYs lost by women ages 15–44 (millions)

a. Includes iron-deficiency anemia for women of reproductive age; breast, ovarian, cervical, and uterine cancer; and genitourinary diseases, excluding nephritis and nephrosis.

Source: Singh and others 2003. Reprinted with the permission of the Alan Guttmacher Institute.

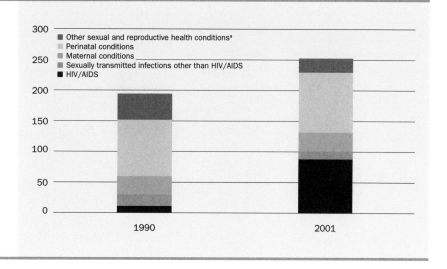

of dying *once a woman becomes pregnant*. The health sector interventions that enable a woman to go through pregnancy and childbirth safely and to have the best chance of having a healthy baby are discussed in the subsection on maternal mortality and morbidity.

A substantial proportion of unwanted pregnancies is ended by induced abortion, whether or not it is legal and whether or not it is safe. Evidence over the past 20 years indicates that increased access to contraception, nonrestrictive legal frameworks on abortion, and appropriate guidelines and training for practitioners can significantly reduce rates of recourse to induced abortion, including unsafe abortion, and rates of abortion-related maternal mortality and morbidity (Alan Guttmacher Institute 1999; Van Look and Cottingham 2002; WHO 2003e; Crane and Smith forthcoming). Still, of the estimated 45 million abortions that take place in the world each year, some 19 million

Governments should review and revise laws, regulations, and practices that jeopardize women's health

occur in countries in which the procedure is unsafe (WHO 2004f). About 95 percent of unsafe abortions—those characterized by the lack or inadequacy of skills of the provider, hazardous techniques, or unsanitary facilities (WHO Division of Family Health 1993)—occur in developing countries, despite the fact that, of countries with populations of more than 1 million, all but two legally permit abortion for one or more indications (Germain and Kim 1998).

Unsafe abortions are estimated to account for more than 68,000 deaths a year (WHO 2004f), about 13 percent of all maternal mortality. Complications of unsafe abortion are the one category of fatal obstetric complications that could be almost totally prevented through the provision of appropriate services (Maine 1991). The world community has repeatedly agreed that where abortion is legal, it should be provided safely and, in all cases, complications of unsafe abortion should be treated through high-quality health services (UN 1994, 1995, 1999a). As abortion is legal in almost every country for at least one reason, and in three-fifths of all countries to preserve the physical and mental health of the woman (WHO 2003e), the international community agreed in 1999 that "health systems should train and equip health service providers and should take other measures to ensure that such abortion is safe and accessible" (UN 1999a, paragraph 63 (iii)). For abortion, as for other areas of sexual and reproductive health, governments and other relevant actors should review and revise laws, regulations, and practices that jeopardize women's health.

The primary health intervention for preventing unwanted or mistimed pregnancies is contraceptive services. Contraceptive prevalence rates have risen steadily since the 1960s (Lule and others 2003), and the global total fertility rate dropped from 5.0 births per woman in 1960 to 2.7 in 2001, making family planning programs among the most important public health success stories of the past 50 years. Nevertheless, according to the United Nations Population Fund (UNFPA), some 350 million women still do not have access to safe and affordable contraception (UNFPA 2002c). The WHO (2004f) estimates that 120 million women who want to space or limit their pregnancies are not using contraception. Recent estimates for developing countries, using a methodology that includes couples using traditional methods, puts the unmet need for effective contraception at about 201 million women, resulting in 76 million unplanned pregnancies each year (Singh and others 2003).

Neither the level of unmet need nor its health impact is evenly distributed. Levels of unmet need are particularly high in Sub-Saharan Africa (figure 3.6). Contraceptive use also varies within countries. In every one of the 45 countries shown in figure 3.7 richer women are more likely to use contraception than poorer women, although the disparity varies dramatically across countries.

Sexually transmitted infections

The inability of women to protect themselves from HIV infection is a function of unavailability of appropriate means of protection (condoms and

Programs that provide only services for sexually transmitted infection fail to reach women

microbicides), poor access to accurate information about sexuality, and the power imbalances in sexual relationships that leave many women vulnerable. In addition to HIV, there are some 340 million new cases of curable sexually transmitted infections each year (WHO 2003d), with massive implications for the health of both women (including infertility and subfertility) and newborns. Syphilis, for example—90 percent of which occurs in developing countries—is an important cause of stillbirth in Sub-Saharan Africa (Gerbase, Rowley, and Mertens 1998; Watson-Jones and others 2002). More than 99 percent of cases of cervical cancer, the second largest cause of female cancer deaths worldwide, are associated with human papillomavirus (Walboomers and others 1999). Women with other sexually transmitted infections are also more likely to contract HIV (UNFPA 2002c).

Services for preventing and treating sexually transmitted infections must be integrated into other reproductive health programs in order to improve access for women. Because women are often asymptomatic or reluctant to seek treatment because of stigma, programs that provide only services for sexually transmitted infection fail to reach them. Programs offering integrated services, including education and counseling, family planning, maternal health services, and diagnosis and treatment of sexually transmitted infection, are more likely to be effective for women, although they often fail to reach men (Lule and others 2003; Askew and Berer 2003).

This fact has important implications, particularly for HIV interventions. To stem the epidemic, the health system must reach sexually active people. The enormous sums of money now being poured into HIV interventions can have their greatest effect only if they build on and strengthen the infrastructure already in place, namely, sexual and reproductive health services (Berer 2004).

Other necessary and effective interventions fall in whole or in part outside the health sector. Sexuality education that stresses partner communication, redress of power imbalances, and promotion of gender equality, as well as programs that address women's educational and economic advancement,

Figure 3.6

Unmet need for contraception by region, 2003

Share of women ages 15–49 at risk of unintended pregnancy (%)

Source: Singh and others 2003. Reprinted with the permission of the Alan Guttmacher Institute.

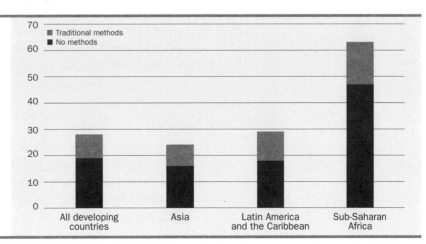

Figure 3.7

Contraceptive prevalence rates for richest and poorest quintiles in 45 countries, mid-1990s to 2000

Percent

Source: UNFPA 2003b.

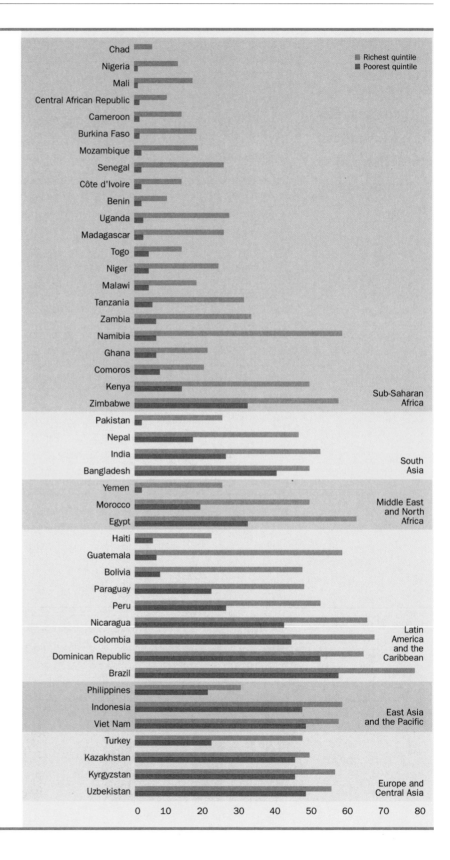

Programs offering integrated services are more likely to be effective for women

have substantial impacts on reproductive and sexual health outcomes, including rates of sexually transmitted infections (Singh and others 2003).

Conflict-affected and displaced populations

More than 40 countries, 90 percent of them low-income nations, are dealing with armed conflict. Implementing reproductive healthcare for a population is never a simple matter; providing such care in areas coping with armed conflict, emergencies, and displacement poses special challenges. People affected by armed conflict have often lost their loved ones, their possessions, their livelihoods, their social status, even their way of life. Maternal and neonatal mortality and morbidity may increase as health services are destroyed or births occur on the roadside during flight (Ahuka, Chabikuli, and Ogunbanjo 2004). Rates of infection of HIV and other sexually transmitted infections may increase with population mixing, exposure to armed men, societal breakdown, and increased sexual assault. Lack of traditional support systems, different cultural pressures, and changing men's and women's roles in society are major barriers to implementing adequate reproductive health programs (McGinn 2000; Doedens and Burns 2001; Purdin 2002). An international working group developed a set of recommendations for providing reproductive health services to address the needs of people living in areas affected by armed conflict (UNHCR 1999) and, for many countries, these recommendations will be a critical part of sexual and reproductive health and rights interventions (see also Bartlett, Purdin, and McGinn 2004).

Maternal mortality and morbidity

Goal 5 sets an ambitious target: reduce the maternal mortality ratio by three-quarters by 2015. Of all the Goals, maternal mortality is the one toward which countries have made the least progress. Ironically, it is also a measure of mortality that can be dramatically, rapidly, and consistently decreased—almost to the point of negligibility—if the appropriate actions are taken. History holds important lessons about the circumstances in which this particular form of mortality declines. More recent experience in the safe motherhood field also tells us a good deal about what works—and what does not—and why.

Precipitous drops in maternal mortality occurred in Scandinavia and Western Europe in the nineteenth century with the deployment of skilled professional midwives. It fell even more precipitously in the United States, Western Europe, and Scandinavia in the 1930s and 1940s with the introduction of key emergency obstetric care techniques (Loudon 1992; Freedman and others 2003; Hogberg 2004). Malaysia and Sri Lanka halved their maternal mortality ratios every 6–12 years during the 1950s–1990s, demonstrating that political commitment to ensure the implementation of a step-by-step program to make services available and utilized can work, even when GDP is relatively low (Pathmanathan and others 2003).

A step-by-step
program to
make services
available
and utilized
can work

Of course, every high-mortality country has a different starting point in terms of the way delivery care is organized and how it interfaces with the health system. The ways in which pregnancy and childbirth are managed within families and communities and the culturally articulated ideas that surround them also differ across countries. Successful maternal mortality reduction strategies will be ones that put local problem solving (within facilities and within communities) at the core of implementation. But to be sustainable, local action must be supported by systemic change in the health system and by clear and strong policy direction and resource allocation from the national level. Given the economic and political environment confronting high-mortality countries today, even the most committed governments require clarity in policy and support from the international health and development communities as a whole.

The analysis of maternal mortality, the range of possible solutions, and the need for priority setting begins with the numbers. Maternal mortality is the death of women from causes related to pregnancy and childbirth.[7] The maternal mortality ratio is the number of deaths per 100,000 live births. It is a measure of the risk of dying once a woman is already pregnant. It can be understood as a measure of the safety of childbirth.

The number of maternal deaths—and therefore the maternal mortality ratio—is difficult to measure accurately. Even in countries with strong vital registration systems, where every death is medically certified, studies show 25–70 percent of maternal deaths are not reported as such (AbouZahr 2003). The WHO, UNICEF, and UNFPA have developed statistical techniques to estimate maternal mortality ratios for most countries in the world. But as the authors of the publication of official UN data explain, the maternal mortality ratio should be used only to give a sense of the scope of the problem. It should not be used to measure short-term trends, and cross-country comparisons should be undertaken only with great caution (WHO, UNICEF, and UNFPA 2004).

Still, the geographic distribution of the approximately 530,000 maternal deaths that occur each year is telling. Sub-Saharan Africa has dramatically higher maternal mortality ratios than any other part of the world (table 3.7). It also accounts for 47 percent of all maternal deaths. Although Asia as a whole has a lower maternal mortality ratio, the region's large size means that it accounts for 48 percent of maternal deaths. Asia is also very diverse, comprising both very high- and very low-mortality countries.

Lifetime risk tells an even more chilling story. This statistic—the chance that a woman will die in pregnancy or childbirth at some point in her life rather than during a single pregnancy—is a function of both the total fertility rate (the number of times a woman gets pregnant) and the maternal mortality ratio (the chance that she will die each time she gets pregnant). While women in developed countries as a whole have a 1 in 2,800 chance of dying in childbirth—with some countries as low as 1 in 8,700—women in Africa have a 1 in 20 chance, and in several countries the lifetime risk exceeds 1 in 10.

Women in Africa have a 1 in 20 chance of dying in childbirth

These dramatic disparities by region are often echoed by significant disparities within countries. Building on the sisterhood method for calculating maternal mortality, Graham and colleagues (2004) use Demographic and Health Survey data to link maternal deaths to data on poverty status. Their analysis of 10 countries with dramatically different maternal mortality ratios, overall levels of human development, and per capita GDP shows that in every country maternal death is associated with poverty-related characteristics. In Indonesia, for example, in 1997 the risk of death was four times higher in the poorest quintile than in the richest.

Data on the proportion of births attended by skilled health personnel also indicate huge disparities. Indeed, among major child and maternal health interventions, the presence of a skilled attendant at delivery is the most inequitably distributed by asset quintile, followed by the use of modern contraception (Gwatkin and others 2003). Education and literacy are, in some countries, even more closely correlated with the presence of a skilled attendant (Kunst and Houweling 2001). Within countries the disparities are often far more extreme. In Chad rich women are 23 times as likely as poor women to be attended during delivery by a skilled health provider; in Bangladesh the difference is a factor of 14. Differences are large in India, where rich women are 10 times as likely to have a skilled birth attendant present, and in Cameroon and Burkina Faso, where the difference is a factor of 3 to 4 (Gwatkin 2004).

Ethnicity sometimes helps explain differentials in access to emergency obstetric care. In Nepal the utilization of emergency obstetric care varies by caste (Institute of Medicine Department of Community Medicine and Family Health 2004). One study found that in mountainous areas, where women in labor can reach emergency care only by being carried, high-caste men were unwilling to transport Dalit (lowest caste) women to the hospital. Dalits also faced opposition from higher caste communities in joining emergency funds meant to reduce the cost barriers to life-saving care (Neupane 2004).

Globally, about 80 percent of maternal deaths are due to direct obstetric complications, primarily hemorrhage, sepsis, unsafe abortion, pre-eclampsia and eclampsia, and prolonged or obstructed labor (figure 3.8). The remaining

Table 3.7

Maternal mortality around the world, 2000

a. Australia, Japan, and New Zealand were excluded from the regional averages and totals.

Source: WHO, UNICEF, and UNFPA 2004.

UN region	Maternal mortality ratio (maternal deaths per 100,000 live births)	Number of maternal deaths	Lifetime risk of maternal death
World	400	529,000	1 in 74
Developed regions	20	2,500	1 in 2,800
Developing regions	440	527,000	1 in 61
Africa	830	251,000	1 in 20
Asia[a]	330	253,000	1 in 94
Latin America and the Caribbean	190	22,000	1 in 160
Oceania[a]	240	530	1 in 83

Some 80
percent of
maternal deaths
are due to
direct obstetric
complications

20 percent of maternal deaths are indirect, that is, they are due to existing medical conditions that are aggravated by pregnancy or delivery.

In countries and areas with high HIV or malaria rates, the proportion of indirect deaths may be far higher, with coinfection with tuberculosis a significant contributing factor. HIV infection may make women more susceptible to direct causes of maternal mortality, including puerperal sepsis, postpartum hemorrhage, and complications of cesarean section. HIV and opportunistic infections such as tuberculosis may also progress more quickly because of pregnancy. Nationally representative surveys in Malawi and Zimbabwe suggest that the risk of pregnancy-related death is eight to nine times higher in HIV-positive than HIV-negative women (Bicego, Boerma, and Ronsmans 2002). Since HIV infection rates in pregnant women in different countries range from less than 1 percent to more than 40 percent (McIntyre 2003), this can affect maternal mortality statistics for the population as a whole (and hence progress toward the Goal). For example, over the past 10 years, pregnancy-related mortality risks increased by a factor of 1.9 in Malawi and 2.5 in Zimbabwe, as HIV prevalence among pregnant women increased (Bicego, Boerma, and Ronsmans 2002). At the country level, therefore, coordination with initiatives for meeting the communicable diseases Goals is critical, since gender-sensitive strategies for the control of HIV, tuberculosis, and malaria will have an impact on maternal mortality as well.

Obstetric complications do not always kill the women who experience them. For every woman who dies, an estimated 30–50 women survive the same complications, but with short- or long-term disabilities, although these numbers are hard to verify (Safe Motherhood Initiative).[8] Short-term morbidity can include hemorrhage, convulsions, cervical tears, shock and fever; long-term, and often chronic, sequelae of childbirth and pregnancy range from infertility to uterine prolapse, depression, and vesico-vaginal fistulae (Fortney and Smith 1996).

Fistulae are holes between the vagina and the urinary tract or between the vagina and the rectum, usually caused by obstructed labor. Unless the fistula is surgically repaired, there is an uncontrollable leakage of urine and

Figure 3.8

**Causes of maternal
death, 2000**

a. Includes ectopic pregnancy, embolism, and anesthesia-related complications.

b. Includes anemia, malaria, and heart disease.

Source: AbouZahr 2003.

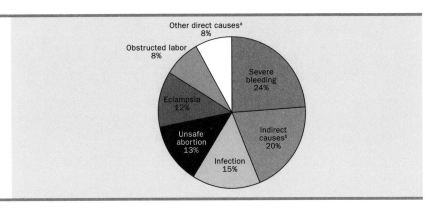

A large proportion of maternal morbidity is treatable

feces through the vagina. The implications for the woman's quality of life are enormous. Many women with this humiliating condition become social outcasts, abandoned by their husbands and families, thrown into deeper poverty, sometimes even committing suicide (Fortney and Smith 1996; Reed, Koblinsky, and Mosley 2000; UNFPA 2003c). The complication can be repaired, but very few centers in Africa provide the service. The same interventions that reduce maternal mortality also reduce the incidence of fistulae and other disabling conditions caused by obstetric complications.

A large proportion of maternal morbidity is treatable. But due to lack of knowledge and social stigma, as well as lack of services, millions of women suffer this burden in silence (Donnay and Weil 2004).

Effective interventions for reducing maternal mortality ratios

During the last half of the twentieth century and in the early years of the Safe Motherhood Initiative, launched in 1987, most program recommendations rested on the hypothesis that obstetric complications could be prevented or predicted by good care during pregnancy and delivery. Recognizing that most women in high-mortality countries deliver at home, early programs focused on training traditional birth attendants in safe and hygienic practices.

Although training programs for traditional birth attendants may improve the routine delivery care that mothers and newborns receive, these interventions proved ineffective in reducing maternal deaths (Rosenfield and Maine 1985; Greenwood and others 1990; Goodburn and others 2000; Smith and others 2000). Neither trained traditional birth attendants nor any other category of minimally trained community health worker can prevent the vast majority of obstetric complications from happening, and once the complication occurs, there is almost nothing traditional birth attendants, by themselves, can do to alter the chance that death will ensue.

Another set of early recommendations was based on the hypothesis that, through antenatal care, obstetric complications could be predicted by screening for known risk factors and that high-risk women could then be carefully monitored and treated. Indeed, women with certain attributes—young age or high parity, for example—do have a higher risk of dying than other women and, in some settings where a functioning health system already exists, attention to high-risk pregnancies can bring already low maternal mortality ratios even lower (Danel and Rivera 2003; McCaw-Binns 2003). But high-risk women account for only a small percentage of all maternal deaths; the vast majority of deaths occur in women with no known risk factors. Thus risk screening programs had little impact on overall maternal mortality levels (Maine 1991; Greenwood and others 1987).

Recognizing these flaws in the early recommendations of the Safe Motherhood Initiative, today the clear consensus internationally is that scarce resources should not be spent trying to predict which women will have

High-quality delivery care has three key elements: a skilled attendant at delivery, access to emergency obstetric care, and a functional referral system

life-threatening complications (Safe Motherhood Initiative).[9] Instead, maternal mortality reduction programs should be based on the principle that every pregnant woman is at risk for life-threatening complications. To reduce the maternal mortality ratio dramatically, all women must have access to high-quality delivery care. That care has three key elements: a skilled attendant at delivery, access to emergency obstetric care, and a functional referral system.

Skilled attendants at delivery. Evidence concerning the effect of skilled attendants at delivery is somewhat muddied by different definitions and by variation across countries in the training of midwives and the regulations governing the procedures they are permitted to perform. In 2004 the WHO, the International Confederation of Midwives, and the International Federation of Gynecology and Obstetrics issued a joint statement with a revised definition of skilled attendant, which is the one used here: "a skilled attendant is an accredited health professional—such as a midwife, doctor or nurse—who has been educated and trained to proficiency in the skills needed to manage normal (uncomplicated) pregnancies, childbirth and the immediate postpartum period, and in the identification, management and referral of complications in women and newborns" (WHO 2004d, p. 1).[10]

There is wide variation in the extent to which skilled attendants are supported and supervised in the broader health system. There is also wide variation in the number of deliveries skilled attendants perform. In a country such as Malaysia, which dramatically lowered maternal mortality in the 1960s and 1970s, midwives were the backbone of the program, each delivering 100–200 babies a year (Pathmanathan and others 2003). But in many other countries, birth attendants deliver far fewer babies. This affects their competence, because specific skills, such as manual removal of the placenta, require regular practice in order to be maintained. In Indonesia, where tens of thousands of community midwives have been trained and deployed to villages around the country, each attendant typically delivers fewer than 36 babies a year. Assessments within three years of their placement found that both their confidence and their competency-based skills were exceedingly low, with only 6 percent scoring above 70, the minimum level considered necessary for competence (Koblinsky 2003a).

The first job of the skilled attendant is to conduct routine deliveries. In this role she can influence maternal mortality levels in two ways. First, she can use safe and hygienic techniques, thereby ensuring that she does not cause a complication through mismanagement of the delivery. The attendant's techniques are certainly important to the health and well-being of each woman, but poor hygiene in routine deliveries accounts for only a small portion of maternal deaths today. Many life-threatening infections are endogenous, due, for example, to delayed treatment of complications such as prolonged labor, ruptured uterus, and retained contraceptive devices (Cunningham and others 1993).

For potentially fatal obstetric complications, a functioning health care system is essential

A second, more promising way in which the skilled attendant can affect maternal mortality levels is by actively managing the third stage of labor in every delivery (McCormick and others 2002). The third stage of labor—the period after the baby is born when the placenta is being expelled—is the period during which most postpartum hemorrhages occur. In many high-mortality settings, postpartum hemorrhage is the leading cause of maternal death. Several large clinical trials provide evidence that the use of manually performed techniques (controlled cord traction and uterine massage) as well as a single dose of an oxytocic drug immediately after delivery can significantly reduce postpartum hemorrhages (WHO 2000a, 2002b). New research on uniject oxytocin, and misoprostol could yield important new technology for this intervention. But the training and competence of the skilled attendant remains crucial. The same techniques of active management of third-stage labor that can prevent some postpartum hemorrhages can also cause serious damage if done incorrectly. This is not just a theoretical risk. Incorrect use of oxytocic drugs, for example, can cause the uterus to rupture, which, in the absence of surgical intervention, can lead to a painful death.

What happens when a routine delivery suddenly, unexpectedly, becomes a complicated one? For most of the potentially fatal obstetric complications, the skilled attendant must have the back-up of a functioning healthcare system in order to save the woman's life. No matter how skilled the attendant is, if she or he is performing deliveries in a setting without the drugs, equipment, and infrastructure to treat the complication—and cannot get the patient quickly to that care—a certain percentage of patients will die. The large majority of maternal deaths entails this kind of unexpected complication.

Access to emergency obstetric care in case of a complication. Even under the very best of circumstances, with adequate nutrition, high socioeconomic status, and good healthcare, a substantial proportion of pregnant women—more than 15 percent—will experience potentially fatal complications (Lobis, Fry, and Paxton forthcoming). But virtually all obstetric complications can be successfully treated. When the emergency obstetric care necessary to treat complications is universally accessible and appropriately utilized, maternal mortality ratios are extremely low and maternal mortality ceases to be a major public health problem.

Emergency obstetric care is generally categorized as either basic or comprehensive care, depending on the functions the facility performs (table 3.8).[11] UN guidelines recommend a minimum of one comprehensive emergency obstetric care facility and four basic emergency obstetric care facilities per 500,000 population. To reduce their maternal mortality ratios by 75 percent, high-mortality countries must substantially improve access to emergency care. It is therefore critical that the indicators for tracking progress toward the Goals include some measure that is sensitive to coverage of emergency obstetric care, as proposed in chapter 5.

One input that is vital to these functions is the presence of skilled health personnel who can perform them. The WHO definition of the competencies of the skilled birth attendant is nearly identical to the functions that must be performed in a basic emergency obstetric care facility (Maine and Paxton 2003). Thus no matter what mix of strategies is pursued, human resources lie at the heart of the solution, as discussed in chapter 4.

Referral systems. Widely available, good-quality emergency obstetric care is necessary but not sufficient to reduce maternal mortality. Appropriate utilization is also necessary. A helpful way to analyze the barriers to utilization is through the "three delays model" (Thaddeus and Maine 1994). Once a complication occurs the key to saving a woman's life is to get her adequate care in time. The delays leading to death can be divided into three categories: delay in deciding to seek care, delay in reaching care, and delay in getting treatment at the facility.

One important element of strategies to reduce delays is the strengthening of the referral system. A wide-ranging literature review by Murray and Pearson, jointly commissioned by this task force and the WHO, reveals widespread "failures" in referral systems, particularly for the poor and marginalized (Murray and Pearson 2004). The review found significant gaps in understanding how referral systems are currently functioning. It also highlighted a fundamental problem in the literature: many studies rely on a conceptualization of the ideal referral system that has a dangerously tenuous relationship to realities on the ground. Moreover, the authors suggest, that ideal may actually be the wrong goal in the case of referral for obstetric emergencies.

The authors point out that maternity referral systems were first conceived at a time when risk-screening was thought to be an appropriate maternal mortality reduction strategy even for high-mortality countries. This conception assumed a stepwise hierarchy of increasingly sophisticated facilities, and it assumed that high-risk women would be referred up the ladder as their pregnancy progressed. Today, however, maternal mortality strategies concentrate

Table 3.8 Signal functions of basic and comprehensive emergency obstetric care services	Basic emergency obstetric care services	Comprehensive emergency obstetric care services
	Administer parenteral[a] antibiotics	All services included in basic emergency obstetric care plus:
	Administer parenteral oxytocic drugs	
	Administer parenteral anticonvulsants for pre-eclampsia and eclampsia	Perform surgery (cesarean section)
a. By injection or intravenous infusion.	Perform manual removal of retained products (for example, manual vacuum aspiration)	Perform blood transfusion
Source: UNICEF, WHO, and UNFPA 1997.	Perform assisted vaginal delivery	

Access to transport is only one part of a far more complex problem

on emergencies. Time is critical. An elegant model of referral from facility to facility could be worse than inefficient. It could be deadly.

Although organized ambulance services appear to be part of the referral system in every country that has achieved major maternal mortality reductions, access to transport is only one part of a far more complex problem. Maternal mortality strategies that address the "second delay" simply by funding and organizing transport fail to grapple with perhaps even more critical systemic issues.

First and foremost is the need for referral facilities that provide 24-hour, 7-day-a-week care within a reasonable distance of where people live. Murray and Pearson conclude that "extensive pyramidal structures of referral systems with multiple tiers of facilities would seem to offer little benefit in the majority of cases for maternity care and may simply delay treatment" (2004, p. 19). In most countries attention should be concentrated on referral within the district-level system. From the perspective of a district health system as a whole, it is the strength of the referral facilities and associated supervision and referral systems that should determine the level of skill that birth attendants must have in order to avert maternal deaths, not vice versa. Murray and Pearson's analysis of case studies from Latin America, East and South Asia, and Sub-Saharan Africa leads them to concur with Koblinsky and Campbell that "the skill level of the attendant needed at the peripheral level…depends upon the ready accessibility and acceptance of referral care" (Koblinsky and Campbell 2003, p. 17). They give the example of Yunnan, China, where accessible referral facilities, a well functioning referral system, and a strong and very active supervision system has meant that semiskilled village doctors can successfully conduct normal births, recognize problems, stabilize patients, and refer them onward for more complex treatment of emergencies. With this system, Yunnan reduced its maternal mortality ratio from 149 to 101 in the 1990s (Koblinsky and Campbell 2003).

However, such results have not been documented for traditional birth attendants. A stated goal of many training programs for traditional birth attendants is to improve their referral of women experiencing obstetric emergencies to facilities that can manage them. A recent meta-analysis of studies evaluating training programs designed to improve referral practices of traditional birth attendants found little effect (Sibley, Sipe, and Koblinsky 2004). Other recent studies explore why traditional birth attendants often fail to refer even patients with obvious complications. They find that fear of losing prestige and future business often get in the way (Bossyns and Van Lerberghe 2004). Interestingly, diffusion of information important for women and their families occurs even without traditional birth attendant training: women with complications are likely to make greater use of facilities once services are improved and barriers to service use decreased, regardless of traditional birth attendant training (Sibley, Sipe, and Koblinsky 2004).

Self-referral can be the choice most likely to save a woman's life

The referral literature connects in important ways to issues often studied under the rubric of "utilization." A paper by Maine and Larsen (2004), commissioned by this task force to review the literature on utilization, finds that studies overwhelmingly focus on the individual characteristics and actions of women and their families. Far less attention is given to the features of the health system that shape their choices. Although the three-delays model has been an extremely effective conceptual device for getting health planners to understand the bigger maternal mortality picture—including social, cultural, and economic determinants and factors outside facilities—it is sometimes used to assume a strictly linear decisionmaking process, with narrow interventions (such as information, education, and communication and community mobilization programs) focused on the decisionmakers themselves, in isolation from the deep systemic problems they face (Maine and Larsen 2004). Even the first delay—the decision to seek care—may be influenced by aspects of the second and third delays. For example, women and their families may choose not to seek emergency care because the nearest facilities are not functioning and they know that at the more distant hospital the doctor is often not there; treatment is uncertain due to shortages of electricity, water, or supplies; or paying for transport from their village will throw them into debt. Yet this is often regarded as the failure of the family to make the right decision.

Murray and Pearson (2004) question the reflexive reaction that sees "bypassing" as a referral failure. In fact, self-referral—going directly to a referral facility, bypassing lower level health centers—can be the choice most likely to save a woman's life; it can also prevent economic ruin for the woman's family. Health system planners are sometimes stuck in a model of stepwise hierarchical referral systems, in which the "wise" use of resources is defined by cost-effectiveness and operational efficiency considerations that are unconnected to the true choices that consumers of the services are facing (Leonard 2000; Mwabu 1989). Bypassing can create low levels of utilization in appropriate lower level facilities as well as dangerous overcrowding and overmedicalization in higher level facilities, as it has in the Dominican Republic (Miller, Tejada, and Murgueytio 2002). But a more comprehensive reconceptualization and systemic approach to referral may be a more appropriate response than attempting to change the behavior of patients (Ganatra, Coyaji, and Rao 1998; Maine and Larsen 2004).

New thinking about referral systems will need to consider some of the major changes that have occurred in recent years, including the relationship between public and private sectors. As chapter 4 shows, in many countries people face a wide array of public and private providers and facilities that are not integrated into a coherent system. Many women move between public and private sectors over the course of a pregnancy, giving birth in a government facility but receiving antenatal care in the nongovernmental sector, for example (Murray and Nyambo 2003).

New thinking
about referral
systems must
consider public
and private
sectors

How should thinking about and planning for referral for maternal, as well as perinatal and childhood, emergencies move forward? Murray and Pearson (2004) suggest that it may be time to think systemically, to recognize that emergencies stemming from many causes—from trauma to complicated malaria or severe diarrhea—share important characteristics in situations where immediate facility-based medical attention makes the difference between life and death. Integrated referral systems deserve serious exploration, particularly in the context of the Millennium Development Goals (Razzak and Kellermann 2002; Bossyns and others 2004; Macintyre and Hotchkiss 1999).

Prioritizing interventions for mortality reduction

Many other interventions promote a healthy pregnancy and contribute to women's overall health and to the birth of healthy newborns. These interventions do not necessarily have a significant impact on maternal death, however. Immunizing a mother with tetanus toxoid, for example, prevents tetanus for both baby and mother, but, while tetanus is a significant cause of neonatal mortality, it accounts for only a tiny proportion of total maternal deaths.

Another example is anemia. It is estimated that about half of pregnant women in developing countries are anemic, a condition often due to malaria or parasites and not simply a lack of iron-rich foods (UNICEF, WHO, and UNU 2001). Recent reviews of the evidence on anemia and maternal mortality find that there is a strong, probably causal relationship between severe anemia and maternal death but little or no evidence of a relationship between mild to moderate anemia and maternal death (Rush 2000; Stoltzfus 2003).[12] Despite this evidence, new estimates conducted for the Global Burden of Disease project posit a continuous and causal relationship between hemoglobin concentration and mortality risk. And although the evidence base was judged to be weak, iron deficiency anemia was guardedly estimated to be a risk factor in some 115,000 maternal deaths, largely due to hemorrhage (Stoltzfus, Mullany, and Black 2004).

Although it is good practice to provide iron and folate to all pregnant women, it is important to recognize that iron supplementation in pregnancy does not, by itself, solve the very serious problem that anemia creates for women in many aspects of their lives (and not just in pregnancy). Nor will iron supplementation during pregnancy be sufficient to prevent the perinatal mortality attributed to maternal nutritional status; that will require attention to women's nutrition throughout their lives. In fact, in the absence of services to treat hemorrhage, iron supplementation is unlikely to reduce maternal deaths substantially, even where a high proportion of women who die during childbirth and unsafe abortions are anemic (Rush 2000). As Rush points out, nutrition and health services function interdependently; in the case of pregnant women, a food supplementation program that is not complemented

Not all interventions are equal in their effect on maternal mortality

by access to health services can even be dangerous, by increasing fetal size in small-stature women in areas without access to cesarean section (Rush 2000).

Antenatal care is a potentially important way to connect a woman with the health system, which, if it is functioning, will be critical for saving her life in the event of a complication. However, the link between receiving antenatal care during pregnancy and accessing an appropriate facility in an emergency is far from automatic (AbouZahr and Wardlaw 2003).[13] In highly malarial areas, antenatal care may also provide an opportunity for treatment or prevention of malaria. But antenatal care, by itself, will not substantially reduce maternal mortality. In many countries in Sub-Saharan Africa, including Kenya, Malawi, and Tanzania, levels of antenatal care coverage are high (more than 85 percent) and maternal mortality ratios are very high (more than 1,000 deaths per 100,000 live births) as well. In fact, maternal mortality can decline dramatically without any increase in antenatal care. During the 1990s Egypt cut its maternal mortality ratio by half (from 174 in 1992 to less than 84 in 2000), while utilization of antenatal care stayed basically level, at just over half of pregnant women (Campbell 2003).

The key point is this: not all interventions are equal in their effect on maternal mortality. Although the World Bank has estimated that full utilization of all interventions would reduce maternal deaths by 74 percent, the contribution that different interventions make to that reduction varies significantly, with emergency obstetric care accounting for the highest contribution by far (figure 3.9) (Wagstaff and Claeson 2004).

We emphasize this point about the relative contributions that different health interventions make to maternal mortality reduction because of the history of maternal mortality programs (Maine and Rosenfield 1999) and because of the task force's core recommendation regarding health systems. Perhaps more than any other major child health or maternal health condition, reducing maternal mortality depends on a facility-based health system that functions.

Figure 3.9

Maternal deaths in relation to use of existing services

Share of maternal deaths averted (%)

Source: Wagstaff and Claeson 2004.

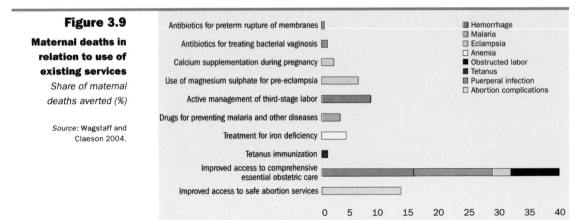

A first-line strategy must include interventions that treat the complications that kill women

When international actors or national governments make policy decisions that—deliberately or not—allow the health system to collapse or when they choose to prioritize investment in vertical programs designed to detour around, rather than engage and strengthen, fragile health systems, they in effect give up on maternal mortality.

In high-mortality settings, where health systems are dysfunctional and failing, investment solely in an intervention deployed outside the health system (for example, trained traditional birth attendants or semiskilled birth attendants)—whose effectiveness in addressing maternal mortality depends on the existence of the health system—represents more than simply an inefficient use of resources. It is arguably a violation of women's very right to health. In making this point, the task force is careful to distinguish between interventions that promote maternal and newborn health and interventions that are necessary to avert maternal death. A strategy designed to address maternal mortality as its true aim—and not just as a welcome, but coincidental, byproduct of a health intervention designed primarily for another purpose (averting newborn death, for example)—must include interventions that prevent and treat the complications that kill women. As a first-line strategy for reducing maternal mortality, anything else arguably fails to meet the fundamental obligations of governments to progressively realize the right to health of millions of women (Freedman 2001; Yamin and Maine 1999).

The maternal mortality ratio is indicative of women's status in a society. But this is not because the standard markers of women's status, such as literacy or income, themselves have a significant impact on maternal mortality.[14] Rather, a society, a global health community, that takes the death of women seriously—that finds it unacceptable that a woman in Africa will, on average, face a 1 in 20 chance of dying in pregnancy—will stop imagining that by addressing child health or even newborn health it has done enough for women. It will, instead, come to grips with prioritizing health system interventions so that the most serious obstacles to reducing maternal mortality receive the most serious attention in maternal mortality strategies.

Getting from here to there: strategic choices and lessons learned

How does a country struggling with high levels of maternal mortality get from where it is today to the ideal situation in which every woman has access to emergency obstetric care, a skilled attendant, and a referral system that ensures that she gets to life-saving care in time to save her life? All three elements are part of a health system. Until the system functions as a system, dramatic reductions will not be possible. But where does a country committed to reducing its maternal mortality and meeting the Goal begin?

In the safe motherhood community today, the issue is often posed as whether to give highest priority to training a cadre of workers with midwifery skills who can attend every birth (since, indeed, every pregnant woman is at

Where should high-mortality countries put their scarce financial, human, and managerial resources?

risk of complications) or to focus on strengthening emergency obstetric care services (including the human resources necessary to staff them) in order to treat the approximately 15 percent of pregnant women who experience complications. The World Bank estimates that if the crude birth rate is 40 per 1,000 people and a skilled attendant manages 200 births a year (far more than most community-based birth attendants manage today), some 60 million births a year occur in developing countries, requiring 400,000 trained and supported skilled birth attendants (Lule and others 2003). This estimate is conservative, if still daunting. Although only 15 percent of pregnant women will need emergency obstetric care services, it is impossible to know which women make up that 15 percent. Under the strategy of emergency obstetric care first, therefore, emergency services need to be accessible to all (albeit not used by all).

In theory, the two interventions—skilled attendants for all births and emergency obstetric care for complicated ones—do not contradict each other. But as strategies in resource-constrained settings they fit less easily together. Ultimately, both interventions appear to be necessary to reach very low maternal mortality levels: in every country with a maternal mortality ratio of less than 50—or even less than 100—a high proportion of births is attended by skilled health personnel and access to emergency obstetric care is widespread. Yet the reality in high-mortality countries today is that policymakers are indeed confronted with a choice between the two interventions, at least as a matter of emphasis or priority setting. Where should they put their scarce financial, human, and managerial resources? How should they sequence these interventions?

Some have looked for guidance to historical examples or to contemporary cases of the few countries or subnational units in which maternal mortality ratios of less than 100 have been achieved. In Malaysia and Sri Lanka, a step-by-step approach, starting with coverage of basic facilities that can deliver emergency obstetric care, followed by a focus on utilization and quality, went hand in hand with the professionalization of midwifery and a governmental commitment to ensuring universal access to health services, including access by the poor and people in rural areas (Pathmanathan and others 2003). Over the course of several decades both countries halved their maternal mortality ratios every 6–12 years, going from more than 500 in 1950 to less than 30 by the early 1990s. Egypt, Honduras, and Yunnan, China, have also succeeded in reducing maternal mortality, cutting rates from about 200 to less than 100 (Koblinsky 2003b).

Although the strategies used in all of these countries (and historically in Western Europe and Scandinavia as well) carry important lessons, it helps to do a reality check against the situation faced today in meeting the MDG target. Thirteen countries are estimated to account for two-thirds of all maternal deaths each year (table 3.9). With the exception of China (which makes the

Thirteen countries are estimated to account for two-thirds of all maternal deaths

list because of the sheer size of its population), virtually every one of these countries has a maternal mortality ratio that exceeds 500, with most closer to 1,000. Looking at the challenge of meeting the Millennium Development Goals on a country-by-country basis, some 46 countries have maternal mortality ratios exceeding 500. Thirty-eight of these countries are in Sub-Saharan Africa, including 17 countries in which maternal mortality ratios exceed 1,000 (table 3.10).

What do maternal mortality ratios of this magnitude tell us about the nature of the health systems in these countries? Is there a difference in the strategies that should be considered by countries with maternal mortality ratios in the 1,000–2,000 range versus those with maternal mortality ratios of 500? Or 200?

In countries in which maternal mortality levels are very high and health systems exceedingly weak, one sometimes hears an argument that goes like this: the vast majority of births (often more than 80 percent) take place at home, very often attended by family members or neighbors; traditional birth attendants or other kinds of minimally trained community health workers are present in communities; the health system is so weak that there is no hope of providing emergency obstetric care or even a true skilled birth attendant in rural areas at any time in the foreseeable future; therefore the strategy should be to provide some additional training to community health workers or traditional birth attendants, making them, in effect, semiskilled attendants.

Table 3.9

Countries with the largest number of maternal deaths, 2000

—Not available.

Note: The 13 countries in the table account for two-thirds of all maternal deaths worldwide (357,000 of 529,000).

Source: WHO, UNICEF, and UNFPA 2004, except skilled attendance, UNDP 2003.

Country	Number of maternal deaths	Maternal mortality ratio (maternal deaths per 100,000 live births)	Lifetime risk of maternal death	Skilled attendance at delivery (percent), 1995–2001
India	136,000	540	1 in 48	43
Nigeria	37,000	800	1 in 18	42
Pakistan	26,000	500	1 in 31	20
Congo, Dem. Rep.	24,000	990	1 in 13	61
Ethiopia	24,000	850	1 in 14	6
Tanzania	21,000	1,500	1 in 10	36
Afghanistan	20,000	1,900	1 in 6	—
Bangladesh	16,000	380	1 in 59	12
Angola	11,000	1,700	1 in 7	23
China	11,000	56	1 in 830	89
Kenya	11,000	1,000	1 in 19	44
Indonesia	10,000	230	1 in 150	56
Uganda	10,000	880	1 in 13	39

Table 3.10

Countries with maternal mortality ratios exceeding 500 deaths per 100,000 live births, 2000 (ranked by maternal mortality ratio)

Note: Figures are intended to give a sense of the scale of the problem. They should not be used to track changes, particularly short-term changes such as those addressed by the Goals.

Source: WHO, UNICEF, and UNFPA 2001.

Country	Estimated number of maternal deaths	Lifetime risk of maternal death	Estimated maternal mortality ratio (maternal deaths per 100,000 live births), 1995	Range of maternal mortality ratio estimates	
				Low	High
Sierra Leone	4,500	1 in 6	2,000	510	3,800
Afghanistan	20,000	1 in 6	1,900	470	3,500
Malawi	9,300	1 in 7	1,800	1,100	2,600
Angola	11,000	1 in 7	1,700	420	3,100
Niger	9,700	1 in 7	1,600	420	3,100
Tanzania	21,000	1 in 10	1,500	910	2,200
Rwanda	4,200	1 in 10	1,400	790	2,000
Mali	6,800	1 in 10	1,200	680	1,700
Central African Republic	1,600	1 in 15	1,100	670	1,600
Chad	4,200	1 in 11	1,100	620	1,500
Guinea-Bissau	590	1 in 13	1,100	280	2,100
Somalia	5,100	1 in 10	1,100	270	2,000
Zimbabwe	5,000	1 in 16	1,100	620	1,500
Burkina Faso	5,400	1 in 12	1,000	630	1,500
Burundi	2,800	1 in 12	1,000	260	1,900
Kenya	11,000	1 in 19	1,000	580	1,400
Mauritania	1,200	1 in 14	1,000	630	1,500
Mozambique	7,900	1 in 14	1,000	260	2,000
Congo, Dem. Rep.	24,000	1 in 13	990	250	1,800
Equatorial Guinea	180	1 in 16	880	220	1,600
Uganda	10,000	1 in 13	880	510	1,200
Benin	2,200	1 in 17	850	490	1,200
Ethiopia	24,000	1 in 14	850	500	1,200
Nigeria	37,000	1 in 18	800	210	1,500
Liberia	1,200	1 in 16	760	190	1,400
Zambia	3,300	1 in 19	750	430	1,100
Guinea	2,700	1 in 18	740	420	1,100
Nepal	6,000	1 in 24	740	440	1,100
Cameroon	4,000	1 in 23	730	430	1,100
Djibouti	180	1 in 19	730	190	1,400
Côte d'Ivoire	3,900	1 in 25	690	170	1,300
Senegal	2,500	1 in 22	690	180	1,300
Haiti	1,700	1 in 29	680	400	970
Timor-Leste	140	1 in 30	660	170	1,200
Lao PDR	1,300	1 in 25	650	160	1,200
Eritrea	930	1 in 24	630	380	890
Sudan	6,400	1 in 30	590	150	1,100

Table 3.10					
Countries with maternal mortality ratios exceeding 500 deaths per 100,000 live births, 2000 (ranked by maternal mortality ratio) *(continued)*				Range of maternal mortality ratio estimates	
Country	Estimated number of maternal deaths	Lifetime risk of maternal death	Estimated maternal mortality ratio (maternal deaths per 100,000 live births), 1995	Low	High
Togo	1,000	1 in 26	570	340	810
Yemen	5,300	1 in 19	570	330	810
Lesotho	380	1 in 32	550	140	1,000
Madagascar	3,800	1 in 26	550	310	780
Gambia	270	1 in 31	540	140	1,000
Ghana	3,500	1 in 35	540	140	1,000
India	136,000	1 in 48	540	430	650
Congo	690	1 in 26	510	160	960
Pakistan	26,000	1 in 31	500	130	940

The task force recognizes the enormous pressure that concerned policy-makers feel to do something for the millions of women who give birth in these circumstances. It also recognizes that a semiskilled worker may have the potential to save a substantial number of newborns who otherwise would die. But it must be clearly stated that a strategy of training tens of thousands of semiskilled workers who will not be backed up by a supervision system, a supply system, or a referral system, is not a strategy that will significantly reduce maternal mortality. In fact, the proliferation of unsupported, unsupervised, semiskilled workers ("certified" after short training courses to manage deliveries) who are deployed in the context of policies that effectively marketize and privatize healthcare has the potential to increase the dangers for pregnant and delivering women. In some cases where such a strategy is being considered, the explicit objective is to train such workers on the assumption that they will set up their own private practices (Mavalankar 1997). Such private provision will be quite outside any government supervision, any effective regulatory system, or even any self-policing professional body.

The task force does not suggest that highly trained specialists are necessary to reduce maternal mortality. Many categories of health personnel can be taught to provide various health services—as long as effective systems of support, supervision, and supplies are established.

All the interventions necessary to save women's lives can be delivered in a district health system—at the primary care and first referral levels. This does not mean that women must give birth in facilities, nor does it mean that traditional birth attendants and other private providers have no place in a delivery system. The case studies of countries that have substantially reduced maternal mortality demonstrate that success is possible with multiple combinations of home and institutional births, attended by different categories of health workers, as long as women have access to emergency obstetric care staffed by skilled health personnel (Koblinsky 2003b).

The time has come for all countries, especially countries with high rates of maternal mortality, to invest in their district health systems as a matter of urgent priority. That system is essential for saving the women's lives. It is essential for saving many newborns and children under five (Petersen and others 2004). It is also essential for coping with other major killers in poor countries, including tuberculosis (Mahendradhata and others 2003) and HIV (Buve, Kalibala, and McIntyre 2003).

Chapter 4

Transforming health systems

Our ability to meet the Millennium Development Goals turns on our ability to think differently and act differently about health systems. The status quo is unacceptable in multiple respects:

- The fragile and fragmented health systems that now exist are unable to ensure availability, access, and utilization of key health interventions in sufficient volume and quality to meet the Goals (Travis and others 2004).
- The costs that people incur in managing (or failing to manage) their health are often catastrophic, deepening poverty (Xu and others 2003).
- As core social institutions, dysfunctional and abusive health systems intensify exclusion, voicelessness, and inequity, while simultaneously defaulting on their potential—and obligation—to fulfill individuals' rights and contribute affirmatively to the building of equitable, democratic societies.

The approach put forward in this chapter responds to the dominant policy packages that have been promoted for health sector reform over the past two decades and to the realities on the ground that have resulted. These prescriptions for reform have been based on the fundamental conviction that healthcare is best delivered to populations through competitive markets, as a commodity to be bought and sold. It is often assumed, almost as common sense, that healthcare distributed on this basis will be not only more efficient, it will also be better, that is, it will lead to improvements in health indicators.

There is little evidence that this assumption is true (Ravindran and Weller forthcoming). In fact, the data reveal no mortality benefits associated with a higher private share of total health spending (Mackintosh and Koivusalo 2004). And in the poorest countries, for the conditions relevant to the child health and maternal health Goals, any benefits that may have accrued to the

Both rich and poor face a pluralistic health market with a wide array of services of varying quality

better-off are offset by the fact that, quite systematically, these reforms have been deeply unequalizing.

Market-based approaches to healthcare: a critique

Deepening inequity has less to do with poor implementation of the reforms (an explanation commonly offered by their advocates) than with inherent weaknesses of market-based approaches to healthcare provision. The projected efficiency of market-based approaches depends on the existence of competition and on symmetry in information between supplier and consumer—both elements generally absent in health systems (Roberts and others 2004). It therefore also depends on a strong and effective system of laws and regulations (the "stewardship" function of government). Where there is market failure, the state is expected to step in as the residual "gap-filler" to offer a set of minimum essential services to those who would not otherwise receive care and whose lack of care would have externalities, that is, ramifications for the broader community (by transmitting infectious diseases, for example).

But this basic approach, championed largely by donors as part of a broader strategy for reforming poorly performing public sector institutions, is ideologically opposed to a strong state presence, including in social sectors. The strategy therefore minimizes the role and, in practice, the legitimacy of the state. Yet, paradoxically, the overall weakening of the state has left it unable to perform the regulatory, governance, and gap-filling functions on which a market-based system depends (recognizing that it was often not even strong enough—or in a few instances interested enough—to perform these functions well in the first place). Indeed, that failure and the chaos and inequity that result tend to have exactly the opposite effect: they further delegitimize the state in the eyes of both the people who make up the health system and the people who look to it to manage health and disease.

The result is that neither the public sector nor the private sector work in the idealized way that market-based approaches theorize. Instead, both rich and poor face a pluralistic market with a wide and chaotic array of services of wildly varying quality. In practice, in high-mortality countries, whether the services are private or public, whether fee exemption schemes are in place or not, healthcare now requires outlays of cash to access. In short, commercialization pervades every part of the system, with consequences for the poor and, ultimately, for society as a whole that are unacceptable and that sabotage any serious effort to meet the Millennium Development Goals.

It is important to state that our rejection of a purely market-based approach to healthcare provision does not imply that markets are not important for economic growth or for any other sector. Indeed, as Mackintosh and Koivusalo put it, "It is well understood that a properly functioning health system is essential to an effective market economy. *To make a health system work in a market economy, however, does not imply simply the commercialization of the*

Humiliation and abuse by the health system is part of the experience of being poor

healthcare sector itself. It requires rather a different starting point for health policy" (Mackintosh and Koivusalo 2004, p. 3) (emphasis added). This chapter argues for a different starting point for health systems as the foundation for scaled-up efforts to meet the maternal health and child health Goals.

Defining health systems

This report adopts the WHO definition of the health system: "all the activities whose primary purpose is to promote, restore, or maintain health" (WHO 2000b). This includes interventions in the household and community and the outreach that supports them, as well as the facility-based system and broader public health interventions, such as food fortification and anti-smoking campaigns. It includes all categories of providers—public and private, formal and informal, for-profit and not-for-profit, allopathic, and indigenous. It also includes mechanisms such as insurance by which the system is financed, as well as the various regulatory authorities and professional bodies that are meant to be the "stewards" of the system.

Equally important, we understand health systems to be a vital part of the social fabric of any society. As such, they "are not only producers of health and healthcare, but they are also purveyors of a wider set of societal norms and values" (Gilson 2003, p. 1461). In societies marked by deep inequality, the experience of neglect or abuse by the health system is part of the very experience of what it means to be poor. Conversely, the existence, legitimacy, and vindication of health claims—demands of entitlement pressed against the web of actors (including the state) that make up the health system—should be seen as valuable assets, among the tools of citizenship in a democratic society (Mackintosh 2001). This understanding of health systems as social institutions grounds the task force's view of health equity and of the role of health systems in reducing poverty.

The literature is replete with anecdotal and quantitative evidence of practices in the health system that communicate norms and values, which then shape the experience of both poverty and citizenship. The Voices of the Poor project undertaken by the World Bank, which included participatory poverty assessments in some 60 countries, consistently found that the poor experience humiliation and abuse at the hands of health systems. In one country, "men, women and young people say over and over again that they are treated 'worse than dogs'. Before they have a chance to describe their symptoms they 'are yelled at, told they smell bad, and [that they are] lazy and good-for-nothing'" (Kern and Ritzen 2001, p. 20).

A study of Lady Health Workers and Lady Health Visitors, who are crucial to the delivery of maternal and child healthcare in parts of Pakistan, showed that the feudal values and gender discrimination that characterize the broader society also shape the demeaning treatment received by female healthcare workers—with consequences for their treatment of patients (Mumtaz and others 2003). The corruption that undermines trust of the state more generally has corrosive—even deadly—effects in the health system when it puts life-saving care out of reach (Afsana 2004; Mamdani and Bangser 2004). Drug leakage rates are reportedly 78 percent in Uganda, one-third of total hospital expenditures are unaccounted for in the Dominican Republic, and senior doctors in Venezuela missed one-third of their contracted hours (Asiimwe and others 1997; Jaen and Paravisini 2001; Lewis, La Forgia, and Sulvetta 1996; McPake and others 2000).

Documentation of the active exercise of citizen rights in the health system is harder to come by. But women's empowerment projects can yield important changes in women's determination and ability to access services, with significant impacts on neonatal and maternal health (Manandhar and others 2004). Rights-based initiatives to implement meaningful complaint and accountability mechanisms have been shown to improve access to services (Mamdani and Bangser 2004; UNICEF 2003b). Especially in the reproductive health field, a rights-based approach has shaped the services provided by NGOs as well. The International Planned Parenthood Federation (IPPF), for example, widely publicizes and posts its Charter on Sexual and Reproductive Rights. The Charter frames IPPF's own services as premised on citizenship rights articulated in human rights law. These shifting foundations for the organization's work have had direct impact on the services it provides (Helzner 2002).

Thinking about health systems

In much of the health policy literature, health systems are treated as "oddly transparent": "a set of rules and formal organizations that can be rewritten, reorganized, and redirected, given the political will" (Mackintosh 2001, p. 176). In this vision of health systems, government becomes the central actor determining outcomes in a policymaking process that is implicitly understood as linear, running from problem identification to policy formulation to policy implementation. The content and flow of the linear process is assumed to be determined by the objective scientific evidence that is marshaled in the process (Keeley and Scoones 1999).

The result is an approach to policymaking and policy research that is overwhelmingly "prescriptive" in style and content. Specific elements of the system are tested against specific outcome objectives, such as cost, coverage, and quality (Mackintosh and Tibandebage 2004). Systems are understood mechanistically, as though recalibrating each moving part has a quantitatively verifiable effect on another part. This mechanistic view has informed the market-based approach to health systems and health policy that has dominated the health field internationally at least since the influential *World Development Report 1993: Investing in Health* (World Bank 1993).

Simply shuffling standard policies, such as user fees, or declaring by fiat the implementation of new programs ignores the very specific organizational cultures that prevail within any given system, not to mention the cultural and social

Strengthening health systems will require large new injections of funds

dynamics of the broader society. A paper commissioned by this task force examines the literature on organizational culture and "values in use" to gain insights into how the operation of such cultures and values determines what actually happens within the system (Gilson and Erasmus 2004). It highlights the dissonance that sometimes exists between official value systems articulated in government policies (such as public service and improving the health of the country) and the implicitly accepted value system that actually influences behavior. One detailed study from Nepal found that in the "implicitly accepted system services themselves are not seen as very important and there is instead an emphasis on things such as distributing and accounting for funds and on seeing the system as a mechanism simply of providing people with an income" (Aitken 1994). Efforts to improve services through the government's formulation and promulgation of ethically based policy statements are subverted in the implementation.

Ultimately, this problem must be addressed by "developing cultural changes alongside structural reform" (Scott and others 2003, p. 105) and recognizing the dynamic, multifaceted nature of structural reform itself (Blaauw and others 2003).

Taking redistribution seriously

Strengthening health systems and meeting the Goals will require large new injections of funds. However, experience tells us that simply pouring money into the system or even allocating funds to seemingly "pro-poor" interventions does not guarantee a more equitable system: "allocation matters greatly, but resources are made effective through the operation of the healthcare system as a whole, and where markets dominate, public resources are employed, diverted, invested and recirculated through them. The distributional outcomes depend on the interactions within the system, and between system and users" (Mackintosh and Tibandebage 2004, p. 162). If we care about equity, about what happens to the poor and vulnerable, about the way in which health systems function as social institutions and their ability to deliver critical health interventions to all citizens, then we need to take redistribution seriously.

This report adopts Mackintosh and Tibandebage's definition of redistribution: "all social processes that create increasingly inclusive or egalitarian access to resources" (Mackintosh and Tibandebage 2004, p. 144). The crux of the problem is not just how to use resources to target a needed intervention to a population that has low access or utilization (what is often labeled a "pro-poor" intervention). Rather, the core issue is how to create a system that encourages, supports, and sustains increasing inclusion, that is, redistribution. Targeted interventions focused on a particular geographic area or population will often be an important element—perhaps an immediate first step—in a broader long-term plan to create the structures that support egalitarian access to resources. For example, in Brazil, where the constitution recognizes health as "a right for all and the duty of the State" (Constitution of Brazil, Article 196), short-term targeting of the poor by

The costs associated with accessing healthcare have led to exclusion

the Family Health Program occurs in the context of a universal health system striving to ensure care for all (Barros, Bertoldi, and Victora 2004).

How do the prescriptions that currently dominate health policy affect redistribution? Mackintosh and Tibandebange (2002, p. 2) contend that marketization of healthcare "exposes and undermines cross-subsidy," as it creates a segmented health system: private services for those who can pay and targeted "gap-filling" for those who cannot.[1] When access to healthcare explicitly depends on the ability to mobilize cash resources, it effectively legitimates exclusion of the poor.

Substantial evidence shows that the costs associated with accessing healthcare have indeed led to exclusion. In one district in Tanzania, for example, transport costs are so prohibitive that "women say that when obstetric emergencies arise, their only option is to 'pray to God'" (Mamdani and Bangser 2004, p. 142). Another study documented children dying when their families were unable to pay for treatment: "a mother… was refused maternal and child healthcare because she was not able to pay a 'fine' of Tshs 700 for not bringing the child back on time" (Mamdani and Bangser 2004, p. 143). Although many countries have fee exemption policies for the very poorest, these policies are rarely implemented, and there is no recourse when services are denied (Mamdani and Bangser 2004; Ravindran, Kikomba, and Maceira forthcoming).

In a marketized system, where exclusion of those who cannot pay is, by definition, deemed legitimate, any cross-subsidy or redistribution that does exist is increasingly seen as an "unrequited gift" from rich to poor. A system that considers subsidy to the poor as an unrequited gift is difficult to sustain, since it turns on the questionable assumptions that government can successfully mandate that those with power and resources shall act benevolently and share their assets with those less fortunate and that a public system openly premised on such benevolent reciprocity between rich and poor will ultimately function equally for all (Mackintosh and Gilson 2002).

By contrast, a system built around healthcare relationships conceived not as gifts but as entitlements may move in a more sustainable direction. Human rights ideas can be used to work toward a system that recognizes and responds to claims. Londono and Frenk (1997), for example, assert that "essential service packages" should be framed not as "minimums" but as a "nucleus of universality" that constitutes a social commitment grounded in citizenship principles. A rights-based approach—one based on entitlement and obligation—can function as a principle not only for national governments and their citizens but within the global community and in transnational relationships as well. As human rights law evolves, it can begin to capture an emerging understanding of the complicity of wealthy countries in the crisis affecting health today, and it can begin to shape a norm of obligation on which claims for action by international actors can be based (International Council on Human Rights Policy and EGI 2003).

**Governments
are ultimately
responsible for
shaping the
health system**

As countries move toward meeting the Goals, how can governments begin to encourage redistribution and inclusion? In fact, redistribution may need to be managed through explicit "social settlements" that permit a level of inequality to persist in order to maintain the stability needed to implement policies that do advance redistribution and equity (Mackintosh 2001). The better-off should not be encouraged to break away from the system; the system needs to work for them, too (Bloom 2001). This has implications for how we think about the balance between "pro-poor, targeted interventions" and "universal coverage" standards as two possible routes for closing gaps in health status.

What are the most policy-relevant next steps that address the issues systematically rather than as "add-on" gap-fillers? In developing strategies to meet the Goals, no country starts from scratch, attempting to build the ideal health system. To meet the Goals, every country must start from where it currently finds itself. In countries with reasonably robust political structures, a low degree of segmentation, a strong national tax base, and an adequate health workforce, moving toward largely public financed and managed health services is a possibility (Bloom and Standing 2001). But in many poor countries, a huge proportion of healthcare is now being delivered through a largely unregulated and diverse private sector. In Viet Nam 60 percent of all outpatient child healthcare is obtained from private providers, including traditional healers and pharmacists. For the poorest 20 percent of children, 90 percent of the care provided to treat acute respiratory infection and diarrhea is private in Chad and Mali and more than 80 percent of care is private in Bangladesh, India, and Pakistan (Bustreo, Harding, and Axelsson 2003).

Most governments cannot and will not become the supplier and funder of a unitary system. But neither should the state view itself merely as the last-resort provider of a safety net for the poor. Governments control budgets, set standards, develop regulations, license and deploy critical personnel, manage infrastructure, and are ultimately responsible for shaping the nature and form of the health system through both bureaucratic and political means. These critical areas of health system functioning deserve far higher priority in health research, fundamental as they are to meeting the grand challenge of actually changing health and healthcare on the ground (Habicht and others 2004).

Drawing on the still slim but growing multidisciplinary body of research and literature in this area, we formulate three basic principles that we believe can usefully inform policymaking that is committed to increasing inclusion and closing the equity gap. In table 4.1 we present the principles, summarizing the rationale underpinning each and identifying potential policy interventions they could generate.

Principle 1: Strengthen government legitimacy
Strong government legitimacy enables a state to take actions that will increase the currency of redistribution and inclusiveness as social norms. When social

Table 4.1

Principles of redistribution and policy responses

Principle	Policy interventions	Rationale
Principle 1: Strengthen government legitimacy.	Improve access to health services: • Encourage progressive financing mechanisms. • Remove regressive user fees. • Improve the quality of care provided by the public sector. Reinforce the commitment to health as a right: • Codify the right to healthcare in law. • Create patient charters. • Widely publicize essential packages of care. • Establish transparent and participatory decisionmaking processes. • Monitor the impact of redistribution policies (through national health expenditure accounts, for example). Improve resource allocation to underserved areas: • Base allocation on measures of equity and capacity to benefit. • Create transparency in allocation and expenditure.	Such policies: • Address inequity by improving access for the poor and marginalized. • Signal commitment to inclusiveness and redistribution. • Demonstrate procedural fairness. • Increase trust and strengthen government's ability to regulate effectively. • Enhance the legitimacy required for the ministry of health to improve its status among other government departments.
Principle 2: Prevent excessive segmentation by enhancing norms of collaboration to improve services in both public and private sectors.	Establish collaborative regulation: • Ensure agreed explicit rules and encourage informal relationships. • Use regulation to check the power of interest groups. Share resources: • Share accurate information. • Share technology. Engage in joint planning. Use financing tools to discourage segmentation: • Provide incentives for the private sector to provide comprehensive care, including preventive and promotive care where probity is established. • Subsidize community insurance for the poor and provide direct transfers to the poor to enhance capacity to pay. Reinforce quality in both public and private sectors: • Reinforce and recognize probity in the private sector where the poor have been included in care. • Promote competition where it acts to root out poor-quality providers. • Use the community to benchmark facilities; "brand" good facilities.	Such policies: • Create and support collaborative professional and institutional cultures. • Normalize a rights-based approach by including stakeholders. • Shape markets to promote inclusion. • Increase trust and communication between public and private sectors, which reduces complexity and transactions costs. • Use negotiated processes to yield rules with increased legitimacy. • Improve cross-subsidization by keeping those who can pay in the system. • Expose the middle class to issues of the poor rather than excluding the poor from the system.

	Principle	Policy interventions	Rationale
Table 4.1 **Principles of redistribution and policy responses** *(continued)*	Principle 3: Strengthen the voice of the poor and marginalized to make claims.	Document, monitor, and publicize disparities in health status and healthcare across population groups. Provide opportunities for asserting claims: • Introduce patients' charters. • Establish an essential health package as an entitlement. • Ensure fair malpractice and nondiscrimination laws. Regulate to ensure appropriate public inclusion in health institution management in both the public and private sectors. Use space opened by consumers' rights movement for advocating claims. Support and encourage existing civil society organizations to help monitor facilities and providers. Ensure government mechanisms exist to improve responsiveness to claims.	Such policies: • Adopt a human rights–based approach to legitimize claims to health. • Improve accountability processes. • Reinforce democratic processes and good governance.

norms support redistribution and inclusiveness, the actual policies to achieve these goals are more likely to be accepted by all segments of society and implemented by "street-level bureaucrats" working within the system (Walker and Gilson 2004). Then the circle is closed: action that truly increases inclusion further enhances legitimacy.

Of course, government legitimacy is, in part, earned through the demonstration of good governance—that is accountability, competence, and respect for human rights and the rule of law (Standing 2004). Legitimacy and demonstrated good governance together increase trust within a system. Trust within the management ranks of the system, among providers, and between providers and patients, all strengthen the state's ability to facilitate a shift in the way society regards issues of redistribution and inclusion. Trust provides a foundation for coordination among relatively autonomous (public and private) providers (principle 2) (Gilson 2003). To cooperate, stakeholders must believe that state action and behavior is fair and that it will be sustained over time (Bloom 2001).

State legitimacy to move the health system toward increased inclusion is enhanced when state policies have "teeth," when they are more than empty rhetoric, when people make claims and those claims are recognized and enforced (linking to principle 3). A basic commitment to health and healthcare as a right, rather than as a commodity to be bought by those with sufficient means, can be codified in law. Doing so not only signals a fundamental social value to be reinforced in public discourse, it can also have concrete effects through the legal system to ensure equitable access to care. Right to health provisions in the South African constitution have been used to obtain broader access to nevirapine for the prevention of maternal-to-child transmission of HIV (Minister of Health v. Treatment Action Campaign 2002). In Venezuela constitutional rights to life and health have been invoked to ensure access to antiretroviral therapy within the public system and to reallocate budgets necessary to implement the policy (Cruz Bermudez et al v. Ministerio de Sanidad y Asistencia Social).

Procedural fairness in government decisionmaking is also central if governments are to make difficult decisions relating to equity and, in turn, expect all sectors of society to support those decisions. The more government signals its values through its decisions, proclamations, speeches, and actions, and the more transparent and inclusive such decisions are, the quicker such values become normalized and part of the accepted discourse of the society. So, for example, where there is evidence of norms of probity in the government sector, they should be highlighted and encouraged. The same is true for practices that tackle discrimination and exclusion or demonstrate responsiveness and accountability to the communities they serve. Such practices do exist somewhere in every country. They should be publicized and rewarded.

Principle 2: Prevent excessive segmentation by enhancing norms of collaboration to improve services in the private and public sectors

Marketization of healthcare tends to undermine redistribution when it severely segments the health system, driving a wedge between those who can pay and those who cannot, thereby exposing (and ultimately driving out) any cross-subsidization between them. Policy interventions that consider the system as a whole and build in mechanisms to encourage collaboration between different parts can enhance norms of inclusion, improve the functioning of both the private and the public sectors, and potentially even isolate and remove the most abusive and poorly functioning providers in either sector. There is increasing evidence that though it is significant, users' income is not the most important determinant of their choice of healthcare provider (Hotchkiss 1998; Ndeso-Atanga 2004). A study of poor people in rural areas of Cameroon showed that when faced with poor-quality care, low income did not rule out the choice of expensive (private) providers over inexpensive government services, particularly when users judged their medical conditions as serious and requiring a motivated provider (Ndeso-Atanga 2004).

A starting point is to enhance a norm of collaboration, both within the public health system and between the private and public sectors. Collaborations do not just happen; they require a supportive policy environment and a meaningful congruency of interests. Most governments in poor countries do not have the capacity to mandate and enforce collaboration through legal regulation.

Collaborative regulation can help shape markets to work in more inclusive ways

The challenge is to find or create situations or institutional arrangements in which there is an alignment of mission or strategy so that collaboration yields added value for both parties (Bloom 2004). The greater the value and more balanced the mutual benefit, the stronger the collaboration (Barrett, Austin, and McCarthy 2002).

Where markets are the driving force in healthcare provision, collaborative regulation can help shape those markets to work in more inclusive ways. For example, within the nongovernmental sector, self-regulatory and collaborative regulatory mechanisms, in which genuinely accessible providers are encouraged to form self-managed associations, can heighten their public profile and enhance their reputation in the community. By publishing benchmark fees and standards of quality of care, these institutions influence public expectations, expanding the information available to users. In this way, self regulation also serves to expose facilities that are dangerous to the poor, differentiating the market in a manner that is beneficial to the poor. This is the idea behind UNICEF's certification of hospitals that meet a set of quality standards as "baby-friendly hospitals." In Bangladesh UNICEF expanded the concept to promote certification of "women-friendly hospitals" as well. In South Africa up to 48 percent of people seeking treatment for sexually transmitted infections access private health services. In an effort to improve the quality of care and address information asymmetry for all patients accessing these services, it has been proposed that general practitioners who agree to adhere to standardized guidelines for the management of sexually transmitted infections receive accreditation (Blaauw and Schneider 2003).

While many governments in developing countries lack inspection capacity, they still have considerable resources that can positively influence the health system. Mackintosh and Tibandebage (2004) suggest that elite hospitals given nonprofit, tax-exempt status can be asked in return for explicit contributions to the capacity, quality, and inclusiveness of the healthcare system as a whole. Government can use incentives, such as access to shared information or technology, or subsidies, or even licensing mechanisms to encourage private providers as individuals or as franchisees of accredited provider networks to set up services in underserved geographic regions (Ravindran and Weller forthcoming; Segall 2000a). Another possibility is to formalize private sector involvement in public sector hospitals. If well managed and carefully monitored, this can be done by cross-subsidizing from private wards in government facilities, providing opportunities for private income to help retain good staff, and improving the quality of care.

Segmentation and lack of collaboration between the private and public sectors can lead to incoherent care. In a number of African countries the private sector is in charge of antenatal care but does not provide delivery care (Berman and Rose 1996). In Tanzania less than 8 percent of private facilities offer delivery services, but 75 percent offer antenatal and postnatal services

(Ravindran, Kikomba, and Maceira forthcoming). In some cases smooth collaboration across the public-private divide can be essential for saving lives. In maternal health, for example, animosity between public and private providers often obstructs optimal referral of obstetric emergencies (Mamdani and Bangser 2004). But, in many cases, the two have common interests and through communication, regulation, and clearer policies could be brought toward better collaboration (Murray and Pearson 2004).

We recognize that many of the policy interventions suggested are susceptible to corruption, perverse incentives, and co-option of self-regulatory bodies by larger corporations in the private sector. A government's ability to control such capture by powerful associations depends on its commitment to dealing with these negative forces and on the extent to which it can be strengthened and legitimized rather than undermined by external agencies and international development policies.

Finally, excessive segmentation of the healthcare system has, in some cases, effectively removed the poor from the public gaze. Blurring the boundaries between sectors not only improves opportunities for cross-subsidization, it also "reduces middle class ignorance of, and distancing from, the problems" (Mackintosh and Tibandebage 2004, p. 165). Indeed, it may be that only when the better-off come to see their own well-being as connected to that of the poor and marginalized will the political conditions be in place for a truly inclusive system and for significantly increased investment in health and healthcare, reconceived as a public good.

Principle 3: Strengthen the voice of the poor and marginalized to make claims

The South Africa and Venezuela "right to health" cases mentioned above were major lawsuits lodged in the formal judicial system to vindicate a broad, population-wide right to health. But, in every healthcare system, there are countless moments when users face obstacles to accessing appropriate healthcare. An inclusive system makes it possible for users to assert claims of entitlement in these moments and then responds to those claims. This is an essential part of accountability in a rights-based system.

Sometimes claims will be formal claims, asserted through legal or regulatory mechanisms. These can be individual claims, as in a malpractice situation. They can also be broader claims for systemic change, such as those asserted through public interest litigation in the Indian legal system, where government policies on issues such as safety of banked blood have been adjudicated. In Latin America, a legal mechanism called *acción de amparo* (protection suit) has been effectively used by NGOs to vindicate a legally enforceable right to health (Yamin 2000).

However, not all accountability involves violation and not all claims involve a process of finding blame and imposing punishment. "Constructive

**Healthcare
financing
presents a
multifaceted
set of issues**

accountability" is about developing an effective dynamic of entitlement and obligation between people and their government and within the complex of relationships that form the system, both public and private (Freedman 2003; George 2003). That dynamic then becomes a crucial building block in the construction of health systems that function first and foremost for the benefit of people.

Building constructive accountability mechanisms into the system requires building the capacity of communities, civil society organizations, and government staff. Sometimes it may require compensating people for the time they devote to what is essentially civic service and that in turn requires specific allocation in the budget (Murthy and others 2003). Building constructive accountability mechanisms may require structural changes in how planning processes occur, priorities are set, and services are delivered. It may entail basic changes in the way information is treated, opening up information about the budget process to NGOs, for example, and providing information about actual spending and movement of funds to the people whose communities are meant to benefit from them (Fundar, International Budget Project, and International Human Rights Internship Program 2004). This requires a shift in the institutional culture that operates in government finance and planning processes and throughout the health system.

In sum: the real challenge in developing countries is for governments to use their powers to influence sectoral development and alter the balance of benefits between social groups in a way that ensures redistribution and equity. The urgency, pace, and scale of the action required to meet the Goals create the risk of adopting quick-fix solutions that merely address symptoms and not fundamental causes. One size does not fit all; "solutions" that may appear "technocratically correct" may not be appropriate unless they are locally responsive. Pritchett and Woolcock (2004) argue that the absence of consensus on how to improve services is appropriate; what is not appropriate is to do nothing.

Healthcare financing

Healthcare financing in developing countries presents a multifaceted set of issues. In the countries where child mortality and maternal mortality are highest, where women have restricted access to contraception and sexual and reproductive health information, the bottom line is an absolute scarcity of resources and a profound failure to ensure that the poor are reached. Healthcare financing is further complicated by broader economic crises, as well as fragmentation of the health system, fragile or absent government bureaucracies, inadequate internal financial control mechanisms, and limited regulatory powers.

Conventional accounting of health systems financing (resource availability, mobilization, allocation and expenditure monitoring) is a necessary first step to addressing these problems. But if we are serious about developing policies that inform redistribution by ensuring inclusion and preventing excessive segmentation (principle 2), this analysis must be broadened to include an

There is a tendency for health benefits to go disproportionately to the wealthy

understanding of the flow of funds throughout the whole health system, from households to the private and public health sectors. What drives these flows? What are the values informing the mobilization and allocation of funds and the distribution of who pays for what, where, and when?

Achieving equity and meeting the Goals represents a major challenge, for several reasons. First, the gap between the amounts of money required to meet the Goals and the amounts currently available is enormous. The Commission on Macroeconomics and Health estimated that an average of $34 per capita a year (2002 prices) would be needed to provide essential health services in low-income countries (Commission on Macroeconomics and Health 2001). Current per capita expenditure in some countries is as low as $1–$10 a year. And these figures represent national averages. Therefore, it is critical to ask questions about distribution across population groups by geography, gender, race, and wealth and across different levels of care. In many countries a disproportionate amount of resources is spent at the tertiary level rather than on primary care.

Second, out-of-pocket expenditures and utilization of private health services are disproportionately high among poorer communities and in poorer countries. And the poorer the country, the more likely this is to be the case (Mackintosh and Koivusalo 2004). Key drivers behind this phenomenon include the lack of commitment to redistribution in health financing policies, inadequate access to public sector services, the poor quality of care received in the public sector, and a loss of trust in the government as a provider of social services. Despite official dictums, including *World Development Report 1993* (World Bank 1993), that basic public health services should be free, all too often they are not. Indeed, out-of-pocket expenditures for maternal health and child health services can be considerable (Toole and others 2003). A recent study of the costs of accessing emergency obstetric care in Bangladesh showed that despite the government's policy of free healthcare, the average cost for an uncomplicated vaginal delivery was the equivalent of a household's monthly income. Costs for an emergency cesarean section could be as high as five times the average household's monthly salary, leading to an acute crisis and further impoverishment (Afsana 2004).

Third, even where government spending has increased, there is a tendency for the benefits to go disproportionately to the wealthy (World Bank 2003b). In Ghana the poorest quintile received only 12 percent of public expenditure on health in 1994, whereas the richest quintile received 33 percent (World Bank 2003b). Studies in several African countries found that public spending on curative care, even care that targets poorer communities, still mostly favors the better-off (Castro-Leal and others 2000).

Public financing policies

How a government chooses to raise funds for health and the mechanisms it uses to set priorities and allocate those funds provide one of the biggest

Revenue generated through user fees has been very limited

opportunities to signal serious intent to redress inequity. Governments generally employ a range of mechanisms to mobilize funds, each with its own trade-offs between equity and efficiency (table 4.2).

Most low-income countries have limited capacity to mobilize tax revenue. Total tax revenue as a percentage of GDP is only 14 percent in low-income countries, far lower than the 31 percent collected in high-income countries (Ravindran, Kikomba, and Maceira forthcoming). The health sector has to compete with all other sectors, especially "productive" sectors, for a share of this modest outlay. Possibilities for increasing the contribution of tax revenue to the health sector may therefore be limited.

In the absence of tax revenue, many developing countries have attempted to finance health through user fees and, increasingly, prepaid community-based insurance schemes. Social health insurance is the predominant health system financing mechanism in Latin America, but it is generally not feasible in Africa or Asia, as it relies on relatively high levels of formal sector employment.

In theory, user fees are supposed to increase efficiency, by sending price signals that encourage adherence to appropriate referral chains and discourage frivolous use of services, thereby reallocating resources to the more cost-effective primary care services. But, in practice, revenue generated through user fees has been very limited. Data from national user fee systems in Sub-Saharan Africa countries in the 1980s and 1990s indicate an average cost recovery level of about 5 percent of recurrent health system expenditures, gross of administrative costs. Where exemption schemes have been introduced in an attempt to protect the poor, they have generally failed (Ravindran, Kikomba, and Maceira forthcoming).

Substantial evidence shows that user fees are a significant barrier, preventing access to maternal and child health services. In Tanzania one study documented several deaths of women denied treatment because of inability to pay, including the death of a woman in a maternity hospital who was unable to pay for an emergency cesarean section (Mackintosh and Tibandebage 2002). Formal fees have also hindered access to hospital care for children, as documented in recent studies from Kenya and Uganda investigating extremely low compliance with pediatric referral to district hospitals in cases of serious child illness. Cost was cited as the most common reason for not obtaining needed care (English and others 2004; Peterson and others 2004).

A study conducted in Cambodia after the introduction and increase in user fees at a district hospital showed decreased utilization rates, especially among those least able to pay. Exemption mechanisms failed, as they strained already limited administrative capacity, and out-of-pocket expenditures soared. The result was a "medical poverty trap" for those unable to access care: untreated illness, reduced access to care, long-term impoverishment, and irrational drug use (Jacobs and Price 2004).

Table 4.2

Key healthcare financing mechanisms

Source: McIntyre 1997.

Financing mechanism	Efficiency	Displacement effects	Equity
General tax revenue	Usually most important source of healthcare finance Relatively efficient Collection costs low relative to revenue Relatively stable but dependent on political decisions	Leaves potential private funding sources untapped (if health services completely tax funded)	Tends to be progressive overall if efficiently paid by all Depends on progressivity of each tax and the combination of taxes (direct taxes tend to be progressive, indirect taxes tend to be regressive)
Dedicated taxes	Relatively efficient Earmarked for health services Revenue can fluctuate if linked to consumption of certain goods	Tend to displace general tax revenue	Tend to be regressive (with the exception of the tax on luxury goods, most consumption taxes are regressive) Can significantly add to tax burden, often in an invisible manner
User fees	Complementary source Tend to have relatively low revenue-generating potential, particularly if reliant on out-of-pocket payments as opposed to targeting the insured High collection and administration costs	Tend to displace general tax revenue	Tend to be highly regressive Adversely affect health service access of the poorest (this problem can be reduced through effective exemption mechanisms or offset by significant and sustained improvements in quality of health services)
Prepaid community schemes	Complementary source Tend to have relatively low and generally inadequate revenue-generating potential Collection and administration costs not excessive	Replace or reduce user fee revenue Cause minimal tax revenue displacement	Tend to be regressive (burden of financing placed on rural poor) May reduce costs of health services for individuals if service quality (especially drug availability) improves
Social health insurance	Can generate significant revenue (depending on size of formal sector and income levels) Administrative costs can be relatively high	May displace general tax revenue Tends to displace voluntary private insurance (which is minimal in poor countries)	Degree of progressivity depends on extent to which contribution structure is income related and on the level of upper limit Can improve equity within insured group Financing burden usually falls on formally employed Creates a two-tier system Public sector resources may be released, which can be targeted to improving services for noninsured

Abolishing user fees signals the government's commitment to improving equity

Abolishing user fees, a step taken by a number of countries in recent years, signals the government's commitment to improving equity and access to care for the poor. It has also resulted in increased utilization—in some cases dramatically so (Burnham and others 2004). In South Africa a 1994 decision to eliminate all user fees for primary healthcare in the public sector was combined with a policy to provide free care to children under the age of six and to pregnant women (McCoy and Khosa 1996). The result was a significant increase in utilization, although the failure to plan adequately for the removal of user fees led to a decrease in quality of care and staff motivation until the systems were improved.

In a small number of countries, health financing reforms have included the introduction or revival of prepayment schemes or community insurance schemes (Ravindran, Kikomba, and Maceira forthcoming). The main objective of prepayment schemes is to keep poor and vulnerable people within the health system, raising additional revenue without imposing financial burden on those who are ill. Such arrangements facilitate risk pooling for those not covered by formal insurance schemes. In addition, unlike most insurance schemes, prepayment schemes normally cover low-cost but high-probability health needs, such as outpatient care. The volume of funds raised with prepayment schemes is often low, however, and the costs of collection and management comparatively high (Ravindran, Kikomba, and Maceira forthcoming). Evidence suggests that these schemes are able to reduce catastrophic expenditure, but only scanty evidence reveals how these systems can be scaled up or what effect they have on equity (Palmer and others 2004). Moreover, because they are usually implemented in rural areas, prepayment schemes can result in a situation in which "the poor simply cross-subsidize the healthcare costs of other poor members of the population" (Bennett, Creese, and Monasch 1998). Significant cross-subsidization is not likely unless the insurance provided in the formal and informal employment sectors can be linked (McIntyre 2004).

Several other financing schemes, most notably in Latin America, have sought to increase use of key maternal and child health services by the poor by offering specific services for free or providing cash benefits conditioned on the use of particular services. In Mexico the Progresa (education, health, and nutrition) program (now Oportunidades) offered cash transfers to eligible families provided they obtained preventive healthcare, participated in growth monitoring and nutrition supplements programs, and attended health education programs. The PAC (basic healthcare program) worked in synergy with Progresa, targeting the most disadvantaged municipalities in Mexico by delivering a cost-effective basic healthcare package. The program reached 10.9 million poor people, most in small, rural communities. The number of Mexicans with no health coverage declined from 10 million in 1995 to 1.5 million in 1999, and the maternal mortality ratio in the six poorest states fell from 72 per 100,000 live births to 59 over the same period (Gertler and Boyce 2001; Marquez and de Geyndt 2003).

**Enforcement
to guarantee
access
sometimes
requires active
civil society
engagement**

In Bolivia a national health insurance plan, called Maternal and Child National Insurance, was developed in 1996, with the main objective of increasing coverage of maternal and child care. The program covers antenatal care; labor and delivery, including cesarean sections and other obstetric emergencies; and postpartum and newborn care. Women and children under five receive services free of charge. According to Demographic and Health Survey statistics, the skilled birth attendants indicator increased from 43 percent in 1994 to 59 percent in 1998 (Seoane and others 2003). Analysis by quintile shows that the poorest segment of the population has increased use of skilled birth attendants and health facilities for delivery (from 11 percent to 20 percent) in just four years. Still, as of 1998 about 80 percent of the poorest people in Bolivia did not have access to services (Koblinsky and Campbell 2003; Seoane and others 2003).

Enforcement to guarantee access under these schemes sometimes requires active civil society engagement. For example, the NGO SENDAS has organized users' committees and mobilized women's groups to ensure implementation of the free maternity care law in Ecuador (Moya and Acurio 2003).

Nevertheless, these types of schemes send important messages about how the state values the right to health.

Priority setting and resource allocation

The allocation and distribution of resources is an intensely political process affected by power struggles among strong stakeholders with disparate agendas. These stakeholders include both different ministries and levels of government and external players. The ability of the state to set priorities and negotiate the allocation of resources in a way that increases equity and meets the needs of stakeholders is a measure of trust in the state, of the state's legitimacy, and of its commitment to procedural justice.

In many instances the formulas used to allocate resources within the health system actually intensify disparities. Analysis of the health budget of Mexico, undertaken by the NGO Fundar, revealed that states with the worst coverage of facilities and the largest deficits in the health workforce—and hence the worst access to emergency obstetric care and the highest maternal mortality ratios—received the lowest per capita allocations from the budget. Rather than allocating resources to close the capacity gap, the budget ended up wrenching it open even wider (Diaz and Freyermuth 2004; Diaz and Hofbauer 2004).

One approach to this general problem has been put forward by Gavin Mooney (2003) in his work on "capacity to benefit" as a key principle in resource allocation. Recognizing that health systems perform social functions beyond the delivery of disease-specific interventions, he outlines the following process for allocating resources for healthcare:

- Establish what good is to be achieved, in collaboration with those who will benefit.

As important as
"what" needs
to be done is
"how" to do it

- See how that good can be made better with the resources available.
- Where regions need help creating the infrastructure needed to do better, adjust the resource allocation formula to allocate funds for this purpose.
- Make due allowance in the allocations for variations in the costs of access across regions.

This process enables values to be translated into funded mandates. It recognizes that some communities are geographically remote and require extra resources to overcome this barrier, and it reinforces the notion that the capacity to benefit from an injection of funds requires a functioning infrastructure and health system to support activities. Lack of capacity in an area must be addressed head-on, not used as part of an efficiency argument not to allocate additional funds.

This approach works in conjunction with a rights-based approach, in which priority setting and resource allocation processes work in collaboration with people to understand better the required choices, to develop and define a vision for change in health systems, and to act upon that vision through organizing, learning, and networking. It explicitly addresses inequality. It also serves as a counter to dominant cost-effectiveness priority-setting mechanisms that result in a collection of basic disease-specific interventions identified as "essential healthcare packages." Even for such a package, implementation requires appropriate mechanisms (public, private sector, bureaucratic) of information, accountability, redress, and pressure. Given the complexity of priority-setting and resource allocation processes, it is critical that such decisions be transparent and "based on fair reasoned and defensible arguments, which must be publicly accessible—so-called accountability for reasonableness" (Segall 2003, p. s17).

Organizing the health system

This task force report sets out a vision of what needs to be done to achieve the child health and maternal health Goals. The interventions and services required to reduce mortality in women and children and to promote sexual and reproductive health have been described. Just as important as what needs to be done, though, is how to do it. The processes through which interventions are delivered ultimately determine the magnitude and the sustainability of their impact. Strengthening the health system is the central process recommended for ensuring universal access to necessary services for women and children and increasing their use of such services. Health systems must provide services in a way that is equitable; marginalization and exclusion of the poor and other disadvantaged groups must end. There must be a fundamental respect for human rights. Health systems are not machines. They are dynamic entities built around human relationships. They are part of the social fabric, an essential context for the assertion of citizenship. They must be respectful of all whom they exist to serve. For these reasons, the way that a health system is organized is critical.

A health system
must be driven
by primary
healthcare

The different levels of primary healthcare

The WHO has called for the strengthening of health systems to be "based on the core principles of primary healthcare as outlined at Alma Ata in 1978," warning that "it is unrealistic to expect the achievement of the Millennium Development Goals without a health system driven by primary healthcare" (WHO 2003b, p. 14). This task force agrees. Furthermore, we support the pyramid-shaped multilevel structure of a health system that can best support a primary healthcare approach.

Maternal health and child health, while similar in many ways, are also fundamentally different. Recent trends in the delivery of child health services have been to move as many of those services as close to the community as possible. From an emphasis on clinic-based care, most experts now believe that the treatment of common but potentially fatal illnesses such as diarrhea and pneumonia can be carried out by relatively unskilled workers within the community. The Integrated Management of Childhood Illnesses strategy, for example, now has a community-based component that is seen as essential to the successful implementation of the entire package of interventions. Of course, these community health workers must be supported and closely supervised by clinically trained staff at first-level facilities, structures that should be easily accessible to a number of neighboring communities with a population that does not exceed the ability of that staff to provide universal care. The management of seriously ill children must be left to these more competent health professionals, and community-level workers, together with primary caregivers, must be able to recognize the signs of severe illness early and make appropriate referrals. Finally, the same is true on one additional level—the presence of an around-the-clock referral hospital is necessary for cases that are so severe that the primary care facility cannot competently deal with them. Child health conditions requiring hospitalization include severe pneumonia requiring oxygen therapy, cerebral malaria, and septicemia.

For the reduction of maternal mortality, the priorities are somewhat reversed. Antenatal care can be provided at the primary healthcare facility, and all births can be attended, even within the community, by a skilled attendant. But most maternal deaths are the result of obstetric complications that occur around the time of delivery. For the most part these complications require a hospital-level intervention, such as a cesarean section, multiple transfusions, or parenteral antibiotics and 24-hour-a-day monitoring.

In other words, although different degrees of emphasis may be placed on different levels of the system for different purposes, reaching the Goals for both child health and maternal health requires strengthening all of the following: household prevention and care-seeking behaviors; the delivery of services within the community by healthcare workers trained to perform a few specific tasks; a competently staffed and adequately supplied clinic that provides outpatient care; and a first-level referral hospital where severe, life-threatening conditions can be

District-level administration of healthcare service delivery can signal national commitment to principles of inclusiveness

managed by health professionals trained to do so. A strong, well functioning health system performs all of these functions. In most settings, all can be ensured within a peripheral administrative unit, typically a district, with appropriate support and supervision from provincial and national authorities (Bulatao and Ross 2003; Campbell 2001; McCoy and others 2004; McCoy and Rowson 2004).

Ensuring equity and inclusiveness—another role of the district health system

Because the district health system is—or at least should be—endowed with significant resources, including adequate quantities of drugs and equipment, appropriate levels of technical expertise, and, perhaps especially, a well functioning hospital, it is well placed to reduce the segmentation of the overall health system by becoming the healthcare "leader" in a specific geographic area (Mackintosh and Koivusalo 2004). In doing so, district-level administration of healthcare service delivery can signal national commitment to principles of inclusiveness and redistribution of resources.

In other words, the management of a district health system should promote good health practices and draw people in for appropriate health services (whether public or private), rather than abandoning them to an often unregulated, unsupervised, unaffordable private healthcare system that ultimately fails the poor. Stronger district health systems, especially better managed district health systems with improved financial integrity and accountability, will also reduce reliance by donors and others on a multiplicity of vertical programs, each with its own redundant management structures (Oliveira-Cruz, Kurowski, and Mills 2003).

We propose that the appropriate response to weak government health services is to pull out all the stops in order to strengthen them, not to further undermine them until they are beyond repair. For some countries this will not be an overly burdensome task, provided that the appropriate resources are made available. In others the process of salvaging the health system will be daunting, but nevertheless possible and, we believe, necessary. If the Goals are to be met in these countries, the implementation of the interventions delineated in this report for reducing child and maternal mortality will need to begin before the process of system strengthening is complete.

The strength of a local health system must come as much from below as from above. Unless people believe that they will receive proper treatment, as individuals as well as patients, utilization rates are unlikely to rise. District health system administrators and service providers must do everything necessary to engender trust in the population they serve (Gilson 2003). Women, the poor, and citizens belonging to minority ethnic groups or practicing minority religions must all be equally served in a respectful manner if the indicators proposed in this report for assessing progress toward the Goals are to move in the right direction and at an appropriate pace. A public healthcare system is

The strength of a local health system must come as much from below as from above

not, after all, worthy of the name unless it is intended to, and is able to, serve all of the public.

Decentralization

There has been a great deal of discussion in the literature, and even some experimentation on the ground, regarding the decentralization of health system functions, at least to the district level. Decentralization creates the potential for greater community involvement in health system management and decisionmaking. It provides a broader array, or at least a more locally tailored array, of consumer choices of services. In theory, realizing this potential could be a formula for increasing inclusivity and trust.

However, in communities in which gross inequities exist in all sectors, greater community control over the health sector may perpetuate them. In many communities strong local interests have been able to control resource allocation for their own narrow purposes, serving their own interests, not those of the community at large.

The data regarding the effects of decentralization on the health of the poor are equivocal (Global Forum for Health Research 2004). The power to decide what needs to be done can, and should, be decentralized if stronger health systems are to develop, but the use of that power needs to be controlled and managed. Local priorities may not reflect national (and international) priorities, and attempts at decentralization have at times been plagued by "a lack of technical, administrative, and financial management expertise and limited awareness of reproductive health problems as public health priorities at the local level" (Langer, Nigenda, and Cantino 2000, p. 671). At other times services as basic as childhood vaccinations have been left off community lists of healthcare priorities. For these reasons, decentralized systems still need to be overseen by national health authorities. Accountability of local authorities to both the public and the central government is critical if equity is to be ensured and national health goals reached. The potential for exacerbating inequities and perpetuating the disenfranchisement of certain groups can be guarded against and the need to respect certain national public health priorities at the local level protected by ensuring a strong, functional partnership between the district health system and more central health authorities.

What has emerged from the research is a set of common denominators of successful decentralization that can be adapted to local contexts (Gilson 2004). These principles can guide the early development of strong systems in countries in which they are in disrepair:

- Communicate a clear and simple vision of the purpose of decentralization. In the context of developing a decentralized district health system, this vision must show that the system is viewed not as a vertical program but as a strategy for all health system development and planning.

Management is a critical aspect of strengthening health systems

- Identify an implementation unit to support health system decentralization. The key function of this unit is to pace the implementation of decentralization at a rate appropriate to the circumstances.
- Develop a mindset at all levels of government that supports decentralization.
- Strengthen coordination by clarifying roles and responsibilities.
- Strengthen supervision, monitoring, evaluation, and accountability.
- Encourage effective leadership throughout the health system. Champions at all levels of the system need to be given the space to take the innovative actions required to make decentralization work.

Health management

Management capacity is a neglected—and now dangerously fragile—part of the overall health system. The structural changes to the health system ushered in by donor-driven neoliberal economic policies and social sector reform agendas create profound and ongoing challenges for health system managers. The newly professed faith in markets and the private sector, together with downsizing and deprecation of the public sector, leave healthcare workers feeling vulnerable, demotivated, undervalued, and cynical (Schaay, Heywood, and Lehmann 1998; Unger, De Paepe, and Green 2003). Diminished service ethics, worsening economic realities, and the tension between managing public interests and private gain have led to a perception—if not a reality—of increased corruption or patronage. Weakened management capacity and the resultant loss of trust in the health system have arguably encouraged vertical programming and donor funding streams that sidestep government channels in order to go directly to "substitute" NGOs (Pfeiffer 2003).

In addition, managers are faced with a complex array of parallel and uncoordinated programs, often introduced top-down without prior consultation, all to be managed with steadily declining resources. For example, a study of management capacity to implement major (and much needed) changes in the huge maternal health programs that have been launched in India reveals a problematically thin management infrastructure (Mavalankar 2003).

To address this situation, managers need a variety of technical skills backed by operational systems. But, just as important are the skills needed to manage the "software" issues in an organization: building trust, shifting organizational culture, and developing organizational networks and relationships (Blaauw and others 2003; Gilson 2003). Successful implementation of policies to promote equity and inclusion requires a focus on human interactions at the micro level, as well as the development of supportive institutional systems for financing, information, and regulation. Development of a rights-based health system that increasingly addresses the systemic barriers to care experienced by poor and vulnerable groups requires managers who are more than administrators, managers who understand a given context and are able to take appropriate action.

**Those
responsible for
policy imple-
mentation, the
health manag-
ers, are seldom
consulted**

Providing an enabling environment to support management

Inclusion in policy development and planning process. Managers have expressed frustration at having to implement, and at times abandon, ill-conceived policies that they played no role in designing (Lehmann and Sanders 2002). Whereas the importance of consultation with communities and health professionals is increasingly recognized in policy development, those responsible for policy implementation, the health managers, are seldom consulted (Penn-Kekana, Blaauw, and Schneider 2004; Unger, De Paepe, and Green 2003). How this consultation should occur is context specific, but that it should occur, even as early as the design phase, is important for sustainability (Faull 1998).

Efficient operational systems and institutional structures. Efficient and appropriately resourced operational systems that are strategically aligned to the goals of the health system are key to effective service delivery. Operational systems include systems for financial management, a support network of supervision, communications, policy guidance, skills training, human resources management, procurement, logistics, and transport (Toole and others 2003). In addition, clear delineation of the responsibilities and delegated authorities between central and local levels is critical to the effective functioning of the district health system. Underpinning all these structures must be an effective information system that is able to provide appropriate, accurate, and timely information to inform management decisions at all levels of healthcare.

The role of many of these systems is to "regularize" activities that are conducted routinely and that require minimal discretion in their execution (Pritchett and Woolcock 2004). Good operational systems free up the health workforce, including managers, to undertake activities that require discretion and individual judgment. For example, good drug procurement and stock control systems enable healthcare workers to spend less time dealing with stockouts and more time managing and communicating with patients. If these basic, routine activities were well executed, managers would be free to pursue important discretionary work such as supervision and maternal and perinatal audits to improve quality of care.

Moving from policies to action

Getting the policies right is a necessary first step for charting better directions for health systems. But moving to the stage of operationalizing policy is the crux of the problem for many health systems—the second half of the battle. The global health landscape is littered with policies that are empty shells—never implemented, monitored, or revised. What allows policies to be operationalized is a complex question, one tied to the strength of the health system.

Moving from policies to action is a major challenge in the maternal, child, and reproductive health fields. Even simple, well documented, evidence-based

Trust must exist among managers, staff, and the community

practices, such as the use of magnesium sulphate for eclampsia, continue to meet resistance in clinical practice in many countries. Why are midwives, nurses, and doctors in many parts of the world unaware of the appropriate interventions for averting maternal deaths, for providing basic HIV/AIDS counseling, for controlling infection? Why is there such ambiguity about and distrust of referral systems (Murray and Pearson 2004)? How can new evidence-based interventions, such as active management of the third stage of labor, trickle down from the WHO into the practices of rural midwives in Malawi?

The answers to these questions lie not just in the pieces of paper, manuals, posters, and booklets that outline norms and protocols. Rather, they lie in a broader notion of "operational systems"—the components that intersect to make a health system. Disseminating the latest international norms requires enlightened managers with good leadership skills who can adapt national guidelines to local contexts. It requires resources that flow in the directions needed and healthcare workers who are flexible and empowered to take up new knowledge, practices, and roles. Trust must exist between managers and staff and between staff and the community. Continuing education and supportive supervision must exist as a vehicle for conveying new information. Logistics for drug supply and referral mechanisms must be mapped out and functional. All of this depends on strong management guided by clear values and trust. Equity must be a guiding principle for those interpreting and implementing policies and deciding who, where, and what is prioritized. Ultimately, the health system must not be regarded as a static venue for delivering a set of interventions but, rather, a dynamic, interactive set of people, innovations, knowledge, and behaviors that, based on a set of guidelines, work to improve health, starting with those who need it most.

A health workforce to meet the Millennium Development Goals

The downward spiral of neglect that plagues so many health systems cannot be reversed without a fresh, long-term approach to creating a viable health workforce.[2]

Strengthening human resources is critical to ensuring inclusive and equitable health systems, for several reasons:

- Health workers—in sheer number, quality, and attitude—profoundly affect health outcomes and the ability to realize health goals (Martinez and Martineau 1998; Narasimhan and others 2004; Padarath and others 2003; Physicians for Human Rights 2004; USAID 2003). Studies indicate that the density of human resources for health, in particular nurses and doctors, is a significant determinant of variation in the rates of infant, under-five, and particularly maternal mortality across countries (Anand and Barnighausen 2004).
- Salaries for healthcare workers generally constitute the greatest share of the health budget, in some countries up to 75 percent. And healthcare workers

constitute a substantial share of the formal labor force in most countries. It is estimated that there are three or more uncounted healthcare workers, including informal, traditional, and community health workers, for every formally trained doctor or nurse (Joint Learning Initiative 2004).

- Healthcare workers' performance is a very tangible manifestation of the values and norms not only of the health system but of the government itself, setting, exemplifying, and promoting the health system's mission and core values. In many instances healthcare workers act as "street-level bureaucrats," with the power to interpret, implement, or sabotage health policies and programs (Gilson and Erasmus 2004).

- Healthcare workers manage all other resources within the health system, and they spearhead performance. The availability of healthcare workers is often the proven constraint to scaling up, limiting HIV/AIDS and tuberculosis treatment, immunization coverage, and other interventions (Mercer and others 2003; Physicians for Human Rights 2004). They determine the absorptive capacity of all other resources (Wyss 2004).

- Despite their importance, "stocks of human resources for health systems are small and in some countries emigration and HIV/AIDS are making it smaller" (Wagstaff and Claeson 2004, p. 111). Recent reports estimate a global shortage of healthcare workers at more than 4 million workers, with Sub-Saharan Africa alone short 1 million healthcare providers (Joint Learning Initiative 2004).

Despite these compelling reasons to focus on healthcare workers, there is a legacy of chronic underinvestment and a failure to adopt a systemwide approach to addressing human resources in health (Joint Learning Initiative 2004). Consequently, most governments and donors deal with different health workforce planning issues in isolation, resulting in patchy and unsustainable solutions (USAID 2003).

Three key problems affecting the health workforce

Three key problems associated with the health workforce have a broad impact on health systems and must be considered when planning an effective health workforce to meet the Goals:

Impact of internal and international migration of healthcare workers. Ironically, "[j]ust as drugs and funds are beginning to flow from the developed to the developing world, the exodus of trained healthcare workers is accelerating in the opposite direction" (Narasimhan and others 2004, p. 1471).

The brain drain of healthcare workers is hitting many developing countries hard, particularly in Sub-Saharan Africa. Half of medical school graduates from Ghana emigrate within 4.5 years of graduation, and 75 percent leave within 9.5 years (Lehmann and Sanders 2002). In South Africa more than 300 specialist

The brain drain of healthcare workers is hitting many developing countries hard

nurses leave every month, many never to return (Physicians for Human Rights 2004). Nearly a third of the health workforce in the United Kingdom comes from other countries (EQUINET 2004). "Millions of healthcare workers are 'acting with their feet,' demonstrating their own response to weaknesses in the system by securing the personal 'best options' for themselves. While this responds to individual demands for security and well-being, it has costs to the healthcare workers, the primary and district level of health systems, the poorest populations and public health sectors in the south" (Padarath and others 2003, p. 4).

Factors driving the brain drain are complex and fundamentally linked to broader health system failures in both "recipient" and "donor" countries (box 4.1) (Physicians for Human Rights 2004). Pull factors include the failure of recipient countries to adequately address their own shortages of nurses and physicians, leading them to recruit from countries already suffering a deficit of qualified workers (Padarath and others 2003; Physicians for Human Rights 2004; USAID 2003). Push factors drive healthcare workers out of a country, and they also operate within a country, causing migration from rural to urban areas and from public to private practice. Skilled workers are also "siphoned off" to vertical programs and

---

Box 4.1

A variety of factors affects the brain drain of healthcare workers

Source: Padarath and others 2003.

Push factors endogenous to the healthcare system
- Low remuneration levels
- Work-related risks, such as exposure to HIVAIDS and tuberculosis
- Unrealistic work loads, as a result of inadequate human resource planning
- Poor infrastructure
- Suboptimal working conditions

Push factors exogenous to the healthcare system
- Crime
- High taxes
- Repressive political environments
- Falling service standards

Pull factors
- Aggressive recruitment
- Better quality of life
- Opportunities for study and specialization
- Better pay

"Stick factors" influencing decision not to emigrate
- Family ties
- Psychological links with home
- Migration costs
- Language and other social and cultural factors

"Stay factors" influencing decision to remain in recipient country
- Reluctance to disrupt family life and schooling
- Lack of employment opportunities in home country
- Higher standard of living in recipient country

HIV/AIDS has contributed to the shortage of health personnel

donor-driven projects, which offer higher status and higher salaries (Mackintosh 2003; Padarath and others 2003; Van Lerberghe and others 2002).

The drivers and characteristics of the health workforce crisis differ from place to place (Dussault and Dubois 2003; Egger, Lipson, and Adams 2000; Kowalewski and Jahn 2001; Padarath and others 2003; Wahba 2004; Wyss 2004; Zurn and others 2002). Imbalances in the workforce take many different forms. These include rural to urban migration; movement away from the public sector into the private sector, particularly in areas where the private sector is more developed (Padarath and others 2003); and imbalances and shortages of appropriate skills within and between different levels of care. A study in Tanzania found that every fourth task that required a skilled health professional was being performed by an unskilled worker (Wagstaff and Claeson 2004).

It is appropriate that skilled personnel concentrate at higher levels of the health system. Of greater equity concern are differences in the distribution of health personnel at the same level of care across districts. These differences are usually driven by inequalities in resource allocation to the districts (McIntyre and others 1995).

Impact of HIV/AIDS. HIV/AIDS has contributed to the shortage of health personnel in many rural and underserved areas, both directly and indirectly. It has caused attrition of HIV-infected healthcare workers and decreased job satisfaction, as services become unbearably stretched and palliative care squeezes out curative care. Healthcare workers face a triple burden from the epidemic—as workers, as patients, and as caregivers. Along with caring for HIV-positive patients at work, many female healthcare workers, like women throughout their countries, are apt to be caregivers for HIV-positive family members at home, and they are susceptible to the virus themselves (Jackson and others 2004). A recent study in South Africa showed an HIV prevalence of 20 percent among younger healthcare workers (Physicians for Human Rights 2004; Shisana and others 2004); in 1997 Malawi lost the equivalent of 44 percent of the nurses it trains in a year to AIDS (Hongoro and McPake 2004). Better training programs that incorporate information on HIV/AIDS treatment and support; flexible work schemes; succession planning (where feasible, from within the same household); support services; and plans to treat people infected with HIV are urgently required (Lehmann and Sanders 2002).

Impact of labor and civil service "reforms." Public sector healthcare workers belong to the civil service and thus have been subject to all of the human resource policies introduced as part of public sector reforms (ILO and WHO 2003; Physicians for Human Rights 2004; USAID 2003). As part of overall structural adjustment policies, health reforms imposed ceilings on staff numbers and salaries while capping investment in higher education and training. "Two decades of health sector 'mis-reforms' treated healthcare workers as a

Strategic health workforce development requires building a "strong action coalition across all stakeholders"

cost burden, not an asset" (Joint Learning Initiative 2004, p. 20). Civil service reforms have had a particularly devastating effect on skilled and experienced healthcare workers in Sub-Saharan Africa, where cuts were skill neutral, focused on reducing absolute numbers rather than retaining the most experienced, skilled personnel (USAID 2003). Beyond sheer numbers, civil service restrictions disallowed important financial and nonfinancial incentives for doctors and nurses who agreed to work in remote rural areas (USAID 2003). Even for those who stayed in the civil service, salaries were often reduced and liberalization of medical practice pushed civil servants into private practice, segmenting the health market and further reducing access of poor people to healthcare.

Proactive health workforce planning is needed to create an inclusive and equitable health system

To meet these challenges a major shift in approaches to human resource planning and management is required. Healthcare workers can no longer be seen as simply cogs in the system, delivering discrete interventions. Instead, the task force advocates proactive health workforce planning and management requiring strong leadership and collaboration with key stakeholders. Plans based on a clear understanding of the nature and distribution of the health workforce must align with the goals and values of the health system and seek innovative solutions to particular problems. Attention to the livelihoods and respect for the rights of healthcare workers must inform planning and management of healthcare workers, particularly if significant inroads are to be made to stanch the brain drain. Supportive systems and policies are required to reinforce this approach; they should also motivate workers. Finally, global players need to support rather than undermine these processes.

The goal is a health workforce that ensures quality care, collaborates across services and sectors, is receptive to the needs of clients, and strengthens equitable health systems.

Strong leadership and collaboration with key stakeholders. Strong, legitimate government with the political will and public commitment to strategic health workforce development is central to the crafting and implementation of health and development policies. This is an inherently "political exercise that goes beyond technical activities and calls for a process of exchange and negotiation between various interest groups" (Dussault and Dubois 2003, p. 8). It requires the building of a "strong action coalition across all stakeholders" (Joint Learning Initiative 2004, p. 5). Professional associations must be engaged, leadership in key fields like nursing and midwifery must be supported, parliamentary committees on healthcare workers must be fostered, and political ingenuity among stakeholders that is directed toward change must be rewarded (Chamberlain and others 2003; Schiffman 2003). In addition, public involvement

**Public
involvement
must be
bolstered to
demand equity-
oriented action**

must be bolstered to demand equity-oriented action and dilute the power of factions resisting change.

Strategies to "delegate" specialist functions to another level of health provider are often resisted by specialists. The doctor-dominated Health Professions Council in Zimbabwe, for example, has denied nurses the right to prescribe drugs privately, even though they do so in the public sector (Bloom and Standing 2001). The hierarchy within nursing is pronounced and formidable (Bloom and Standing 2001). Registered nurses' lobbies in Ghana, Kenya, Malawi, and Zambia strongly resisted and ultimately banned attempts to create "enrolled nurses," who have less training than registered nurses (Dovlo 2004). But such opposition is not universal. In India, for example, in order to make emergency obstetric care more widely available, the Federation of Obstetric and Gynecology Societies of India (a national association of some 20,000 obstetricians and gynecologists) has taken up an initiative to train nonspecialist doctors (medical officers) in providing emergency obstetric care, including cesarean section. The government of India welcomed this initiative, which it plans to support (India, Ministry of Health and Family Welfare 2004).

Expanded cadre of mid-level workers. In many countries achieving equity in the distribution of healthcare workers will require a significant number of additional skilled professionals. Given the cost and long lead time to train physicians (as well as the diminished ability of many developing countries to retain them in the public sector), countries have two viable ways to obtain more skilled staff. The first is a massive scale-up in the training and deployment of nurses and midwives, together with an expansion of their scope of practice, including the right to diagnose, prescribe, and dispense medication. In many countries nurses' skills have been upgraded to allow them to perform surgical procedures and administer anesthesia (Dickinson 2003; Kowalewski and Jahn 2001).

The second, often complementary, option is to develop "alternative" or "substitute" healthcare workers. In some developing countries bold measures have been taken to ensure that the structure of the health workforce meets the true needs of the people. The "scope of practice" of the health workforce, previously modeled on the structure of the health workforce in developed countries, is now being adapted to reflect local demands. Substitute cadres typically have less academic training, including shorter preservice training. But in some settings they can perform clinical tasks at a level equivalent to nurses and physicians (Dovlo 2004; Kowalewski and Jahn 2001; Rana and others 2003; Thairu and Schmidt 2003; Vaz and others 1999). The appeal of using alternative cadres is the cost savings, the shorter period needed for training, and the potential for better and wider distribution to a population in need. Country-specific alternative cadres are also less likely to find employment in the international labor market, because their job titles and qualifications are not internationally recognized (Dovlo 2004). They may therefore be less likely to emigrate. Any

Nonphysician teams have been used to deliver critical services effectively

strategy to use alternative cadres must include plans for monitoring, evaluating, supervising, and regulating these cadres to ensure high-quality care and to protect patients' and workers' rights.

Focus on skilled birth attendants. No human resource plan should be considered complete without explicit attention to the training, accreditation, deployment, supervision, and monitoring of skilled birth attendants. Too often the need for and unique characteristics of this type of worker are missing from international and national agendas (WHO 2002c).

In maternal and reproductive health, alternative cadres have been used to deliver critical services effectively. Evidence has shown that nonphysician teams can be trained to undertake functions at the first referral level, including emergency operations (Kowalewski and Jahn 2001). Paraprofessionals have been trained to perform cesarean sections in Burkina Faso and Mozambique, provide anesthesia in a few African countries, and perform sterilizations in Bangladesh and India. Mid-level providers have been trained to provide abortion and postabortion services, including manual vacuum aspiration in Kenya, South Africa, and Uganda (Dickson-Tetteh and others 2000; Kiggundu 1999; Yumkella and Githiori 2000). In Ethiopia, Nepal, and Tanzania midwives provide all basic emergency obstetric functions.

Whether skilled attendants are based in the community or in a facility, their ability to manage the complications that kill women depends on their ability to access a functioning health system. Desperately needed initiatives to expand the number of skilled attendants must therefore be linked to and properly sequenced with initiatives to strengthen the health system (especially emergency obstetric care services) and improve workforce policies. The converse is also true: health system and health workforce strategies must give careful attention to the unique role of skilled attendants.

Long-term investments in the health workforce. While the training of mid-level and substitute workers are medium-term investments, sustainable long-term investments in health workforce development require the adoption of an "education pipeline" approach. This approach focuses on the country's basic and secondary educational systems, ensuring that sufficient numbers of students with a solid secondary-level education go on to become health professionals.

The perennial lack of healthcare workers in rural areas suggests that training programs must select and recruit people who reflect the demographics of the people most in need of care. In many places this means recruiting ethnic minorities and people with rural backgrounds (Wyss 2004). It may also mean that training institutions are best situated in rural communities.

To this end, it is essential that the ministries of education and finance be part of human resource planning. Maternal and child health can be the losers when ministry of education priorities are at odds with those of the ministry of

It is essential that the ministries of education and finance be part of human resource planning

health. In Uganda, for example, health training institutes are under the purview of the ministry of education and a bias toward general medical practitioners does not match the desperate need for nurse-midwives (Ssengooba, Oliveira-Cruz, and Pariyo 2004). In addition, the literature implies that ministry of education jurisdiction over tertiary educational institutions may be skewing the supply of health professionals away from primary healthcare (Dovlo 2004).

Finally, strengthening the health workforce requires a long-term investment in information and management systems to effectively monitor the health workforce dynamics—distribution, trends, pay differentials between cadres, posting and transfer mechanisms, and information on vacancies. Comprehensive human resource management systems must include qualitative monitoring and evaluation using clinical audits, healthcare workers' assessments of their working environment, evaluation of the referral system, monitoring of the level and reasons for brain drain, and clear evaluations of career paths. More detailed analyses, such as the WHO's Workload Indicators of Staffing Need tool, which allows finer tuning of the exact number and skill mix of staff in each district and health center, have been used with success in Papua New Guinea, Tanzania, and elsewhere (WHO 1998).

Focus on the human rights and livelihoods of healthcare workers. Given the massive migration of healthcare workers, the impact of HIV/AIDS, and deep dissatisfaction with working environments, a plan for the health workforce must start with a focus on the human rights and livelihoods of healthcare workers themselves. Governments must ensure a viable career in the health sector, for both men and women—one with proper accreditation, training, continuing education, opportunities for promotion, and livable wages. Rwanda's effort to place healthcare workers at the front of the queue for antiretroviral treatment represents a proactive approach to protecting healthcare workers (Rwanda, Ministry of Health 2003).

In most countries, the majority of frontline workers, especially nurses and midwives, are women. The pressures that confront women workers stem from deeper social dynamics, such as gender hierarchies and class structures. These issues cannot be addressed immediately, but the specific expression of those dynamics within the clinical setting—such as sexual harassment—can (Mumtaz and others 2003). Gender-sensitive career paths (allowing women to move in and out of the labor market), personal security, nondiscrimination in working conditions, and promotions are essential to any systemic human resources plan.

Many of the problems experienced by healthcare workers as a whole are particularly acute for community health workers, whose livelihoods and rights are often overlooked. These workers are usually trained but seldom retrained; they work as volunteers or are given small, irregular allowances; they receive little supervision; and they have almost no job security, as any commitment to

A systemic approach requires a careful rethinking of motivation and incentives that affect performance

them ends as abruptly as does the donor funding (Flores and McCoy 2004; USAID 2003). Yet the literature is clear that "adequate and sustained remuneration is essential to maintain the interest of the Community Health Worker and to ensure the stability of a program" (Lehmann, Friedman, and Sanders 2004, p. 25). Adequate training and supervision are also critically important to the sustainability of community health worker programs; a poorly managed program disconnected from a strong health system may well do more harm than good (Bloom and Standing 2001). Unsupported, community health workers may become involved in predatory practices, setting up in the private sector to offer services they are not trained or competent to provide or demanding informal fees in the public sector for services that are meant to be free (Pangu 2000).

Rethinking the motivation and incentive mechanisms. Moving from a dry culture of personnel administration to a systemic approach to sustaining a health workforce requires a careful rethinking of motivation and incentives that affect performance. If the "most precious possession of any health service is the dedication and inner motivation of its healthcare workers," then the health system must nurture their ability to exercise that dedication and inner motivation (Pangu 2000; Segall 2000a, p. 62). Too often healthcare workers are paid too little (or too infrequently) to have their employment in the public sector count as a viable career. As a result, they turn to moonlighting in the private sector (Pangu 2000; Physicians for Human Rights 2004; Segall 2000b; USAID 2003). The evidence on coping strategies used by healthcare workers is a testament to the depth of the problem, including the negative impact of such strategies on provider-client trust and worker morale (Ferrinho and others 2004; Van Lerberghe and others 2002). In addition, failure to address nonmonetary incentives—such as having adequate supplies, running electricity, and water in the health clinic and sufficient staff to reduce workloads—contributes to low morale and reduces the motivation to solve problems and provide responsive services (Mackintosh 2003; McCoy and others 2004).

Various approaches have been proposed to provide incentives and reward performance. A number of countries have moved toward results-oriented management and performance management, with mixed results. Linking pay, bonuses, and other financial incentives to individual performance depends on the ability to measure clearly delineated outputs. But measuring health outputs is extremely complex and not without problems (Ssengooba, Oliveira-Cruz, and Pariyo 2004). False reporting, skewing of management focus to ensure good output measures, increased competition among colleagues, and lack of monitoring capacity reduce the potential effectiveness of this approach. In contrast, cooperative behavior can be stimulated when incentives are shared by staff. Studies of the Republic of Korea and Taiwan (China) suggest that groupwide incentives work well for public health staff (Khaleghian and Das Gupta 2004).

**Solving the
problems of
the health
workforce in
poor countries
is a global
responsibility**

Nonmonetary incentives include ongoing training and education (Bloom and Standing 2001; Physicians for Human Rights 2004; UNAIDS 2003), as well as more rapid advancement within careers and public acknowledgment of service (Kowalewski and Jahn 2001). Accreditation and membership in professional associations are also important means of improving motivation and incentives that are often lacking for professions such as midwifery.

Also important are the "software" issues of motivating and retaining staff. These include ensuring an organizational culture that is supportive, encourages dialogue, and gives voice to front-line workers who implement systems changes (Penn-Kekana, Blaauw, and Schneider 2004).

Greater accountability of global players. Solving the problems of the health workforce in poor countries is a global responsibility. Donors must shift toward funding long-term investments rather than providing short-term, front-end input into specialized training programs. They should commit to funding health programs that are located within the health system rather than vertical programs that siphon off skilled healthcare workers. All parties should be open to new thinking about the health workforce, including new ideas about the kind of worker most suited to handle the health issues in each developing country (Biscoe 2001; USAID 2003).

Donors and governments alike must look outside the health sector to determine how civil service policies, including IMF conditionalities on such policies, affect the health workforce. The IMF and World Bank must encourage countries to use Poverty Reduction Strategy Papers and medium-term expenditure frameworks to promote the cross-sectoral work of human resource planning.

While country-level commitment to follow-through on strengthening the health workforce is critical, even poor countries with strong human resource policies have porous boundaries, allowing exit by skilled personnel to "greener pastures" and entrance for privatizing forces that threaten to further dismantle public systems. Rich countries must examine the ways in which their own policies contribute to dangerous imbalances.

Clearly, global leadership, technical assistance, and coordinated development assistance are needed to create a new vision for healthcare workers in the poorest regions of the world. In particular, the unique role of the skilled birth attendant must be explicitly included in the emerging international reckoning on the crisis in the global health workforce. Currently, the global human resource initiatives, the safe motherhood community, and the WHO do not speak with a unified voice on this issue. Disappointingly, a recent World Bank publication on strengthening health systems in order to meet the Millennium Development Goals points to the importance of human resources but does not identify the specific healthcare workers essential to reducing maternal and neonatal mortality (World Bank 2003b). And the Joint Learning Initiative on human resources for health and development does not emphasize the need for skilled birth attendants (Joint Learning Initiative 2004). These critical strands of global discourse must be unified if real change is to occur on the ground. Thus any initiative—regional, national, or global—that addresses the health workforce or human resource development in keeping with the priorities set by the Goals must include a particular emphasis on pregnancy and delivery care and the skilled birth attendant.

Chapter 5

Monitoring Goals 4 and 5: targets and indicators

The purpose of targets and indicators is to monitor and measure progress toward meeting the Goals. But they are important for other reasons as well: in the public health field, what we count is often what we do. Indicators should not only reflect movement toward the Goals, they should encourage implementation of priority, evidence-based interventions. Equally important is the need to ensure that inappropriate indicators—or the inappropriate use of acceptable indicators—do not distort program or policy priorities. In addition, movement toward the target or indicator should occur in a fashion that promotes equity, so that marginalized groups, including the poor, progress toward better health outcomes at a pace that is faster compared to that of better-off groups. Finally, in the Millennium Development initiative, indicators are the basis for accountability.

The task force proposes several modifications to the targets and indicators for the child mortality and maternal health Goals. These modifications will help spur progress as countries adapt the Millennium Development Goals to their specific settings, working to incorporate them into poverty reduction strategies, and as the international community moves toward the major review of progress in achieving the Goals scheduled for 2005. Table 5.1 outlines the target and indicators proposed for each goal. The suggested modifications are explained in the sections that follow.

What lies behind the averages? Monitoring equity

If MDG initiatives are to increase equity, the targets and indicators must incorporate an equity focus in their construction. For the global Millennium Development initiative as a whole, the task force proposes reframing the targets broadly to emphasize prioritization of the most disadvantaged and to encourage "faster progress among the poor and other marginalized groups" (as shown in table 5.1).

Table 5.1	Goal	Targets	Indicators
Proposed targets and indicators for the child health and maternal health Goals *Note:* Proposed modifications appear in italics.	Goal 4: Reduce child mortality	Reduce by two-thirds, between 1990 and 2015, the under-five mortality rate, *ensuring faster progress among the poor and other marginalized groups*	Under-five mortality rate Infant mortality rate Proportion of 1-year-old children immunized against measles *Neonatal mortality rate* *Prevalence of underweight children under 5 (see Goal 1 indicator)*
	Goal 5: Improve maternal health	Reduce by three-quarters, between 1990 and 2015, the maternal mortality ratio, *ensuring faster progress among the poor and other marginalized groups* *Universal access to reproductive health services by 2015 through the primary health-care system, ensuring faster progress among the poor and other marginalized groups*	Maternal mortality ratio Proportion of births attended by skilled health personnel *Coverage of emergency obstetric care* *Proportion of desire for family planning satisfied* *Adolescent fertility rate* *Contraceptive prevalence rate* *HIV prevalence among 15- to 24-year-old pregnant women (see Goal 6 indicator)*

Particular attention should be paid to disadvantaged groups and geographically constrained areas, and data should be disaggregated accordingly. Obtaining baseline information on key equity indicators is feasible even in countries in which the data are poor. As a paper commissioned by the task force shows, multiple dimensions of inequity can be established using data collected in Demographic and Health Surveys and Multiple Indicator Cluster Surveys (Wirth and others 2004).

Indicators should be adapted to the local context, where possible identifying the specific disparities that policies and programs will aim to narrow. For example, a country might specify in its indicators that progress in maternal mortality for indigenous groups and groups in particular provinces, in addition to the poor, should be explicitly monitored. In all countries, it will be important to disaggregate all non-sex-specific indicators by gender.[1]

Several countries, such as Viet Nam, have already included equity considerations in their interpretations of the Millennium Development Goals, adding new goals, such as reducing vulnerability, improving governance for poverty reduction, reducing ethnic inequality, and ensuring pro-poor infrastructure development (Swinkels and Turk 2002). The task force endorses these country-led efforts and recommends that targets and indicators be framed in equity-sensitive terms wherever possible.

Goal 4: Child health, neonatal mortality and nutrition.

The current child health indicators are the under-five mortality rate, the infant mortality rate, and the proportion of one-year-old children immunized against measles.

There is increasing recognition that neonatal mortality (defined as death during the first 28 days of life) represents a significant proportion of child mortality—globally, an estimated 37 percent—and that the child health Goal will not be reached unless neonatal mortality is addressed. The causes of neonatal death are different from the causes of death among older children. Programs and policies at all levels must be adjusted to reflect the different strategies necessary to reduce neonatal mortality. To encourage explicit attention to such actions, the task force recommends that the neonatal mortality rate be added as a fourth indicator to Goal 4.

The underlying role of malnutrition in a large proportion of child mortality must also be stressed. The Goals currently include an indicator on the prevalence of underweight children under five years of age (the indicator falls under Goal 1 on eradicating extreme poverty and hunger). Although underweight children may be an appropriate indicator of poverty and hunger, this measure is as much a reflection of health and the health system as it is a reflection of other important goals. Child malnutrition is in part a result of low birthweight, maternal malnutrition, improper feeding practices, frequent illness in infancy and early childhood, and micronutrient deficiencies—all problems that are within the purview of the health system (Sethuraman, Shekar, and Burz 2003). For this reason, the indicator on prevalence of underweight children should be echoed in the child health Goal in country-level implementation of the Goals.

Goal 5: Improving maternal health

The maternal health Goal is currently backed by one target (reduction of the maternal mortality ratio by three-quarters between 1990 and 2015) and two indicators (the maternal mortality ratio and the proportion of births attended by skilled health personnel). The maternal mortality ratio is extremely difficult to measure accurately, as the wide range of uncertainty in table 3.10 conveys.[2] The WHO therefore states that, while maternal mortality ratios help convey the scale of the problem, they cannot be used to track trends in maternal mortality.

The second indicator, the proportion of births attended by skilled health personnel ("skilled attendants") is also subject to multiple measurement problems (see chapter 3). Moreover, as detailed in a task force background paper (Freedman and others 2003), the proportion of skilled attendants does not vary consistently with maternal mortality ratios: particularly in very high-mortality countries, there is huge variation in the use of skilled attendants and little statistical correlation between the two indicators. Hence skilled attendants cannot be assumed to be a proxy for maternal mortality reduction.

The task force recommends adding an indicator that explicitly tracks the coverage of emergency obstetric care

The indicator is nevertheless important, as it is the only indicator in all of the Goals that explicitly relates to human resources. Skilled attendants will be a critical component of any strategy for reducing maternal mortality, and it is therefore important that it be included in the MDG indicators.

But the skilled attendant indicator should not be used by itself to track the reduction in maternal mortality ratio. If the core strategy for reducing maternal mortality relates to strengthening the facility-based health system, an indicator that tracks an intervention such as skilled attendants that can be (and often is) deployed *outside of that system* can lead to distortions in policy and program.

The task force therefore recommends that an indicator that explicitly tracks the coverage of emergency obstetric care be added. In 1997 UNICEF, the WHO, and UNFPA issued a set of process indicators designed to assess the availability and utilization of emergency obstetric care (UNICEF, WHO, and UNFPA 1997). For the purpose of monitoring the Goals, the task force recommends the use of the first indicator in this series, which sets a minimum standard of one comprehensive and four basic functioning emergency obstetric care facilities per 500,000 population.

The full set of emergency obstetric care process indicators gives a broad sense of a key aspect of health system development at the national level; it can also be used to sharpen policymakers' understanding of gaps in facility functioning. Over the past five years, dozens of countries have used these process indicators. A paper commissioned by the task force reviews this experience and contains the most comprehensive look at these data currently available (Paxton and others 2004). A second paper commissioned for the task force is a case study of Bangladesh. That study combines data on facility functioning generated by use of the emergency obstetric care process indicators with geographic mapping techniques to determine not only linear distance to facilities but also travel time, yielding a more nuanced picture of accessibility (Balk, Storeygard, and Booma 2004).

The ability to make evidence-based statements about the level of maternal mortality and its causes has been identified as a key factor in mobilizing the political will to address maternal mortality in many countries that have engineered dramatic declines (Koblinsky 2003b; Pathmanathan and others 2003). The invisibility—the phantom quality—of the death of women in pregnancy and childbirth is, in fact, one more dimension of the social devaluation of women (Graham and Hussein 2004). A strong, policy-relevant set of indicators for maternal mortality reduction is not just a sop to statisticians; it is a potentially powerful way to frame political demands for the fulfillment of women's right to the conditions necessary to survive pregnancy and childbirth.

New target: reproductive health

In operationalizing Goal 5, there is a serious problem of "fit" between the Goal and the target. Improving maternal health requires a policy vision and

To dramatically reduce maternal mortality and meet the target, emergency care must be accessible and utilized

programmatic interventions that include but go beyond those needed to reduce maternal mortality. In this respect, the maternal health Goal is markedly different from the child health Goal. The difference lies in the relationship between health and death. For infants and children, the biological causes of poor health are the same as the biological causes of most deaths. Child mortality can therefore be understood with a cumulative model: assaults of illness and poor health (such as infection and malnutrition) increasing in number or severity ultimately lead to death. Programs and policies that address the most important causes of poor health and poor development in children will, by definition, also address the causes of death.

Maternal health and maternal death have a fundamentally different relationship to each other. Pregnancy is not an illness. Yet the care a woman receives during pregnancy and delivery can influence how she experiences those events, both physically and emotionally, and so can do much to optimize her health. A woman's care during pregnancy and delivery can also have enormous influence on the survival and early health status of the child she bears. But, somewhat counterintuitively, most of the elements of routine care during pregnancy have little impact on the chance that a woman will experience a life-threatening obstetric complication—and once a woman does experience a complication, the routine care given in pregnancy will not save her life. To dramatically reduce maternal mortality and meet the target, emergency care must be accessible to and utilized by pregnant women who experience complications.

Consequently, the strategies for reducing maternal mortality and meeting the target will be quite different from the strategies for protecting and promoting other aspects of maternal health and meeting the maternal health Goal overall. Those aspects are best captured by the broader concept of sexual and reproductive health endorsed at the Cairo and Beijing conferences. Protecting and promoting sexual and reproductive health has ramifications not just for health but also for multiple other Goals, including poverty reduction (UNFPA 2002c) and gender empowerment. Although sexual and reproductive health requires action in multiple sectors, health sector interventions are at the core of sexual and reproductive health strategies.

To ensure that development strategies built around the Goals capture the nonmortality aspects of sexual and reproductive health, the task force proposes adding a target modeled on the target endorsed by the global community during the International Conference on Population and Development and International Conference on Population and Development + 5 conferences, with the additional modification of ensuring that priority is given to the critical issue of equity.

> New Target for Maternal Health Goal 5: Universal access to reproductive and sexual health services through the primary healthcare system by 2015, ensuring faster progress among the poor and other marginalized groups.

A new proposed target: universal access to reproductive and sexual health services through the primary healthcare system by 2015

The Task Force on Education and Gender Equality has also endorsed universal access to reproductive health services through the primary healthcare system by 2015 as a critical aspect of women's capability (UN Millennium Project 2005b). That task force views access to reproductive health services as an essential component of the capabilities domain of gender equality and essential to human well-being and to sexual and reproductive health and rights.

Indicators for sexual and reproductive health and rights

How best to measure access to reproductive health services is a subject of considerable debate. In the reproductive health field, there is a long history of dissatisfaction with indicators that have distorted programs by focusing only on contraceptive coverage and fertility rates. Coercion and discrimination in population programs that center on contraceptive delivery is not an historical artifact. It continues to be a live issue in many parts of the world today (Miranda and Yamin 2004; Murthy 2003). Transition from a demographic to a reproductive health and woman-centered paradigm, including its rights dimensions, requires that any indicator for measuring progress in access to contraceptive services include indicators that focus on users of those health services, their needs as they (and not the state or any other actor) understand and express them, and the ability of the health system to meet those needs.

The UN Millennium Project has identified an indicator that measures and monitors women's ability to bring into effect their stated fertility preferences as a key reproductive health-related measure of gender equality. The UN's Division on the Advancement of Women, the WHO, UNICEF, and the United Nations Population Fund (UNFPA) strongly support the addition of this indicator to the Millennium Development Goals. Choices about the number, timing, and spacing of one's children are related to consensus human rights, poverty alleviation, maternal health and child health, nutritional status, women's social and economic participation, and other aspects of the Goals (Bernstein 2004; UN 2002).

As in other areas, the choice of indicators is complicated by data availability (or lack thereof) and methodological problems. There is no perfect single indicator for sexual and reproductive health and rights. The task force therefore supports the Millennium Project's proposal to use a set of indicators, noting that these measures are to be used together and not as independent measures of progress.

The first new indicator is the Proportion of Desires (for family planning) Satisfied (PDS). This measure conveys the proportion of women who wish to space or limit childbearing and who utilize effective means of doing so. The indicator measures how well a country is able to satisfy the family planning desires of women both to space births and to limit further fertility—an outcome on which countries too often fail miserably (Ravindran and Mishra 2000). This indicator has the advantage of being useful in different cultural contexts, since it does not prejudge the expressed preferences of the women for large or small

**The first
proposed new
indicator is the
Proportion of
Desires (for
family planning)
Satisfied**

families but monitors their ability to translate their preferences into action (for more detailed information on the construction of the indicator and its advantages over "unmet need," see Bernstein 2004). Analyses testing the indicator show a strong association between the measure and poverty status: the poor are least likely to be able to act on their preferences (Bernstein 2004; UN 2002).

The second new indicator is the adolescent fertility rate. Adolescents are of particular concern because of their unique vulnerabilities, their greater likelihood of dying in childbirth or having unsafe abortions, and the fact that their births are more likely to be unintended and premature (UN Millennium Project 2005b).

Finally, given the huge toll that unsafe abortion has on health and on mortality, countries should also consider taking steps to track the prevalence and outcomes of unsafe abortions.

Monitoring health systems

A central argument of this report is that a new and different focus on health systems is needed to meet the Goals. Although health has a strong presence in the Millennium Development Goals, the Goals are disease- or health status-based—improve maternal health, reduce child mortality, reduce HIV/AIDS, malaria, and tuberculosis—and all of the indicators track and reflect discrete interventions or outcomes. None reflects progress in strengthening health systems. This is a potentially serious problem. Short-term, disease-specific interventions are not necessarily the building blocks for long-term development of the health system. In fact, in some cases short-term interventions may even retard progress toward long-term goals. It is therefore essential that the indicators reflect some key aspects of health system strengthening. For example, the introduction of the emergency obstetric care indicator could possibly function as a "tracer," or sentinel marker, for a functioning health system more generally (Knippenberg, Soucat, and Van Lerberghe 2003).

Fortunately, within the international health field, attention is now being paid to the challenge of measuring the equity and strength of health systems. The task force supports the WHO's initiative to develop meaningful health systems indicators that are sensitive to equity concerns (WHO 2004c). Those health systems indicators will be most useful when they are integrated into policy and budget cycles and can inform tools for accountability.

In many countries over the past several decades, health systems have borne the brunt of macroeconomic policies determined outside the health sector and of well intentioned disease-specific initiatives designed to have a quick impact on health status. Far too often, the threat to health system functioning posed by such policies goes unnoticed until the damage is done. In other cases, the damage can be (and is) anticipated, but it remains invisible or suppressed in the policymaking process. Although some civil society groups are able to sound the alarm about the likelihood of detrimental impact, the information and data to conduct a serious assessment are often missing or inaccessible.

The task force proposes the development of a health system impact statement

This is a serious issue of accountability that must be addressed. The task force proposes the development of a health system impact statement modeled on similar tools, such as environmental impact statements, used in other sectors.

Monitoring the Goals: the role of health information

The measurement of progress toward the Goals is only as accurate as the data allow. In the case of maternal mortality and skilled birth attendance in particular, the data are grossly inadequate, with many countries having no reliable data on these measures.

Vital statistics and civil registration systems

While modeling and population-based surveys can augment our understanding of general levels and trends, they are not a substitute for strong, country-owned vital statistics and civil registration systems. Information is a theme echoed by other task forces of the UN Millennium Project. This task force seconds the call for information, starting with a simple accounting of who is born and who dies, as a critical crosscutting investment necessary for reaching the Goals. In Sub-Saharan Africa the void in health information is immense: fewer than 10 countries have viable vital registration systems (Evans and Stansfield 2004). And yet, these systems—which count and accurately classify every birth and death—are precisely what are needed to accurately measure trends in infant, child, and maternal mortality over short periods of time (Campbell 1999).

Population-based surveys

Population-based surveys provide useful snapshots of health data. They are particularly important in countries in which vital registration systems are weak. In many cases, surveys such as Demographic and Health Surveys supply the data for gauging national levels of maternal mortality and resulting trends between surveys. Such surveys can play a powerful role in spurring action or political will, as was the case in Indonesia after the 1994 survey revealed an unexpectedly high maternal mortality ratio (Schiffman 2003). In addition, surveys such as Multiple Indicator Cluster Survey and Demographic and Health Surveys may well be the primary means of measuring many of the MDG indicators. Such surveys often contain data on ethnic group, region, age, sex, the educational level of mothers, and wealth quintile and thus lend themselves to equity analyses that would reveal how population groups fare relative to one another on key outcomes, including the health Goals. In keeping with this report's focus on equity, the task force advocates more extensive use of population-based surveys for this purpose.

Confidential enquiries into maternal deaths

A simple accounting of maternal deaths, a difficult task in and of itself, is only the start of a well conceived strategy for reducing maternal mortality. The

A simple accounting of maternal deaths is only part of a well conceived strategy

death toll must be explained, through a careful evaluation of the avoidable factors that lead to maternal deaths (WHO 2004a).

Several approaches are available for investigating the causes of individual maternal deaths, including community-based maternal death reviews (often called verbal autopsies) in settings in which most births take place at home; facility-based maternal death reviews; confidential enquiries into maternal deaths; surveys of severe morbidity; and clinical audits. The rationale for each approach and its advantages and disadvantages are outlined in a WHO report entitled "Beyond the Numbers" (WHO 2004a).

Importantly, the defining characteristic of all these approaches is the emphasis on confidentiality in order to ensure open, detailed reports of the sequence of events culminating in a maternal death or "near-miss" event (a severe obstetric complication that requires interventions to save the mother's life) (WHO 2004a). In countries that have enjoyed some success in reducing maternal mortality, confidential enquiries or audits have been identified as a key tool in raising public awareness and pointing to avoidable factors that provided a starting point for action. Often maternal death notification processes or maternal perinatal audits are put in place at the district or provincial level as a quality of care mechanism designed to reduce avoidable maternal deaths (Jackson and others 2004; McCoy and others 2004; Supratikto and others 2002). Near misses are another important source of information on the quality of care provided by the health system in instances of obstetric emergencies.

Chapter 6

Global policy and funding frameworks

Equitable and well functioning health systems depend on supportive policy environments and funding mechanisms at both the national and international levels. For low-income countries the international policy environment and external financial support are closely intertwined, either directly, through policy conditions on the receipt of external loans and grants, or indirectly, from the type of policy advice, technical assistance, or project and program support that particular donors offer.

Health systems in low-income countries are already highly dependent on external support from a variety of sources, including UN specialized agencies, funds, and programs; the World Bank and regional development banks; bilateral donors; international NGOs; and private foundations. To reach the health-related Goals, low-income countries will need even greater financial support and more coherent and visionary technical support from external sources. Inevitably, even in countries that have acted boldly to take control over the process, health systems will continue to be strongly influenced by the policy agendas and priorities of major donors.

This chapter considers some of the main policy and funding frameworks for donor support to the Goals. It examines inherent tensions within these frameworks that obstruct the strengthening of health systems and identifies how these frameworks could better support long-term investments in equitable and effective health systems.

Influence of international financial institutions

While the World Bank is the largest single donor to the health sector, in aggregate bilateral donors provide the largest portion of official development assistance to health sectors in low-income countries. Direct loans and grants to the health sector by development banks, particularly the World Bank,

**Low-income
countries will
need even
greater financial
support from
external sources**

have increased in recent years, but they still represent a small percentage of
the banks' overall assistance to low- and middle-income countries (Michaud
2003).[1] Considerable technical and program support is provided by UN specialized agencies and funds, such as the WHO, UNICEF, and UNFPA.

The IMF provides no direct support to the health sector. But together
with the development banks (often referred to collectively as the international
financial institutions), it wields significant direct and indirect influence over
the health sectors in low- and middle-income countries—and all other key
sectors for that matter—through the policy conditions attached to the various
types of loans they provide.

Because their support to countries is mainly in the form of loans, the main
counterpart agency for the international financial institutions is the ministry
of finance, typically one of the most powerful ministries in the government.
This partnership tends to reinforce the influence of the international financial
institutions over other ministries, including the ministry of health.

The IMF also exerts influence over borrowing governments through its
functional role as the international institution that evaluates countries' macroeconomic frameworks for absorbing official development assistance and other
external finance. At least since the debt crisis of the 1980s, there has been an
understanding among donors that financial assistance to a low-income country
is contingent on IMF approval of the country's macroeconomic situation. IMF
approval is also a condition for debt rescheduling by official and commercial
lenders, and it influences the ratings assigned to a country's external debt by
credit rating agencies, which significantly affect the country's access to commercial loans and international capital markets.

At the policy level, the IMF and World Bank play dominant roles in donor
consultative groups. Recently, they have also taken the lead in coordinating
external debt relief and promoting national Poverty Reduction Strategy Papers
(PRSPs) as a development planning tool. In addition, the World Bank plays a
leading role in policy research and the development of various assessment tools
for use by development planners.

In terms of the content of their policy prescriptions, the IMF and World
Bank previously took the lead in promoting the so-called Washington consensus, which prioritized fiscal discipline, financial and exchange rate liberalization, trade liberalization and foreign direct investment, privatization, deregu-
lation, and protection of property rights (Williamson 1993). This agenda has
been tempered in recent years by a direct emphasis on poverty reduction, which
highlights the need to improve poor people's opportunities, empowerment,
and security (World Bank 2000). The international financial institutions focus
on economic growth as the key long-term driver for poverty reduction and for
achieving the Goals, as reflected in recent World Bank publications on infrastructure, trade, and private sector development, including *World Development
Report 2005* (IMF and World Bank 2004a; World Bank 2004c).

The challenge is to seek opportunities to shift the dominant discourse toward sustainable, inclusive health systems

In the health sector the World Bank has been extremely influential in conceptualizing healthcare as a marketable (and tradable) commodity (World Bank 2003b) and in promoting various reforms based on principles of health economics, cost-effectiveness analysis, and the experience of industrialized countries such as New Zealand, the United Kingdom, and the United States (Kumaranayake and Walker 2002; Lee and Goodman 2002; Standing 2002b; World Bank 1993). This approach contrasts with the arguments set forth in this report, which acknowledges healthcare as a right and conceptualizes health systems as fundamentally social institutions that should strive to promote equity and inclusion as core values and health policymaking as a political process in which participation of the people directly affected is an important goal. Given the significant influence of the IMF and World Bank on health policies at the national level, the challenge for the health sector and all health stakeholders is to seek opportunities to shift this dominant discourse and use the development assistance frameworks in a manner that supports long-term investments in sustainable, inclusive health systems.

Debt relief, poverty reduction, and public expenditure management

Much international development assistance in recent years has been focused on a few closely linked initiatives promoted by the international financial institutions and bilateral donors. These initiatives include external debt relief, mainly through the Heavily Indebted Poor Countries (HIPC) initiative; Poverty Reduction Strategy Papers; and public financial management (involving public expenditure reviews and medium-term expenditure frameworks). These initiatives now form the framework for external assistance to low-income countries, including support for pursuing the Goals.

At the same time, the international financial institutions, the UN system, and bilateral donors (acting through the Development Assistance Committee of the Organisation for Economic Co-operation and Development) have begun to harmonize their policies and procedures and to align their assistance programs in individual countries, in order to reduce the considerable burden on recipient countries of managing official development assistance. Taken together, these initiatives are leading the development banks and some other donors to move away from financing individual projects toward providing more programmatic support to governments. This trend can be seen in the emergence of sectorwide approaches in health and other sectors and new instruments for providing general budget support to governments (such as the World Bank's Poverty Reduction Support Credits). Meanwhile, some new donor funding mechanisms, such as the United States' Millennium Challenge Account, are also more selective about the countries they support.

All of these processes have implications for the health Goals and for health systems. As these processes evolve and are adapted in individual countries, they present new opportunities and challenges for ministries of health and other

The actual relief obtained from the HIPC initiative has been less than needed

key stakeholders in health systems. The international financial institutions and other donors have critical roles to play in ensuring that health systems are strengthened and made more inclusive through these processes.

External debt relief and the HIPC initiative

The HIPC initiative, launched by the IMF and World Bank in 1996, is an external debt reduction program for poor countries with "unsustainable debt burdens." In principle, debt relief frees up scarce resources that HIPC governments can reallocate to health, education, and other sectors. Although the benefits of debt relief have likely been significant, in practice, it has not yet been possible to quantify the direct benefits of the HIPC initiative to the health sector. Countries that have qualified for full or partial HIPC relief increased their poverty-reducing expenditures from 6.5 percent of GDP in 1999 to 7.9 percent of GDP in 2003, which is about three times the amount the countries spent on debt service. Although the definitions of "poverty-reducing expenditures" vary across countries, basic healthcare is commonly included (IMF and International Development Agency 2004).

The HIPC initiative has been criticized on several grounds, including the criteria used to identify HIPCs, the macroeconomic and other conditions imposed, and the slow pace of implementation. In particular, macroeconomic and other targets set for debt relief may restrict some HIPCs from accessing additional external resources, especially loans, for health and other social spending; from hiring additional healthcare workers; and from raising healthcare workers' salaries. In Zambia, for example, the UN Special Envoy for HIV/AIDS in Africa complained publicly in June 2004 that IMF prescriptions for HIPC debt relief were preventing the health ministry from hiring more staff, at a time when 20 percent of municipal districts had no doctors or nurses. Oxfam has also argued that without the fiscal surplus targets required by the IMF, several HIPCs could already have doubled their health budgets (Oxfam 2003). These concerns are likely to remain, especially as the IMF and World Bank establish a more formal debt sustainability framework for HIPCs and other low-income countries under conditions of inadequate donor support (IMF and World Bank 2004b).

The HIPC initiative is significant not only for the 25 countries that have received debt relief but also because the initiative has triggered other processes, such as the Poverty Reduction Strategy Papers, that affect a much larger number of countries. Regrettably, the process for obtaining HIPC relief has been complicated and time consuming, and the actual relief obtained has been less than needed (due in part to the number of creditors not yet participating). For countries still in the process of qualifying for debt relief, it will be important for the IMF to be as flexible as possible in setting macroeconomic targets and other conditions that are consistent with achieving the health Goals.

PRSPs need to focus on more ambitious, MDG-based poverty reduction scenarios

Poverty Reduction Strategy Papers and the Goals

Poverty Reduction Strategy Papers (PRSPs), introduced in 1999 as one of the core requirements for HIPC debt relief, have become a requirement for all concessional loans from the World Bank and the IMF. Poverty reduction strategies are also now agreed upon as the main country-level framework for low-income countries to map out plans to achieve the Goals.

This means that substantially more attention needs to be given to the poverty reduction strategy process if the Goals are to be met. While many observers have viewed the principles underlying the PRSP approach as a basis for improving participatory, outcome-focused, comprehensive national planning and priority setting to better serve poor and marginalized groups, including through improvements in basic healthcare (World Bank 2004a), in practice, the PRSP process has varied considerably from country to country.

Recent studies have confirmed that in many countries the PRSP process has improved governments' capacity to conduct poverty analysis and opened up space for greater involvement of civil society groups in the national planning process (IMF Independent Evaluation Office 2004; World Bank Operations Evaluation Department 2004). But these studies also confirmed that the poverty reduction strategy process has predominantly been externally driven. Macroeconomic assumptions and targets underlying the PRSPs have generally been insulated from the consultation and timetables for the production of the PRSP, and PRSPs often have not coincided with the development of national plans and sector strategies. Country ownership of the PRSP process and the building of in-country capacity for poverty analysis and pro-poor planning has often been limited by the IMF and World Bank's emphasis on producing "high-quality" PRSP documents—typically with the assistance of consultants. Ministries of finance and planning have led the process, with varying levels of involvement by line ministries and nongovernmental groups and little input from legislative bodies. Finally, many donors have not yet aligned their country programs with countries' PRSP priorities and are unwilling or unable to provide firm, multiyear commitments of assistance.

All of these problems represent obstacles to achieving the Goals. But the most significant problem is the tension over whether the PRSP is intended to map a country's poverty reduction "needs" (as proposed by the UN Millennium Project) or to identify priorities for poverty reduction within a country's "available resources." The latter approach has previously been endorsed by the IMF and World Bank, which have encouraged countries to avoid structuring their PRSPs as "wish lists," but now these institutions have endorsed the need for PRSPs to include more ambitious poverty reduction strategy scenarios for when increased donor resources are forthcoming. It is important for these more ambitious scenarios to be MDG-based, because priority-setting based on "realistic" projections of resource availability can lead to modest, incremental changes in public expenditures that may have little impact on poverty

It is vital that health ministries and other health stakeholders continue to engage in the PRSP process

reduction and progress toward the Goals—and will let donors justify maintaining low levels of assistance.

Challenges for the health sector. The World Bank's recent evaluation of the PRSP process concluded that the first generation of strategies overemphasized public investment in social sectors such as health and paid insufficient attention to growth-related activities. This conclusion is at odds with desk surveys of PRSPs by the WHO, UNFPA, DFID, and others, which have generally found the treatment of health and poverty to be uneven and often superficial (Laterveer, Niessen, and Yazbeck 2003; UNFPA 2002a; Walford 2002; WHO 2004e). With respect to population, reproductive health, and adolescent health issues, the World Bank itself recently found that PRSPs pay a "reasonable level of attention" to these issues but that "the scope and quality of the inclusion varies enormously" (World Bank 2004b).

The WHO's second synthesis report on health in PRSPs found that many do not systematically analyze the health situation of poor people and the barriers that prevent poor women in particular from accessing reproductive healthcare. PRSPs generally recommend expanding coverage of basic health services, especially in rural areas, and providing fee exemptions for the poor, but they include little analysis of why similar approaches have failed in the past. The WHO also found that although health spending is rising in all countries in nominal terms, projected changes in health spending as a proportion of GDP are typically small and health is not generally increasing in importance within the priority sectors identified for poverty reduction. Although the IMF and World Bank have recently called for scaling up to accelerate progress toward the Goals and their leadership has been vocal on the need for a dramatic scale-up of official development assistance, their country-level processes are not yet advocating the major increases in public health spending (including large increases in donor spending) needed to achieve the Goals. Instead, they tend to recommend better targeting of proven interventions (such as skilled attendants at births to reduce maternal mortality) to reach poor and vulnerable groups, accompanied by improvements in health policies and institutions (IMF and World Bank 2004a; Wagstaff and Claeson 2004).

Despite the uneven treatment of the health Goals, health equity, and health systems in PRSPs, it is vital that health ministries and other health stakeholders continue to engage in the process, as the poverty reduction strategy becomes the main vehicle for making progress toward the Goals and aligning donor assistance. At the same time, the merger of the poverty reduction strategy process with the national planning process could inadvertently diminish the attention paid to healthcare and health systems, since the health sector historically has had a low priority in most national plans and budgets.

In this policy environment, health ministries and other health stakeholders are likely to face challenges arguing for substantial, long-term public

Medium-term expenditure frameworks require substantial capacity to implement

investments in the health sector. They will need to be forceful in articulating to their ministries of finance and planning not only the particular health needs and constraints of poor people but also the impoverishing effect of ill health on the majority of the population in the absence of an equitable, well financed, and well managed health system. Within the poverty reduction strategy framework, it will also be important for donors to maintain and improve their direct support to health systems, ideally through coordinated support of a national health sector strategy that is founded on principles of inclusion, equity, and rights.

Public expenditure management and medium-term expenditure frameworks

Public expenditure reviews and medium-term expenditure frameworks form the third set of initiatives making up the framework for external assistance to low-income countries. Both have been widely promoted by the international financial institutions and some bilateral donors through loans and technical assistance.

Public expenditure reviews and medium-term expenditure frameworks are highly technocratic processes, typically introduced and supported by consultants and driven mainly by national finance or planning ministries. Health and other line ministries play an important but subordinate role, although this role can be enhanced where the medium-term expenditure frameworks approach is "piloted" in a few sectors. In Cambodia and Ghana, for example, the medium-term expenditure framework process was first piloted in health and one or two other sectors (Holmes and Evans 2003).

In theory, a medium-term expenditure framework aligns national policies, planning, and budgeting within a medium-term perspective (usually three to five years). The national finance ministry, the planning ministry, or both first estimate the government's total "resource envelope" for the period and establish sector allocations within that envelope. Line ministries then develop estimates of the current and future costs of their sector priorities, usually through an iterative process involving negotiation between central and line ministries. These sector costs are then reconciled with the estimates of available resources.

In practice, the medium-term expenditure framework approach has proved difficult to implement because of the substantial capacity required in all ministries and offices concerned. The results have been mixed (Le Houerou and Taliercio 2002; Oxford Policy Management 2000). Some countries, such as South Africa, are quite far along in fully institutionalizing the framework, while others, such as Burkina Faso, Cameroon, and Ghana, are at early and faltering pilot stages (Holmes and Evans 2003). Case studies confirm that the medium-term expenditure framework is effective where there is clarity about the objectives and priorities of government policy, realistic forecasting of the resources available for allocation and planning, and analysis directly linked to the allocation of resources (Conway and others 2002).

It will be very important for health ministries to be knowledge-able about the medium-term expenditure framework process

The medium-term expenditure framework has been criticized as a top-down, nonparticipatory approach, in which finance and planning ministries generally control the process and determine the indicative and final allocations to sectors. There has been criticism of the inflexibility of the "resource envelope" calculation that typically starts the process. This inflexibility can be particularly hard on the health sector, because health ministries tend to have relatively weak positions within government, especially compared with finance and planning ministries. This is compounded when donors, NGOs, and other funders of the health system do not provide medium-term estimates of their commitments. External assistance tends to be fragmented among a large number of multilateral and bilateral donors, international and national NGOs, and global health initiatives, most of which have their own planning and funding cycles. These commitment gaps effectively shrink the health ministry's "external resource envelope" for planning purposes and inhibit the ministry from fully costing the priorities in its health sector strategy. This can lead to a mismatch between a comprehensive health sector strategy—which is often developed with donor support—and the health sector medium-term expenditure frameworks.

Challenges for the health sector. With the introduction of the PRSP, medium-term expenditure frameworks have taken on a new life, with international financial institutions, some bilateral donors, and indeed the UN Millennium Project now promoting them as the "budget side" of the PRSP (Holmes and Evans 2003; IMF and World Bank 2004c; UN Millennium Project 2005a). Despite their mixed success in implementation, medium-term expenditure frameworks are likely to become even more important as donors shift toward general budget support rather than project or sector support to some low-income governments (through general loans or block grants to support a PRSP, for example). In this case donors are likely to rely on the medium-term expenditure frameworks as the budget framework for their assistance. Critical to this process are mechanisms for tracking health sector budgetary allocations and spending through the medium-term expenditure framework, in order to be able to hold governments accountable for realizing health needs. In South Africa initiatives to monitor government allocations and expenditures relating to children, women, and HIV/AIDS have served to hold government accountable to their stated priorities as well as their legal obligations (Streak 2004).

In this policy environment it will be very important for health ministries to be knowledgeable about the medium-term expenditure framework process and to be active in negotiating with their finance and planning ministries and with donors for steadily increasing allocations of resources to the health system. The international financial institutions and other donors to the health sector have a critical role in helping health ministries navigate through this challenging process. At a minimum, and as a matter of urgency, they should provide multiyear commitments to the health sector for incorporation in the medium-term expenditure frameworks.

Poverty reduction loans can restrict social sector spending

Poverty reduction loans and poverty and social impact assessments

With the introduction of the HIPC and PRSP processes in many countries, both the IMF and World Bank have "adjusted" their structural adjustment loan facilities to better support poverty reduction. These "adjusted" poverty reduction loans (the IMF's Poverty Reduction and Growth Facility loans and the World Bank's Poverty Reduction Support Credits) are intended to support a country's poverty reduction program, as outlined in its poverty reduction strategy.

Poverty reduction loans and other forms of direct budget support to low-income countries—such as that contemplated in DFID's new poverty reduction budget support policy (DFID 2004)—provide mechanisms for donors to directly support national poverty reduction strategies, including the PRSPs (and therefore national Millennium Development Goals, to the extent they are reflected in a country's poverty reduction strategy). While supporting government ownership of the poverty reduction strategy, these direct financing mechanisms also have the potential to reduce the administrative costs to low-income governments of negotiating and implementing multiple projects funded by the same donor. In this respect, these general budget support mechanisms can be seen as a continuation of the trend away from project-based support, which began with the introduction of sector investment programs and later sector-wide approaches.[2]

By their nature general poverty reduction loans do not provide direct funding to health or other sectors. For example, the Poverty Reduction Support Credit funding mechanism provides for the transfer of funds from the World Bank to a single government account. Unless specifically negotiated and included in the Poverty Reduction Support Credit documents, there is no mechanism to ensure that any portion of the Poverty Reduction Support Credit will be allocated to the health sector (or any other sector).

Poverty reduction loans have also been criticized for containing stringent macroeconomic targets that can restrict social sector spending, including bans on hiring additional healthcare workers and raising healthcare workers' salaries (EURODAD 2003; Oxfam 2003, 2004; Stewart and Wang 2003). Although intended to support national priorities for poverty reduction, Poverty Reduction and Growth Facility loans and Poverty Reduction Support Credits, like the structural adjustment loans before them, also support a wide range of public sector and economic reforms that can have negative as well as positive impacts on health systems. For example, the Ghana Poverty Reduction Support Credit negotiated in 2003 with the World Bank includes a number of policy conditions related to governance, public sector management, and health. While there are general references in the document to "improving staff motivation and health worker incentives," the Poverty Reduction and Growth Facility arrangement negotiated in parallel with the IMF includes a strict ceiling on the public wage bill. As a condition for the release of additional funds by the IMF in July 2004, Ghana had to roll back part of an agreed wage increase

Macroeconomic targets should allow as much flexibility as possible for the health sector

to registered nurses and other core public servants in order to stay within the wage bill ceiling. Ghana is thus another country in which needed investments in the health system are subordinated to macroeconomic targets resulting from inadequate donor financing (IMF 2004; IDA 2003).

Challenges for the health sector

Poverty Reduction Support Credits and other forms of general budget support appear to provide relatively limited, indirect support for health systems. In the absence of a strong national commitment to the health sector—reflected in steady and substantial allocations of budget to the health ministry—development banks and other donors should continue to provide direct support to the health ministry. Even within Poverty Reduction Support Credits, provisions can be included to ensure a certain level of health expenditures and to address significant barriers to healthcare access, especially for women and other disadvantaged groups. Macroeconomic targets that are conditions for Poverty Reduction and Growth Facility loans, Poverty Reduction Support Credits, or other forms of direct budget support to low-income countries should be as flexible as possible. Health sector expenditures (especially for human resources) should be exempted from these targets on the basis that they are poverty-reducing expenditures necessary to achieve the health-related Goals.

In response to criticisms of the economic reforms they have promoted, the IMF and World Bank, with support from bilateral donors such as DFID, have been developing tools for analyzing the poverty and social impact of these reforms. Poverty and Social Impact Analyses analyze the distributional impact of a policy reform, especially on poor and vulnerable groups (World Bank 2003a). The first set of pilot Poverty and Social Impact Analyses undertaken by the World Bank and DFID did not directly address health sector issues. There is considerable potential for using them to analyze the poverty and social impact of health sector policies or proposed changes in those policies.[3] Similar tools could also be developed to analyze the impact of broader policy changes—for example, fiscal targets, public sector reforms, or trade liberalization measures—on the health system. These tools should analyze broader distributional and equity effects on the health system, not simply the effects on the poorest groups in the population. It is also important for civil society organizations, development institutions, and others to undertake these types of impact assessments.

Donor coordination and harmonization

For some time the international financial institutions, organizations within the UN system, bilateral donors, and international NGOs have acknowledged the significant burden on low-income countries of negotiating and implementing separate programs and projects, accommodating visits by headquarters teams and liaising with their in-country offices, and complying with their separate procurement, disbursement, and reporting requirements. This problem is especially

It is imperative that donors provide firmer, longer term commitments of support to the health sector

acute in the health sector, where numerous UN agencies and programs, most bilateral donors, the World Bank and regional development banks, and an expanding number of international and national NGOs are active (Buse and Walt 1997; Peter and Chao 1998). Low-income country governments, including health and other line ministries, can also be caught between competing interests and conflicting priorities of these external actors. The health sector is particularly vulnerable to these types of conflicts, given the professional debates and ideological differences on matters such as the efficacy of certain vaccines, approaches to family planning and HIV/AIDS prevention, access to safe abortion services, and healthcare financing schemes (Mayhew 2002; Walt and others 1999).

At the international level, the Rome Declaration on Harmonization, adopted in 2003 by heads of multilateral and bilateral development institutions, the international financial institutions, and partner countries, has spurred a number of efforts to harmonize donor practices and better coordinate their in-country activities in alignment with national and sector priorities. This includes continued efforts by the United Nations to strengthen in-country coordination of its agencies and programs through the UN Development Group.

Within countries, various steps are being taken to improve the functioning of donor coordination groups, NGO coordination groups, and sector working groups (which often include government and civil society representatives) (Aid Harmonization and Alignment 2004). Some donors have also been testing various types of joint funding and support of sectorwide programs, and more recently they have been experimenting with joint development assistance frameworks and joint funding of the poverty reduction strategy through direct budget support.

Challenges for the health sector. In the health sector, donors and ministries of health have experimented with different forms of coordination and joint activity to reduce administrative costs and improve health outcomes. These efforts have included geographical zoning of donor activities, lead agency and sector working group arrangements, joint and parallel funding of programs such as the Integrated Management of Childhood Illness and the Safe Motherhood Initiative, and various levels of participation in sectorwide programs (Buse and Walt 1997; Walt and others 1999).

Although progress is being made in several countries to harmonize donor procedures and shift from project-based to programmatic funding in the health sector, a number of key donors continue to operate outside these coordination mechanisms and to finance stand-alone projects with separate implementation units, management information systems, and reporting requirements. It is extremely important that these agencies better align their activities with the national health strategy or health sector plan and harmonize their procedures with other donors. It is also imperative that donors and large international NGOs provide firmer, longer term commitments of support to the health sector, so that ministries of health, in coordination with other ministries, can develop longer

Donors and large NGOs must refrain from "poaching" health managers from the public health system to supervise their projects

term investment plans for the health sector. This is particularly true in human resource development, where there is an urgent need for donors to support long-term, cross-sectoral human resource planning for health systems.

Donors and large NGOs also need to examine more critically their own practices relating to salary supplements, per diems for short training courses, and other incentives provided to health ministry staff. They must also refrain from "poaching" health managers from the public health system to supervise their projects, which can debilitate and demoralize the daily functioning of public health systems. In Mozambique, for example, donor and NGO practices caused such severe problems that a code of conduct to regulate their practices was ultimately created (Pfeiffer 2003).

International financial institutions and other donors also need to more effectively support the strengthening of health ministries' regulatory functions. These functions are essential to ensure some level of equity and inclusion in an increasingly fragmented and commercialized health sector.

Sectorwide approaches need to be promoted

Sectorwide approaches in the health sector, vigorously promoted by the World Bank, the WHO, DFID, and other donors, are at various stages of implementation in about 20 countries (IMF and World Bank 2004a). The sectorwide approach is a fluid concept, but it generally consists of a collaborative program of work for government, donors, and other stakeholders, including the joint development of sector policies and strategies, medium-term projections of available resources and likely expenditures, establishment of common management systems, and institutional improvements and capacity building in the sector (Cassels 1997). In practice, sectorwide approaches to health have evolved quite differently across countries. The successes they have enjoyed and the challenges they have faced have varied, depending on the local political context, the institutional climate within donor organizations and government, the level of interest of individual health ministry officials and donor representatives, relationships between local actors, and other factors. Variations in funding arrangements for health sectorwide approaches are particularly large, ranging from parallel funding of specific activities or programs to various pooling or basket arrangements.

In general, implementation of these sectorwide approaches has proceeded more slowly and involved greater financial and human investments by both government and donors than proponents expected. There is an ongoing tension between the sectorwide approach, which aims to coordinate health initiatives, particularly at the district level, and old and new vertical health programs (including new global health initiatives, such as the Global Fund to Fight AIDS, Malaria and Tuberculosis) (Peter and Chao 1998).

Some NGOs have complained that they have been excluded from sectorwide approaches and have lost direct funding from donors who have shifted their health sector budgets into sectorwide programs (Reality of Aid 2004).

The sectorwide approach provides a framework for long-term health sector planning

Although sectorwide approaches appear to be strengthening the planning, budgeting, and management systems within health ministries and to be raising levels of funding to the health sector, there is so far little evidence that they have improved the delivery of health services or the health status of poor and marginalized groups (Toole and others 2003).

It is unclear why they have not yet improved health services. Since all these sectorwide approaches are relatively new mechanisms, it may simply be too early to observe positive impacts at the service delivery level. It could also be that most have concentrated on systems improvements at the central level and have not tackled access, equity, and quality of care issues at the district and local levels. This is an important issue that merits further monitoring and analysis.

Despite its slow and uneven progress, the sectorwide approach is the only model of sector coordination that directly promotes government ownership and alignment of donor support with national sector priorities and processes (Walt and others 1999). In contrast to other types of coordination, the sectorwide approach also provides a broad platform for addressing fundamental health system weaknesses and constraints as well as a flexible framework in which health ministries can work with donors, NGOs, and other stakeholders to make the long-term improvements in their health systems that will allow them to meet the Goals.

Concerns have been raised about the absence of emphasis on maternal mortality in donor-supported sectorwide approaches, even where maternal health problems are significant (Hill 2002). Goodburn and Campbell (2001) nevertheless argue for continued promotion of "safe motherhood" through sectorwide approaches, for two reasons. First, there is a greater potential for increased funding to address maternal mortality, because of the considerable resources invested by donors in sectorwide approaches. Second, given the dependence of emergency obstetric care on health systems, linking maternal health programs to sectorwide approaches at an early stage "may mean that the implications of proposed solutions to providing better care can be tested and considered in an integrated fashion" (Goodburn and Campbell 2001, p. 919).

In light of the challenging economic and policy environment in which health systems now operate, a health sectorwide approach or other sector support mechanism can provide health ministries in low-income countries with the long-term technical, financial, and political support they need to improve access to quality healthcare, especially for vulnerable groups. Health ministries and their sectorwide approach partners should also strongly encourage more donors and nongovernment providers of healthcare to participate in the approach to the fullest extent their charters permit.

Other global initiatives' impact on the health sector

The liberalization of trade, spurred by multilateral, regional, and bilateral trade agreements, can have direct and indirect effects on health systems (Koivusalo 2003; Ranson and others 2002). Considerable attention has focused on the

New disease-specific initiatives can strain fragile health systems

liberalization of health services under the WTO General Agreement on Trade in Services (GATS) and similar trade agreements (Drager and Fidler 2004; PAHO 2002; UNCTAD 1997) and on the mandated patenting of pharmaceutical drugs under the WTO Agreement on Trade-Related Aspects of Intellectual Property Rights (TRIPs Agreement) (Correa 2002). Other trade agreements, such as the WTO Agreements on the Application of Sanitary and Phytosanitary Measures and Technical Barriers to Trade, also limit governments' flexibility to adopt health regulations and standards that are deemed "trade restrictive." While much attention has focused on these WTO agreements, health sectors have been opening to cross-border investment and other forms of commercialization for some time, under health sector reform programs, regional and bilateral trade agreements, and various public-private arrangements.

Large private funders, such as the Bill & Melinda Gates Foundation, and new funding mechanisms, such as the Global Fund to Fight AIDS, Tuberculosis and Malaria, are injecting much-needed resources into health research and health sector activity in low-income countries, mainly to combat specific diseases. But some of these new disease-specific initiatives, administered through vertical programs, can strain fragile health systems and divert healthcare workers from primary care to disease-specific activities. Where large-scale programs for HIV/AIDS treatment are being introduced, reproductive healthcare may be seriously compromised, because the healthcare workers providing reproductive health services are among those most likely to be recruited for new HIV/AIDS programs. Concerns have also been raised about the extent to which the new global disease initiatives skew the allocation of global resources for health research and development (toward new drug therapies, for example, rather than toward microbicides that could prevent HIV infections in large numbers of women worldwide) and crowd out other potential sources of funding that could strengthen health systems. Health system impact assessments, codes of conduct, and other measures are needed to ensure that these new health initiatives support rather than undermine health systems, especially at the district and community levels (Buse and Walt 2002; Unger, De Paepe, and Green 2003).

Ultimately, the kind of transformational change required to meet the Goals at the national level requires that finance and planning ministries and the officials of international financial institutions with whom they negotiate have a profoundly different appreciation of the importance of health and health systems for economic growth, poverty reduction, and the building of democratic societies. While acknowledging the importance of efficiency and effectiveness in the functioning of the health system, the task force argues against the deeply unequalizing economic approach to health systems that focuses on competitive markets as the predominant framework for healthcare delivery. Fundamental rethinking and significant new investment are required to build equitable, well functioning health systems.

Chapter 7

Conclusions and recommendations

The essential conclusion of the task force is that the Millennium Development Goals for child mortality and maternal health are attainable—but not without extraordinary effort. The technical interventions for achieving these Goals exist; they must now be implemented at a scale and in a manner that will reach those who need them most. Access to safe, effective, and affordable interventions must be provided to all, through functioning health systems; barriers to the utilization of competent, professionally delivered services must be lowered or eliminated.

The principal recommendations for achieving these ambitious goals are as follows:

1. Health systems, particularly at the district level, must be strengthened and prioritized in strategies for reaching the child health and maternal health Goals. Doing so demands a radical shift in the way health systems are addressed:

- Health systems must be understood not only as mechanisms for delivering technical interventions but also as core social institutions that are indispensable for reducing poverty, social exclusion, and inequity and advancing democratic development and human rights.
- For health systems to increase inclusion and close the equity gap, policies implemented in the context of good governance must:
  - Strengthen rather than undermine government legitimacy.
  - Prevent excessive segmentation of the health system.
  - Increase the power of the poor and other marginalized groups to make claims for healthcare.

2. Strengthening health systems will require considerable additional funding.
- To progress at the speed required to meet the Goals in the poorest countries, both bilateral donors and international financial institutions must

vastly increase foreign assistance to the health sector for the foreseeable future.

- User fees at the primary care level should be abolished; health system financing should not be an additional burden on the backs of already impoverished populations.
- Countries should be encouraged to shift additional funds into the social sectors, to the extent possible.

3. The health workforce must be developed according to the goals of the health system, with the rights and livelihoods of healthcare workers addressed.

- These principles must also inform strategies to address brain drain, low morale, and loss of productivity due to illness and death (often from HIV/AIDS), factors that are limiting the ability of governments to provide their populations with access to good-quality healthcare.
- Effective management and operational systems that seek to improve quality and increase trust in the health system should accompany the development of the health workforce.
- Medium- to long-term plans for building a cadre of skilled birth attendants—the health workers key to reducing maternal deaths—must form an explicit part of all health workforce plans.
- "Scope of profession" regulations and practice must be changed to empower mid-level providers, including skilled birth attendants, to perform life-saving procedures safely and effectively.

4. Sexual and reproductive health and rights are essential to meeting all the Goals, including those on child health and maternal health.

- Countries should take steps to ensure universal access to sexual and reproductive health services.
- Initiatives addressing the HIV/AIDS pandemic should be integrated with sexual and reproductive health and rights programs.
- Adolescents must receive explicit attention with services that are sensitive to their increased vulnerabilities and designed to meet their needs.
- In circumstances where abortion is not against the law, such abortion should be safe. In all cases women should have access to quality services for the management of complications arising from abortion.
- Governments and other relevant actors should review and revise laws, regulations, and practices, including on abortion, that jeopardize women's health.

5. Effective intervention to reduce child mortality requires scaling up availability and utilization to 100 percent of the population in poor countries.

- Child health interventions must be increasingly offered within the community. Policies need to be reformulated to allow services to be delivered as close to patients as possible. Community health workers need to be trained and permitted to encourage preventive behaviors, to care for a larger proportion of nonsevere childhood illnesses, and to ensure early referral to appropriate facilities for the treatment of severe illnesses.

- More attention must be paid to child nutrition, including micronutrients, as the relationship between nutritional status and mortality is becoming increasingly evident.
- Governments must increase investments in interventions aimed at reducing neonatal deaths.

6. Maternal mortality strategies should focus on building a functioning health system that ensures access to emergency obstetric care for all women who experience complications.

- The system should supply, support, and supervise the skilled birth attendants who should be the backbone of that system, whether they are based in facilities or in communities.
- Strategies to ensure skilled attendants for all deliveries must be premised on integration of the skilled attendant into a functioning district health system.
- Skilled attendant strategies cannot be allowed to substitute for strategies to strengthen the health system, including emergency obstetric care.

7. Information systems are an essential element in building equitable health systems.

- Indicators of health system functioning—including equity—must be developed alongside disease-specific indicators and then integrated into policy and budget cycles.
- Health information systems must able to provide appropriate, accurate, and timely information that is used to inform management and policy decisions.
- Countries must take steps to strengthen vital registration systems.

8. The targets and indicators of Goals 4 and 5 should be modified as follows:

- All targets should be framed in equity-sensitive terms, providing that the rate of progress toward the target be faster among the poor and other marginalized groups than for the better-off.
- For Goal 4 on child mortality:
  - Neonatal mortality rate should be added as an indicator.
  - Prevalence of underweight children under-five (now an indicator for Goal 1) should be monitored.
- For Goal 5 on maternal health:
  - "Coverage of emergency obstetric care" should be added as an indicator for the maternal mortality target.

- "Universal access to reproductive health services" should be added as a new target.
- The full set of indicators to meet Goal 5 include:
  - Contraceptive prevalence rate.
  - Proportion of desire for family planning satisfied.
  - Adolescent fertility rate.
  - HIV prevalence among 15- to 24-year-old pregnant women.
  - Coverage of emergency obstetric care.
  - Proportion of births attended by skilled health personnel.
  - Maternal mortality ratio.

9. Global institutions are critical partners. Poverty reduction strategy processes and funding mechanisms should support and promote actions that strengthen rather than undermine equitable access to good-quality healthcare. To do so, global institutions will need to:

- Commit to long-term investments.
- Remove restrictions on funding of salaries and other recurrent costs.
- Align funding from donors and international financial institutions with national health programs to meet the Goals.
- Allow health stakeholders to fully participate in the development of funding plans.

Notes

Executive summary

1. This task force report limits its focus and recommendations to the health sector. For the full complement of strategies to meet the maternal health and child health Goals, these recommendations should be linked to the recommendations of other task forces and to *Investing in Development: A Practical Plan to Achieve the Millennium Development Goals* (UN Millennium Project 2005a).

Chapter 2

1. If couples using traditional methods of contraception are excluded from the calculation of unmet need, the figure declines to 134 million women (Singh and others 2003).

2. South Asia has a particularly rich heritage of integrated primary care projects run by NGOs such as the International Center for Diarrhoeal Disease Research, Bangladesh (Chakaria), Gonoshashthya Kendra, and the Bangladesh Rural Advancement Committee (BRAC) in Bangladesh; the Comprehensive Rural Health Project (Jamkhed) and SEARCH (Gadchiroli) in India; and HANDS and the Aga Khan Foundation in Pakistan (Hossain and others 2004).

Chapter 3

1. Although figure 3.1 appears to end with childbearing, cycling back to birth, sexuality, and aspects of reproductive health continue to be important determinants of well-being and illness through menopause and into old age.

2. Some studies, most of them conducted in Europe and the United States, link fathers' health-related behaviors, such as smoking and drug use, and occupational hazards, such as chemical exposures, to child health (Wen and others 2002; Parker and others 1999; Ji and others 1997). The extent of impact of these aspects of fathers' lives on child health in low and middle-income countries is unknown and rarely explored.

3. Nationally representative surveys were conducted between 2001 and 2004 in Bangladesh, the Philippines, Thailand, and Viet Nam. Sixteen counties in metropolitan Beijing were surveyed in October–November 2003. An abbreviated survey was conducted in May–July 2003 in Indonesia. Samples sizes ranged from 27,000 to 175,000 households.

4. The proportion of lives saved was adjusted for countries with a high prevalence of HIV/AIDS, where breastfeeding could increase mortality.

5. Recognizing the need to improve local access to priority interventions, a recent WHO/UNICEF policy statement (WHO and UNICEF 2004b) urges countries to train community-based health workers in the diagnosis of pneumonia in children and to allow them to treat with antibiotics, an intervention that had been restricted to health facilities. As resistance to existing antimalarials spreads, many countries will soon adopt artemisinin-based combination therapy (ACT) as their first-line treatment for malaria. Because of the cost of this intervention and the fear of inducing resistance to ACT through overuse, malaria diagnosis and treatment, which has traditionally been done within the community, may increasingly become restricted to the facility level.

6. Although this report has emphasized that the Goals for reducing child and maternal mortality can be achieved through the widespread application of existing interventions, the role of research to develop new and improved interventions should not be minimized. New vaccine and drug development, including the development of new vaccines for the prevention of common childhood illnesses, more heat-stable vaccines, new antibiotics and other drugs that can be given in shorter and easier-to-administer courses, and other innovations can only help accelerate progress toward the Goal. The crying need for operational research—studying how to bring new interventions to the target populations in an acceptable and affordable manner—goes without saying.

7. The WHO definition is "the death of a woman while pregnant or within 42 days of termination of pregnancy, irrespective of the duration and the site of the pregnancy, from any cause related to or aggravated by the pregnancy or its management, but not from accidental or incidental causes" (WHO 1992).

8. See www.safemotherhood.org.

9. See www.safemotherhood.org.

10. A "skilled attendant" refers to the person attending the delivery. "Skilled attendance" sometimes refers to trained personnel plus the enabling conditions of emergency obstetric care and a referral system. To avoid confusion between "skilled attendants" and "skilled attendance," recent publications use the phrase "skilled care" to refer to these three elements (see www.safemotherhood.org/resources/publications.html).

11. *Essential obstetric care* is sometimes used interchangeably with *emergency obstetric care*. For the sake of clarity, this report uses *emergency obstetric care* to refer to the interventions for treating obstetric complications and *essential obstetric care* to refer to the broader range of services, including the management of routine pregnancies (Koblinsky 1999).

12. Rush also discusses the methodological problems in attributing deaths to anemia, which is different from the question of whether anemia increases the risk of death.

13. A study in Bangalore, India, found that the presence of an auxiliary nurse midwife in the area was associated with lower use of professional delivery care (by a doctor or midwife at a facility), both overall and in complicated cases (Nanda 2003).

14. The World Bank's analysis of factors associated with maternal mortality reduction shows that health sector interventions have a far stronger explanatory power than literacy or wealth (Lule and others 2003).

Chapter 4

1. Of course, policy that is explicitly designed to create such a system can nevertheless result in the organized/unorganized markets described by Bloom and Standing (2001), in which the poor do indeed end up paying, often driving them further into impoverishment, and are more likely to receive goods and services of poor quality.

2. The term *health workforce* is used here to mean all people formally employed in providing healthcare rather than the broader term human resources for health, which refers to all people engaged in the promotion, protection, or improvement of population health (WHO 2002a; Joint Learning Initiative 2004).

Chapter 5

1. For more on disaggregation and the Goals, see http://hdr.undp.org/mdg/default.cfm.

2. The obstacles to measuring the maternal mortality ratio and the various methodologies used to arrive at the estimates published by the WHO are explained in the publication of the official data and widely documented in the literature (WHO, UNICEF, and UNFPA 2004).

Chapter 6

1. The World Bank is nevertheless now among the top four individual sources of development assistance for health, along with USAID, the WHO (if extrabudgetary contributions are added to its regular budget), and the Global Fund to Fight AIDS, Tuberculosis and Malaria. The Bill & Melinda Gates Foundation is the next highest source of funding, followed by UNICEF and UNFPA.

2. Poverty Reduction and Growth Facility loans and Poverty Reduction Support Credits are direct descendants of Enhanced Structural Adjustment Facilities and Structural Adjustment Loans, which existed in parallel with sector projects and policy loans.

3. A Poverty and Social Impact Analysis is being planned to examine the impact of health user fees in Kenya (IMF and World Bank 2004c).

References

AbouZahr, Carla. 2003. "Global Burden of Maternal Death and Disability." *British Medical Bulletin* 67 (1): 1–11.

AbouZahr, Carla, and Tessa Wardlaw. 2003. *Antenatal Care in Developing Countries: Promises, Achievements and Missed Opportunities: An Analysis of Trends, Levels and Differentials, 1990–2001.* WHO and UNICEF, Geneva.

Afsana, Kaosar. 2004. "The Tremendous Cost of Seeking Hospital Obstetric Care in Bangladesh." *Reproductive Health Matters* 12 (24): 171–80.

Aguilar, A. M., R. Alvarado, D. Cordero, P. Kelly, A. Zamora, and R. Salgado. 1988. *Mortality Survey in Bolivia: The Final Report. Investigating and Identifying the Causes of Death for Children Under Five.* Report of the Basic Support for Institutionalizing Child Survival (BASICS) Project. USAID (U.S. Agency for International Development), Washington, D.C.

Ahmad, O. B., A. D. Lopez, and M. Inoue. 2000. "The Decline in Child Mortality: A Reappraisal." *Bulletin of the World Health Organization* 78 (10): 1175–91.

Ahuka, O. L., N. Chabikuli,, and G. A. Ogunbanjo. 2004. "The Effects of Armed Conflict on Pregnancy Outcomes in the Congo." *International Journal of Gynecology and Obstetrics* 84 (1): 91–2.

Aid Harmonization and Alignment. 2004. Country Implementation Tracking Tool. Website. [www.aidharmonization.com].

Aitken, J. M. 1994. "Voices from the Inside: Managing District Health Services in Nepal." *International Journal of Health Planning and Management* 9 (4): 309–40.

Alan Guttmacher Institute. 1998. *Into a New World: Young Women's Sexual and Reproductive Lives.* New York.

———. 1999. *Sharing Responsibility: Women, Society and Abortion Worldwide.* New York.

Aleman, J., I. Brannstrom, Jerker Liljestrand, R. Pena, L. A. Persson, and J. Steidinger. 1998. "Saving More Neonates in Hospital: An Intervention towards a Sustainable Reduction in Neonatal Mortality in a Nicaraguan Hospital." *Tropical Doctor* 28 (2): 88–92.

Alliance for Safe Children and UNICEF. 2004. *Child Injury in Asia: Time for Action.* Issue Paper. Alliance for Safe Children and UNICEF East Asian and Pacific Regional Office, Bangkok.

Anand, S., and T. Barnighausen. 2004. "Human Resources and Health Outcomes: Cross-Country Econometric Study." *The Lancet* 364 (9445): 1603–9.

An-Na'im, Abdullahi. 1992. "Toward a Cross-Cultural Approach to Defining International Standards of Human Rights: The Meaning of Cruel, Inhuman or Degrading Treatment of Punishment." In Abdullahi An-Na'im, ed., *Human Rights in Cross-Cultural Perspective: A Quest for Consensus.* Philadelphia: University of Pennsylvania Press.

Asiimwe, D., B. McPake, F. Mwesigye, M. Ofumbi, L. Oertenblad, P. Streefland, and A. Turinde. 1997. "The Private Sector Activities of Public-Sector Health Workers in Uganda." In S. Bennet, B. McPake, and A. Mills, eds., *Private Health Providers in Developing Countries: Serving the Public Interest?* London: Zed Books.

Askew, Ian, and Marge Berer. 2003. "The Contribution of Sexual and Reproductive Health Services to the Fight Against HIV/AIDS: A Review." *Reproductive Health Matters* 11 (22): 51–73.

Balk, D., A. Storeygard, and G. Booma. 2004. "Access to Maternal Healthcare Facilities in Bangladesh." Background paper for the United Nations Millennium Project Task Force on Child Health and Maternal Health. CIESIN (Center for the International Earth Science Information Network), Columbia University, New York.

Bang, A. T., R. A. Bang, S. B. Baitule, M. H. Reddy, and M. D. Deshmukh. 1999. "Effect of Home-Based Neonatal Care and Management of Sepsis on Neonatal Mortality: Field Trial in Rural India." *The Lancet* 354 (9449): 1955–61.

Barnett, B., and J. Stein. 1998. *Women's Voices, Women's Lives: The Impact of Family Planning.* Family Health International, Research Triangle Park, N.C.

Barrett, Diana, James Austin, and Sheila McCarthy. 2002. "Cross-Sector Collaboration: Lessons from the International Trachoma Initiative." In M. R. Reich, ed., *Public-Private Partnerships for Public Health.* Cambridge, Mass.: Harvard Center for Population and Development Studies.

Barros, A. J. D., A. D. Bertoldi, and C. G. Victora. 2004. "The Family Health Program in Brazil: Coverage and Access." PowerPoint presentation at the "Reaching the Poor with Effective Health, Nutrition, and Population Services: What Works, What Doesn't, and Why?" conference, February 18, Washington, D.C.

Bartlett, L. A., Susan Purdin, and Therese McGinn. 2004. "Forced Migrants: Turning Rights into Reproductive Health." *The Lancet* 363 (9402): 76–7.

Barua, A., and K. Kurz. 2001. "Reproductive Health-Seeking by Married Adolescent Girls in Maharashtra, India." *Reproductive Health Matters* 9 (17): 53–62.

Beaton, G. H., R. Martorell, K. J. Aronson, and others. 1993. *Effectiveness of Vitamin A Supplementation in the Control of Young Child Morbidity and Mortality in Developing Countries.* State of the Art Series, Nutrition Policy Discussion Paper 13. UN ACC/SCN (United Nations Administrative Committee on Coordination, Standing Committee on Nutrition), Geneva.

Bellagio Study Group on Child Survival. 2003. "Knowledge into Action for Child Survival." *The Lancet* 362 (9380): 323–7.

Bennett, S., A. Creese, and R. Monasch. 1998. *Health Insurance Schemes for People Outside Formal Sector Employment.* ARA Paper 16, Division of Analysis, Research and Assessment. WHO, Geneva.

Berer, Marge. 2003a. "HIV/AIDS, Sexual and Reproductive Health: Intimately Related." *Reproductive Health Matters* 11 (22): 6–11.

———. 2003b. "Integration of Sexual and Reproductive Health Services: A Health Sector Priority." *Reproductive Health Matters* 11 (21): 6–15.

———. 2004. "HIV/AIDS, Sexual and Reproductive Health: Intersections and Implications for National Programmes." *Health Policy and Planning* 19 (Suppl. 1): i62–70.

Berman, P., and L. Rose. 1996. "The Role of Private Providers in Maternal and Child Health and Family Planning Services in Developing Countries." *Health Policy and Planning* 11(2): 142–55.

Bernstein, Stan. 2004. "A Proposal for Including a Measure of Unmet Need for Contraception and Adolescent Fertility or Early Marriage Levels as Indicators of the Reproductive Health Component of Gender Equality." Background paper prepared for the UN Millennium Project. New York. [http://unstats.un.org/unsd/mi/techgroup/subgroups/IAEG%20submission%20on%20unmet%20need%20v3.pdf 2004].

Bhan, Gautam, Nita Bhandari, Sunita Taneja, Sarmila Mazumder, and Rajiv Bahl. 2005. "The Effect of Maternal Education on Gender Bias in Care-Seeking for Common Childhood Illnesses." *Social Science & Medicine* 60 (4): 715–24.

Bhutta, Z. A., G. Darmstadt, B. Hasan, and R. Haws. 2005. "Community-based Interventions for Improving Perinatal and Neonatal Health Outcomes in Developing Countries: Review of the Evidence." *Pediatrics* 115: 519–617.

Bicego, George, J. Ties Boerma, and Carine Ronsmans. 2002. "The Effect of AIDS on Maternal Mortality in Malawi and Zimbabwe." *AIDS* 16 (7): 1078–81.

Biscoe, Gillian. 2001. *Human Resources: The Political and Policy Context.* Geneva: World Health Organization.

Blaauw, Duane, and Helen Schneider. 2003. "Improving the Management of Sexually Transmitted Infections in the Private Sector in South Africa." In N. Söderlund, P. Mendoza-Arana, and J. Goudge, eds., *The New Public/Private Mix in Health: Exploring the Changing Landscape.* Geneva: Alliance for Health Policy and Systems Research.

Blaauw, Duane, Lucy Gilson, Loveday Penn-Kekana, and Helen Schneider. 2003. "Organisational Relationships and the 'Software' of Health Sector Reform." Background paper. Disease Control Priorities Project (DCPP) Capacity Strengthening and Management Reform. Centre for Health Policy, School of Public Health, University of Witwatersrand, Johannesburg, South Africa.

Black, R., S. Morris, and J. Bryce. 2003. "Where and Why Are 10 Million Children Dying Every Year?" *The Lancet* 361 (9376): 2226–34.

Bloom, Gerald. 2001. "Equity in Health in Unequal Societies: Meeting Health Needs in Contexts of Social Change." *Health Policy* 57 (3): 205–24.

———. 2004. *Private Provision in Its Institutional Context: Lessons from Health.* DFID Health Systems Resource Center. London.

Bloom, Gerry, Henry Lucas, Adebiye Edun, Mungai Lenneiye, and John Milimo. 2000. *Health and Poverty in Sub-Saharan Africa.* IDS Working Paper 103. Institute for Development Studies, University of Sussex, Brighton, U.K.

Bloom, Gerry, and Hilary Standing. 2001. *Pluralism and Marketisation in the Health Sector: Meeting Health Needs in Contexts of Social Change in Low- and Middle-Income Countries.* IDS Working Paper 136. Institute for Development Studies, University of Sussex, Brighton, U.K.

Borghi, J., Kara Hanson, C. A. Acquah, G. Ekanmian, V. Filippi, C. Ronsmans, R. Brugha, E. Browne, and E. Alihonou. 2003. "Costs of Near-Miss Obstetric Complications for Women and Their Families in Benin and Ghana." *Health Policy and Planning* 18 (4): 383–90.

Bossyns, Paul, and Wim Van Lerberghe. 2004. "The Weakest Link: Competence and Prestige as Constraints to Referral by Isolated Nurses in Rural Niger." *Human Resources for Health* 2 (1). [www.human-resources-health.com/content/2/1/1].

Bossyns, Paul, Wim Van Lerberghe, R. Abache, and M. S. Abdoulaye. 2004. "Unaffordable or Cost-Effective? Introducing an Emergency Referral System in Rural Niger."

Braveman, P., and S. Gruskin. 2003. "Defining Equity in Health." *Journal of Epidemiology and Community Health* 57 (4): 254–58.

Braveman, P., B. Starfield, and H. J. Geiger. 2001. "World Health Report 2000: How It Removes Equity from the Agenda for Public Health Monitoring and Policy." *British Medical Journal* 323 (7314): 678–81.

Brazil. 1988. *Constitution of the Federative Republic of Brazil.*

Brinkerhoff, D. W. 2004. "Accountability and Health Systems: Toward Conceptual Clarity and Policy Relevance." *Health Policy and Planning* 19 (6): 371–79.

Bruce, Judith. 1990. "Fundamental Elements of the Quality of Care: A Simple Framework." *Studies in Family Planning* 21 (2): 61–91.

Bruce, Judith, and Shelley Clark. 2003. "Including Married Adolescents in Reproductive Health and HIV/AIDS Policy." Paper prepared for the WHO/UNFPA/Population Council Technical Consultation on Married Adolescents, December 9–12, Geneva. [www.popcouncil.org/pdfs/CMImplications.pdf].

Bryce, J., S. el Arifeen, George Pariyo, Claudio F. Lanata, Davidson R. Gwatkin, J. P. Habicht, and The Multi-Country Evaluation of the IMCI Study Group. 2003. "Reducing Child Mortality: Can Public Health Deliver?" *The Lancet* 362 (9378): 159–64.

Bulatao, R. A., and J. A. Ross. 2003. "Which Health Services Reduce Maternal Mortality? Evidence from Ratings of Maternal Health Services." *Tropical Medicine and International Health* 8 (8): 710–21.

Burnham, G. M., G. Pariyo, E. Galiwango, and F. Wabwire-Mangen. 2004. "Discontinuation of Cost Sharing in Uganda." *Bulletin of the World Health Organization* 82 (3): 187–95.

Buse, K., and G. Walt. 1997. "An Unruly Mélange? Coordinating External Resources to the Health Sector: A Review." *Social Science and Medicine* 45 (3): 449–63.

———. 2002. "Globalization and Multilateral Public-Private Health Partnerships: Issues for Health Policy." In K. Lee, K. Buse, and S. Fustakian, eds., *Health Policy in a Globalising World*. Cambridge, U.K.: Cambridge University Press.

Bustreo, F., A. Harding, and H. Axelsson. 2003. "Can Developing Countries Achieve Adequate Improvements in Child Health Outcomes without Engaging the Private Sector?" *Bulletin of the World Health Organization* 81 (12): 886–94.

Buve, A., S. Kalibala, and J. McIntyre. 2003. "Stronger Health Systems for More Effective HIV/AIDS Prevention and Care." *International Journal of Health Planning and Management* 18 (Supp): S41–51.

Campbell, Oona M. R. 1999. "Measuring Progress in Safe Motherhood Programmes: Uses and Limitations of Health Outcome Indicators." *Reproductive Health Matters* Special issue: Safe Motherhood Initiative: Critical Issues: 31–42.

———. 2001. "What Are Maternal Health Policies in Developing Countries and Who Drives Them? A Review of the Last Half-Century." In V. De Brouwere and W. Van Lerberghe, eds., *Safe Motherhood Strategies: A Review of the Evidence*. Antwerp: ITG Press.

———. 2003. "Egypt, 1992–2000." In M. Koblinsky, ed., *Reducing Maternal Mortality: Learning from Bolivia, China, Egypt, Honduras, Indonesia, Jamaica and Zimbabwe*. Washington, D.C.: World Bank.

Cassels, A. 1997. "A Guide to Sector-Wide Approaches for Health and Development: Concepts, Issues and Working Arrangements." World Health Organization, Danida (Danish International Development Agency), and Department for International Development, European Commission–sponsored report. WHO, Geneva.

Castro-Leal, F., J. Dayton, L. Demery, and K. Mehra. 2000. "Public Spending on Healthcare in Africa: Do the Poor Benefit?" *Bulletin of the World Health Organization* 78 (1): 66–74.

Caulfield, L. E., M. de Onis, M. Blossner, and R. E. Black. 2004. "Undernutrition as an Underlying Cause of Child Deaths Associated with Diarrhea, Pneumonia, Malaria, and Measles." *American Journal of Clinical Nutrition* 80: 193–98.

Chamberlain, J., R. McDonagh, A. Lalonde, and S. Arulkumaran. 2003. "The Role of Professional Associations in Reducing Maternal Mortality Worldwide." *International Journal of Gynecology and Obstetrics* 83 (1): 94–102.

Chowdhury, M., and others. 1997. "Control of Tuberculosis by Community Health Workers in Bangladesh." *The Lancet* 350 (9072):169–72.

Commission on Macroeconomics and Health. 2001. *Macroeconomics and Health: Investing in Health for Economic Development.* World Health Organization. Geneva.

Conway, T., M. Foster, A. Fozzard, and F. Naschold. 2002. *How, When and Why Does Poverty Get Budget Priority: Poverty Reduction Strategy and Public Expenditure in Five African Countries.* Overseas Development Institute. London.

Copelon, Rhonda, and Rosalind Petchesky. 1995. "Toward an Interdependent Approach to Reproductive and Sexual Rights as Human Rights: Reflections on ICPD and Beyond." In M. Schuler, ed., *From Basic Needs to Basic Rights: Women's Claim to Human Rights.* Washington, D.C.: Institute for Women, Law and Development.

Correa, Carlos M. 2002. "Public Health and Intellectual Property Rights." *Global Social Policy* 2 (3): 261–78.

Correa, Sonia. 1994. *Population and Reproductive Rights: Feminist Perspectives from the South.* London: Zed Books Ltd.

Cottingham, J., and C. Myntti. 2002. "Reproductive Health: Conceptual Mapping and Evidence." In G. Sen, A. George, and P. Ostlin, eds., *Engendering International Health.* Cambridge, Mass.: MIT Press.

Crane, B., and C. H. Smith. Forthcoming. "Safe Abortion: An Essential Strategy for Achieving the Millennium Development Goals to Improve Maternal Health, Empower Women, and Reduce Poverty." Background paper prepared for the UN Millennium Project. New York.

Cruz Bermudez et al. v. Ministerio de Sanidad y Asistencia Social (MSAS). Case No. 15789, Supreme Court of Venezuela.

Cunningham, F. Gary, Paul C. MacDonald, Norman F. Gant, Kenneth J. Leveno, and Larry C. Gilstrap III. 1993. *Williams Obstetrics,* 19th Edition. Norwalk, Conn.: Appleton & Lange.

Dadhich, J. P., and Vinod Paul. 2004. State of India's Newborns. *Saving Newborn Lives Report.* New Delhi: Save the Children.

Daga, S. R., A. S. Daga, R. V. Dighole, R. P. Patil, and H. L. Dhinde. 1992. "Rural Neonatal Care: Dahanu Experience." *Indian Pediatrics* 29 (2): 189–93.

Daga, S. R., A. S. Daga, S. Patole, S. Kadam, and Y. Mukadam. 1988. "Foot Length Measurement from Foot Print for Identifying a Newborn at Risk." *Journal of Tropical Pediatrics* 34 (1): 16–19.

Danel, I., and A. Rivera. 2003. "Honduras, 1990–1997." In M. Koblinsky, ed., *Reducing Maternal Mortality: Learning from Bolivia, China, Egypt, Honduras, Indonesia, Jamaica and Zimbabwe.* Washington, D.C.: World Bank.

Daniels, Norman, J. Bryant, R. A. Castano, O. G. Dantes, K. S. Khan, and S. Pannarunothai. 2000. "Benchmarks of Fairness for Healthcare Reform: A Policy Tool for Developing Countries." *Bulletin of the World Health Organization* 78 (6): 740–50.

Darmstadt, G. L., Z. A. Bhutta, S. Cousens, T. Adam, N. Walker, and L. de Bernis. 2005. "Evidence-based, Cost-effective Interventions: How Many Newborn Babies Can We Save?" *The Lancet* 365 (9463): 977–88.

Datta, N. 1985. "A Study of Health Problems of Low Birth Weight Babies in a Rural Community and the Feasibility of Intervention Package Likely to Improve Their Health Status." Ph.D. thesis, Postgraduate Institute of Medical Education and Research, Chandrigarh, India.

Datta, N., V. Kumar, L. Kumar, and S. Singh. 1987. "Application of Case Management to the Control of Acute Respiratory Infections in Low-Birth-Weight Infants: A Feasibility Study." *Bulletin of the World Health Organization* 65 (1): 77–82.

Daulaire, Nils, Pat Leidl, Laurel Mackin, Colleen Murphy, and Laura Stark. 2002. *Promises to Keep: the Toll of Unintended Pregnancies on Women's Lives in the Developing World*. Washington, D.C.: Global Health Council.

Dehne, K., and G. Riedner. 2001. "Adolescence, a Dynamic Concept." *Reproductive Health Matters* 9 (17):11–15.

DFID (U.K. Department for International Development). 2004. *Poverty Reduction Budget Support*. DFID Policy Paper, London.

Diaz, Daniela, and Graciela Freyermuth, eds. 2004. *Muerte Materna y Presupuesto Público*. Mexico City: Fundar, Centro de Análisis e Investigación.

Diaz, Daniela, and Helena Hofbauer. 2004. "The Public Budget and Maternal Mortality in Mexico: An Overview of the Experience." Fundar, Centro de Análisis e Investigación, Mexico City.

Diaz, Margarita, Ruth Simmons, Juan Diaz, Carlos Gonzales, Maria Yolanda Makuch, and Debora Bossemerer. 1999. "Expanding Contraceptive Choice: Findings from Brazil." *Studies in Family Planning* 30 (1): 1–16.

Dickinson, Clare. 2003. *Reducing Maternal Mortality: System and Institutional Approaches*. DFID Health Systems Resource Centre, London.

Dickson-Tetteh, K., L. M. Mavuya, M. Gabriel, K. Rees, D. L. Billings, and T. D. N. King. 2000. "Abortion Care Services Provided by Registered Midwives in South Africa: A Report on the Midwifery Training Program." Reproductive Health Research Unit and Ipas. Johannesburg.

Dixon-Mueller, Ruth. 1993. *Population Policy and Women's Rights: Transforming Reproductive Choice*. London: Praeger.

Doedens, Wilma, and Kate Burns. 2001. "Challenges to Reproductive Health in Emergencies." *WHO Health in Emergencies Newsletter* 10: 1–2.

Donnay, F., and L. Weil. 2004. "Obstetric Fistula: The International Response." *The Lancet* 363 (9402): 71–72.

Dovlo, D. Y. 2004. "Using Mid-Level Cadres as Substitutes for Internationally Mobile Health Professionals in Africa: A Desk Review." *Human Resources for Health* 2 (1): 7. [www.human-resources-health.com/content/2/1/7].

Dowsett, G. W. 2003. "Some Considerations on Sexuality and Gender in the Context of AIDS." *Reproductive Health Matters* 11 (22): 21–29.

Drager, Nick, and David P. Fidler. 2004. "GATS and Health-Related Services: Managing Liberalization of Trade in Services from a Health Policy Perspective." WHO Trade and Health Notes. World Health Organization, Geneva.

Dussault, Gilles, and Carl-Ardy Dubois. 2003. "Human Resources for Health Policies: A Critical Component in Health Policies." *Human Resources for Health* 1 (1): 1–16. [www.human-resources-health.com/content/1/1/1].

Egger, D., D. J. Lipson, and Orvill Adams. 2000. "Achieving the Right Balance: The Role of Policy-Making Processes in Managing Human Resources for Health Problems." World Health Organization, Geneva.

el Arifeen, S., L. S. Blum, D. M. E. Hoque, E. K. Chowdhury, R. Khan, R. Black, C. G. Victora, and J. Bryce. 2004. "Integrated Management of Childhood Illness (IMCI) in Bangladesh: Early Findings from a Cluster-Randomised Study." *The Lancet* 364 (9445): 1595–1602.

English, M., F. Esamai, A. Wasunna, F. Were, B. Ogutu, A. Wamae, R. W. Snow, and N. Peshu. 2004. "Assessment of Inpatient Paediatric Care in First Referral Level Hospitals in 13 Districts in Kenya." *The Lancet* 363 (9425): 1948–53.

EQUINET. 2004. "Equity in the Distribution of Health Personnel." Paper presented at the Regional Research Review Meeting, April 15–17, Johannesburg.

EURODAD (European Network on Debt and Development). 2003. Is PRGF Maximising Finance for Poverty Reduction? Website. [www.eurodad.org/articles/default.aspx?id=460].

Evans, T., and B. Stansfield. 2004. "Health Information in the New Millennium: A Gathering Storm?" *The Lancet* 81 (12): 856.

Faull, Norman. 1998. *Competitive Capabilities.* Cape Town, South Africa: Juta.

Ferrinho, Paulo, Maria Carolina Omar, Maria de Jesus Fernandes, Pierre Blaise, Ana Margarida Bugalho, and Wim Van Lerberghe. 2004. "Pilfering for Survival: How Health Workers Use Access to Drugs as a Coping Strategy." *Human Resources for Health* 2 (4). [www.human-resources-health.com/content/2/1/4].

Fikree, Fariyal, and Omrana Pasha. 2004. "Role of Gender in Health Disparity: The South Asian Context." *British Medical Journal* 328 (7443): 823–26.

Filmer, Deon, Jeffrey S. Hammer, and Lant H. Pritchett. 2000. "Weak Links in the Chain: A Diagnosis of Health Policy in Poor Countries." *World Bank Research Observer* 15 (2): 199–224.

Flores, Walter, and David McCoy. 2004. "Maternal and Child Health and Equity in Guatemala." Background paper for the UN Millennium Project Task Force on Child Health and Maternal Health. New York.

Fortney, J. A., and J. B. Smith. 1996. *The Base of the Iceberg: Prevalence and Perceptions of Maternal Morbidity in Four Developing Countries.* Research Triangle Park, N.C.: Family Health International.

Frasca, T. 2003. "Men and Women—Still Far Apart on HIV/AIDS." *Reproductive Health Matters* 11 (22): 12–20.

Freedman, Lynn P. 1995. "Censorship and Manipulation of Family Planning Information: An Issue of Human Rights and Women's Health." In Sandra Coliver ed., *Article 19, The Right to Know: Human Rights and Access to Reproductive Health Information.* Philadelphia: University of Pennsylvania Press.

———. 2001. "Using Human Rights in Maternal Mortality Programs: From Analysis to Strategy." *International Journal of Gynecology and Obstetrics* 75 (1): 51–60.

———. 2003. "Human Rights, Constructive Accountability and Maternal Mortality in the Dominican Republic: A Commentary." *International Journal of Gynecology and Obstetrics* 82 (1): 111–114.

Freedman, Lynn P., Meg Wirth, R. J. Waldman, M. Chowdhury, and Allan Rosenfield. 2003. "Millennium Development Project Task Force 4 Background Paper on Child Health and Maternal Health." UN Millennium Project, New York. [www.unmillenniumproject.org/documents/tf4interim.pdf].

Freedman, Lynn P., and Stephen L. Isaacs. 1993. "Human Rights and Reproductive Choice." *Studies in Family Planning* 24 (1): 18–30.

Friedman, H. R. 1994. "Reproductive Health in Adolescence." *World Health Statistics Quarterly* 47 (1): 31–35.

Fundar, International Budget Project, and International Human Rights Internship Program. 2004. *Dignity Counts: A Guide to Using Budget Analysis to Advance Human Rights.* Mexico City.

Ganatra, Bela, K. J. Coyaji, and V. N. Rao. 1998. "Too Far, Too Little, Too Late: A Community-Based Case-Control Study of Maternal Mortality in Rural West Maharashtra, India." *Bulletin of the World Health Organization* 76 (6): 591–98.

George, Asha. 2003. "Using Accountability to Improve Reproductive Healthcare." *Reproductive Health Matters* 11 (21): 161–70.

Gerbase, Antonio C., Jane T. Rowley, and Thierry E. Mertens. 1998. "Global Epidemiology of Sexually Transmitted Diseases." *The Lancet* 351 (Supplement 1): S2–4.

Germain, Adrienne, and T. Kim. 1998. *Expanding Access to Safe Abortion: Strategies for Action.* International Women's Health Coalition. New York.

Gertler, P., and S. Boyce. 2001. *An Experiment in Incentive-Based Welfare: The Impact of PROGRESA on Health in Mexico.* [Retrieved October, 2004, from www.worldbank. org/research/projects/service_delivery/paper_gertler1.pdf].

Gilson, Lucy. 2003. "Trust and Development of Healthcare as a Social Institution." *Social Science and Medicine* 56 (7): 1453–68.

———. 2004. "The State of Decentralisation in the South African Health Sector, 2003." In The Local Government and Health Consortium, eds., *Decentralising Health Services in South Africa: Constraints and Opportunities.* Durban: Health Systems Trust.

Gilson, Lucy, and Ermin Erasmus. 2004. "Values in Use and Organisational Culture: Exploring the Relevance to Health Systems Development." Background paper for the UN Millennium Project Task Force on Child Health and Maternal Health. New York.

Global Forum for Health Research. 2004. *Strengthening Health Systems: The Role and Promise of Policy and Systems Research.* Geneva: Alliance for Health Policy and Systems Research.

Goodburn, E. A., M. Chowdhury, R. Gazi, and others. 2000. "Training Traditional Birth Attendants in Clean Delivery Does Not Prevent Postpartum Infection." *Health Policy and Planning* 15 (4): 394–99.

Goodburn, Elizabeth, and Oona Campbell. 2001. "Reducing Maternal Mortality in the Developing World: Sector-Wide Approaches May Be the Key." *British Medical Journal* 322 (7291): 917.

Graham, W. J., A. E. Fitzmaurice, J. S. Bell, and J. A. Cairns. 2004. "The Familial Technique for Linking Maternal Death with Poverty." *The Lancet* 363 (9402): 23–27.

Graham, W. J., and J. Hussein. 2004. "The Right to Count." *The Lancet* 363 (9402): 67–68.

Greenwood, A. M., B. M. Greenwood, A. K. Bradley, K. Williams, F. C. Shenton, S. Tulloch, P. Byass, and F. S. Oldfield. 1987. "A Prospective Study of the Outcome of Pregnancy in a Rural Area of the Gambia." *Bulletin of the World Health Organization* 65 (5): 635–43.

Greenwood, A. M., A. K. Bradley, P. Byass, B. M. Greenwood, R. W. Snow, S. Bennett, and A. B. Hatib-N'Jie. 1990. "Evaluation of a Primary Care Programme in the Gambia: The Impact of Traditional Birth Attendants on the Outcome of Pregnancy." *Journal of Tropical Medicine & Hygiene* 93 (1): 58–66.

Gwatkin, Davidson. 2004. "Looking beyond the averages, in order to ensure that poor women benefit fully from progress toward reproductive health goals." Paper prepared for ICPD at 10 conference. In Bos, Eduard. 2004. "Improving Maternal Health: The Need to Focus on Reaching the Poor." Presented at "Seminar on the relevance on population aspects for the achievement of the Millennium Development Goals," United Nations, November 17–19, New York.

Gwatkin, Davidson R., A. Bhuiya, and C. G. Victora. 2004. "Making Health Systems More Equitable." *The Lancet* 364 (9441): 1273–80.

Gwatkin, D. R., Shea Rutstein, Kiersten Johnson, Eldaw Abdalla Suliman, and Adam Wagstaff. 2003. *Initial Country-Level Information about Socio-Economic Differences in Health, Nutrition, and Population.* 2nd Edition. Washington, D.C.: World Bank and UNFPA (United Nations Population Fund).

Habicht, Jean-Pierre, Jef Leroy, Gretel Pelto, Stefano Bertozzi, Jennifer Bryce, and Juan Rivera. 2004. "Prioritizing Research to Meet the MDGs Requires Structural and Funding Change: Beyond the 10/90 Gap." Presentation at the session on "Child

Health and Nutrition: The Effectiveness of Child Health and Nutrition Programs," Global Forum for Health Research, November 16–20, Mexico City.

Hall, J. J., and R. Taylor. 2003. "Health for All Beyond 2000: The Demise of the Alma-Ata Declaration and Primary Healthcare in Developing Countries." *Medical Journal of Australia* 178 (1): 17–20.

Hanson, Kara. 2002. "Measuring Up: Gender, Burden of Disease, and Priority Setting." In G. Sen, A. George, and P. Ostlin, eds., *Engendering International Health: The Challenge of Equity.* Cambridge, Mass.: Massachusetts Institute of Technology Press.

Healthy Newborn Partnership. 2004. "Report of a Meeting." Report prepared at Advancing Newborn Health within Existing Programmes to Meet Millennium Development Goals for Both the Child and the Mother, February 23–25, Addis Ababa.

Heise, Lori L., Mary Ellsberg, and M. Gottemoeller. 1999. "Ending Violence against Women." Population Reports Series L, Number 11. Johns Hopkins University School of Public Health, Population Information Program. Baltimore, Md.

Helzner, Judith. 2002. "Transforming Family Planning Services in the Latin American and Caribbean Region." *Studies in Family Planning* 33 (1): 49–60.

Hill, Peter S. 2002. "Between Intent and Achievement in Sector-Wide Approaches: Staking a Claim for Reproductive Health." *Reproductive Health Matters* 10 (20): 29–37.

Hobcraft, I. 1993. "Women's Education, Child Welfare and Child Survival: A Review of the Evidence." *Health Transition Review* 3 (2): 159–75.

Hogberg, Ulf. 2004. "The Decline in Maternal Mortality in Sweden: The Role of Community Midwifery." *American Journal of Public Health* 94 (8): 1312–20.

Holmes, M., and A. Evans. 2003. "A Review of Experience in Implementing Medium Term Expenditure Frameworks in a PRSP Context: A Synthesis of Eight Case Studies." Draft discussion report. Overseas Development Institute, London.

Hongoro, C., and B. McPake. 2004. "How to Bridge the Gap in Human Resources for Health." *The Lancet* 364 (9443): 1451–56.

Hossain, S. M. Moazzem, Abbas Bhuiya, Alia Rahman Khan, and Iyorlumun Uhaa. 2004. "Community Development and Its Impact on Health: South Asian Experience." *British Medical Journal* 328 (7743):830–33.

Hotchkiss, D. R. 1998. "The Tradeoff Between Price and Quality of Services in the Philippines." Social Science and Medicine 46 (2): 227–42.

IDA (International Development Association). 2003. "Program Document for a Proposed Credit in the Amount of SDR 63.9 million (US$88 million equivalent) and Proposed Grant in the Amount of SDR 26.9 million (US$37 million equivalent) to the Republic of Ghana for a Poverty Reduction Support Credit and Grant." Report 25995-GH. Washington, D.C.

ILO (International Labour Organization) and WHO (World Health Organization). 2003. "Public Service Reforms and Their Impact on Health Sector Personnel: Case Studies on Cameroon, Colombia, Jordan, Philippines, Poland, Uganda." Geneva. [www.ilo.org/public/english/dialogue/sector/papers/health/pubserv1.pdf].

IMF (International Monetary Fund). 2004. "Ghana: Second Review Under the Poverty Reduction and Growth Facility and Request for Waiver of Nonobservance of Performance Criteria-Staff Report." Staff statement, press release on the executive board discussion, and statement by the executive director for Ghana. IMF Country Report 04/210. Washington, D.C.

IMF (International Monetary Fund) and International Development Association. 2004. "Heavily Indebted Poor Countries (HIPC) Initiative: Status of Implementation." Washington, D.C. [www.imf.org/external/np/hipc/2003/status/091203.pdf].

IMF (International Monetary Fund) Independent Evaluation Office. 2004. "Report on the Evaluation of Poverty Reduction Strategy Papers (PRSPs) and The Poverty Reduction and Growth Facility (PRGF)." Washington, D.C.

IMF (International Monetary Fund) and World Bank. 2002. "Review of the PRSPs Approach: Main Findings." International Development Association and IMF. Washington, D.C.

———. 2004a. "Global Monitoring Report 2004: Policies and Actions for Achieving the MDGs and Related Outcomes." Development Committee (Joint Ministerial Committed of the Board of Governors of the Bank and the Fund on the Transfer of Real Resources to Developing Countries) DC2004-0006. Washington, D.C.

———. 2004b. "Note on the Status of Implementation of the HIPC Initiative and Further Considerations on an Operational Framework for Debt Sustainability in Low-Income Countries." DC2004-0015. Washington, D.C.

———. 2004c. "Poverty Reduction Strategy Papers—Progress in Implementation." Washington, D.C.

India, Ministry of Health and Family Welfare. 2004. *Annual Report, 2003–2004.* New Delhi.

Institute of Medicine Department of Community Medicine and Family Health. 2004. *Utilization of Emergency Obstetric Care in Selected Districts in Nepal.* Kathmandu.

International Council on Human Rights Policy and EGI (Ethical Globalization Initiative). 2003. *Duties Sans Frontières: Human Rights and Global Social Justice.* Geneva: International Council on Human Rights Policy.

Jackson, D., A. Ntuli, A. Padarath, and C. Day. 2004. "Vulnerable Health Systems: Perilous Motherhood. A Case Study of Maternal Mortality in One Region of the Eastern Cape Province, South Africa." Background paper for the UN Millennium Project Task Force on Child Health and Maternal Health. New York.

Jacobs, Bart, and Neil Price. 2004. "The Impact of the Introduction of User Fees at a District Hospital in Cambodia." *Health Policy and Planning* 19 (5): 310–21.

Jaen, M. H., and D. Paravisini. 2001. "Capture and Penalties in Venezuala's Public Hospitals." In R. Di Tella and W. D. Savedoff, eds., *Diagnosis Corruption: Fraud in Latin America's Public Hospitals.* Washington, D.C.: Inter-American Development Bank.

Ji, Bu-Tian, Xiao-Ou Shu, Martha S. Linet, Wei Zheng, Sholom Wacholder, Yu-Tang Gao, Da-Ming Ying, and Fan Jin. 1997. "Paternal Cigarette Smoking and the Risk of Childhood Cancer among Offspring of Nonsmoking Mothers." *Journal of the National Cancer Institute* 89 (3): 238–43.

Joint Learning Initiative. 2004. *Human Resources for Health: Overcoming the Crisis.* Harvard University Global Equity Initiative.

Jones, G., Richard Steketee, R. Black, Z. A. Bhutta, S. Morris, and The Bellagio Child Survival Study Group. 2003. "How Many Child Deaths Can We Prevent This Year?" *The Lancet* 362 (9377): 65–71.

Keeley, James, and Ian Scoones. 1999. "Understanding Environmental Policy Processes: A Review." IDS Working Paper 89. Institute for Development Studies, University of Sussex, Brighton, U.K. [www.ids.ac.uk/ids/bookshop/wp/wp89.pdf].

Kern, A., and J. Ritzen. 2001. "Dying for Change: Poor People's Experience of Health and Ill-Health." WHO and World Bank, Geneva.

Khaleghian, Peyvand, and Monica Das Gupta. 2004. *Public Management and the Essential Public Health Functions.* Policy Research Working Paper 3220. Washington, D.C.: World Bank.

Kiggundu, C. 1999. "Decentralising Integrated Postabortion Care in Uganda: A Pilot Training and Support Initiative for Improving the Quality and Availability of Integrated RH Service." Ministry of Health, PRIME, Ipas, and DISH. Kampala, Uganda.

Knippenberg, R., A. Soucat, and Wim Van Lerberghe. 2003. "Marginal Budgeting for Bottlenecks: A Tool for Performance Based Planning of Health and Nutrition Services for Achieving the Millennium Development Goals." PowerPoint presentation. World Bank, UNICEF (United Nations Children's Fund), and WHO, Washington, D.C. and Geneva.

Koblinsky, Marge. 1999. "Essential Obstetric Care and Subsets—Basic and Emergency Obstetric Care: What's the Difference." MotherCare Policy Brief 1. John Snow Inc., Arlington, Iowa.

————. 2003a. "Indonesia, 1990–1999." In M. Koblinsky, ed., *Reducing Maternal Mortality: Learning from Bolivia, China, Egypt, Honduras, Indonesia, Jamaica and Zimbabwe.* Washington, D.C.: World Bank.

————, ed. 2003b. *Reducing Maternal Mortality: Learning from Bolivia, China, Egypt, Honduras, Indonesia, Jamaica and Zimbabwe.* Washington, D.C.: World Bank.

Koblinsky, Marge, and O. Campbell. 2003. "Factors Affecting the Reduction of Maternal Mortality. In M. Koblinsky, ed., *Reducing Maternal Mortality: Learning from Bolivia, China, Egypt, Honduras, Indonesia, Jamaica and Zimbabwe.* Washington, D.C.: World Bank.

Koenig, Michael A., Mian Bazle Hossain, and Maxine Whittaker. 1997. "The Influence of Quality of Care upon Contraceptive Use in Rural Bangladesh." *Studies in Family Planning* 28 (4): 278–89.

Koivusalo, Meri. 2003. "The Impact of WTO Agreements on Health and Development Policies." Globalism and Social Policy Programme Policy Brief 3. STAKES (National Research and Development Center for Welfare and Health, Finland). Helsinki.

Konare, Alpha Oumar. 2004. "New Year's message of H.E. Mr. Alpha Oumar Konare, Chairperson of the Commission of the African Union." [www.africa-union.org/home/new%20year%20message.htm].

Kowalewski, M., and A. Jahn. 2001. "Health Professionals for Maternity Services: Experiences on Covering the Population with Quality Maternity Care." In V. De Brouwere and W. Van Lerberghe, eds., *Safe Motherhood Strategies: A Review of the Evidence.* Studies in Health Services Organization and Policy, 17. Antwerp: ITG Press.

Kramer, M. S. 1987. "Intrauterine Growth and Gestational Duration Determinants." *Pediatrics* 80 (4): 502–11.

Krieger, Nancy. 2001. "Theories for Social Epidemiology in the 21st Century: An Ecosocial Perspective." *International Journal of Epidemiology* 30 (4): 668–77.

Krieger, Nancy, and Sofia Gruskin. 2001. "Frameworks Matter: Ecosocial and Health and Human Rights Perspectives on Disparities in Women's Health—The Case of Tuberculosis." *Journal of the American Medical Women's Association* 56 (4): 137–42.

Kumaranayake, Lilani, and Damian Walker. 2002. "Cost-Effectiveness Analysis and Priority-Setting: Global Approach without Local Meaning?" In K. Lee, K. Buse, and S. Fustakian, eds., *Health Policy in a Globalising World.* Cambridge, U.K.: Cambridge University Press.

Kunst, A. E., and T. Houweling. 2001. "A Global Picture of Poor-Rich Differences in the Utilisation of Delivery Care." In W. Van Lerberghe and V. De Brouwere, eds., *Safe Motherhood Strategies: A Review of the Evidence.* Studies in Health Services Organization and Policy 17. Antwerp: ITG Press.

Kwast, B. E., R. W. Rochart, and W. Kidane-Mariam. 1986. "Maternal Mortality in Addis Ababa, Ethiopia." *Studies in Family Planning* 17 (1): 288–98.

Kyaddondo, David, and Susan Reynolds Whyte. 2003. "Working in a Decentralized System: A Threat to Health Workers' Respect and Survival in Uganda." *International Journal of Health Planning and Management* 18 (4): 329–42.

The Lancet. 2004. "Editorial: The Mexico Statement: Strengthening Health Systems." 364 (9449): 1911–12.

The Lancet Neonatal Survival Series Group. Forthcoming. Tentative observations based on ongoing work.

Langer, A., G. Nigenda, and J. Cantino. 2000. "Health Sector Reform and Reproductive Health in Latin America." *Bulletin of the World Health Organization* 78 (5): 667–76.

Laterveer, Leontien, Louis W. Niessen, and Abdo S. Yazbeck. 2003. "Pro-Poor Health Policies in Poverty Reduction Strategies." *Health Policy and Planning* 18 (2): 138–45.

Lawn, Joy E., Simon Cousens, and J. Zupan. 2005. "4 Million Neonatal Deaths: Where? When? Why? *The Lancet* 365 (9462): 891–900.

Lawn, Joy E., Simon Cousens, Zulfiqar Bhutta, Gary L. Darmstadt, J. Martines, Vinod Paul, Rudolf Knippenberg, H. Fogstad, P. Shetty, and R. Horton. 2004. "Why Are 4 Million Newborn Babies Dying Each Year?" *The Lancet* 364 (9450): 399–400.

Le Houerou, Philippe, and Robert Taliercio. 2002. "Medium Term Expenditure Frameworks: From Concept to Practice—Preliminary Lessons from Africa." World Bank Africa Region Working Paper Series 28. Washington, D.C.

Lee, Kelley, and Hilary Goodman. 2002. "Global Policy Networks: The Propagation of Healthcare Reform since the 1980s." In K. Lee, K. Buse, and S. Fustukian, eds., *Health Policy in a Globalising World*. Cambridge, U.K.: Cambridge University Press.

Lehmann, Uta, I. Friedman, and David Sanders. 2004. "Review of Utilisation and Effectiveness of Community-Based Health Workers in Africa." JLI Working Paper 4-1. Joint Learning Initiative for Human Resources for Health and Development. Harvard University.

Lehmann, Uta, and David Sanders. 2002. "Human Resource Development." In P. Ijumba, A. Ntuli, and P. Barron, eds., *South African Health Review*. Durban, South Africa: Health Systems Trust.

Leonard, Kenneth. 2000. "Incentives and Rural Healthcare Delivery: Cameroon I." In D. Leonard, ed., *Africa's Changing Markets for Health and Veterinary Services*. New York: St. Martin's Press.

Lewis, M. A., G. M. La Forgia, and M. B. Sulvetta. 1996. "Measuring Public Hospital Costs: Empirical Evidence from the Dominican Republic." *Social Science & Medicine* 43 (2): 221–34.

Link, Bruce, and Jo Phelan. 1995. "Social Conditions as Fundamental Causes of Disease." *Journal of Health and Social Behavior* (extra issue): 80–94.

Lobis, Samantha, Deborah Fry, and Anne Paxton. Forthcoming. "Emergency Obstetric Care in the United States: Availability, Access and Utilization." On file with author.

Londono, J. L., and J. Frenk. 1997. "Structured Pluralism: Towards an Innovative Model for Health System Reform in Latin America." *Health Policy* 41 (1): 1–36.

Loudon, Irvine. 1992. *Death in Childbirth: An International Study of Maternal Care and Maternal Mortality 1800–1950*. New York: Oxford University Press.

Luke, Nancy, and Kathleen M. Kurz. 2002. "Cross-Generational and Transactional Sexual Relations in Sub-Saharan Africa: Prevalence of Behavior and Implications for Negotiating Safer Sexual Practices." AIDSMark Project. ICRW (International Center for Research on Women) and Population Services International, Washington, D.C.

Lule, E., N. Oomman, J. Epp, and G. N. V. Ramana. 2003. "Achieving the Millennium Development Goal of Improving Maternal Health: Determinants, Interventions and Challenges." Health, Nutrition, and Population Discussion Paper, draft. World Bank, Washington, D.C.

Machel, J. 2001. "Unsafe Sexual Behaviour Among Schoolgirls in Mozambique: A Matter of Gender and Class." *Reproductive Health Matters* 9 (17): 82–90.

Macintyre, K., and D. Hotchkiss. 1999. "Referral Revisited: Community Financing Schemes and Emergency Transport in Rural Africa." *Social Science and Medicine* 49 (11): 1473–87.

Mackintosh, L. S. 2003. "A Study on the Factors Affecting the Retention of Midwives in Malawi." Dissertation submitted to the University of Liverpool, School of Tropical Medicine, International Health Division. Liverpool, U.K.

Mackintosh, Maureen. 2001. "Do Healthcare Systems Contribute to Inequalities." In D. A. Leon and G. Walt, eds., *Poverty, Inequality and Health: An International Perspective*. Oxford, U.K.: Oxford University Press.

Mackintosh, Maureen, and Lucy Gilson. 2002. "Non-Market Relationships in Healthcare." In J. Heyer, ed., *Group Behavior and Development: Is the Market Destroying Cooperation?* Oxford, U.K.: Oxford University Press.

Mackintosh, Maureen, and Meri Koivusalo. 2004. "Health Systems and Commercialisation: In Search of Good Sense." Paper prepared for the UNRISD conference on Commercialization of Healthcare, March 2004, Geneva.

Mackintosh, Maureen, and Paula Tibandebage. 2002. "Inclusion by Design? Rethinking Healthcare Market Regulation in the Tazanian Context." *Journal of Development Studies* 39 (1): 1–20.

———. 2004. "Inequality and Redistribution in Healthcare: Analytical Issues for Developmental Social Policy." In T. Mkandawire, ed., *Social Policy in a Development Context*. Palgrave, Basingstoke.

Mahendradhata, Y., M. L. Lambert, A. Van Deun, F. Matthys, M. Boelaert, and P. Van der Stuyft. 2003. "Strong General Healthcare Systems: A Prerequisite to Reach Global Tuberculosis Control Targets." *International Journal of Health Planning and Management* 18 (Supp.): S53–65.

Mahy, M. 2003. "Measuring Child Mortality in AIDS-Affected Countries." Paper UN/POP/MORT/2003/15, prepared for Workshop on HIV/AIDS and Adult Mortality in Developing Countries, September 8–13, New York.

Maine, Deborah. 1991. *Safe Motherhood Programs: Options and Issues*. New York: Center for Population and Family Health, Columbia University.

Maine, Deborah, Lynn Freedman, Farida Shaheed, and Schuyler Frautschi. 1994. "Risk, Reproduction and Rights: The Uses of Reproductive Health Data." In R. Cassen, ed., *Population and Development: Old Debates, New Conclusions*. Washington, D.C.: Overseas Development Council.

Maine, Deborah, and Mandi Larsen. 2004. "Blaming the Victim? The Literature on Utilization of Health Services." Background paper prepared for the UN Millennium Project Task Force on Child Health and Maternal Health. United Nations, New York.

Maine, Deborah, and Anne Paxton. 2003. "Evidence-Based Strategies for Prevention of Maternal Mortality." In R. Johanson and S. Daya, eds., *Evidence-Based Obstetrics*. Oxford, U.K.: Blackwell Publishing.

Maine, Deborah, and Allan Rosenfield. 1999. "The Safe Motherhood Initiative: Why Has It Stalled?" *American Journal of Public Health* 89 (4): 480–82.

Malhotra, A., and Rekha Mehra. 1999. *Fulfilling the Cairo Commitment: Enhancing Women's Economic and Social Options for Better Reproductive Health*. International Center for Research on Women. Washington, D.C.

Mamdani, Masuma, and Maggie Bangser. 2004. "Poor People's Experiences of Health Services in Tanzania: A Literature Review." *Reproductive Health Matters* 12 (24): 138–53.

Manandhar, D. S., David Osrin, B. P. Shreshtha, N. Mesko, J. Morrison, K. M. Tumbahangphe, S. Tamang, S. Thapa, D. Shreshtha, B. Thapa, J. R. Shreshtha, J. Borghi,

Hilary Standing, M. Manadha, A. M. Costello, and MIRA Makwanpur Trail Team. 2004. "Effect of a Participatory Intervention with Women's Groups on Birth Outcomes in Nepal: Cluster-Randomized Controlled Trial." *The Lancet* 364 (9438): 970–79.

Marquez, P., and W. de Geyndt. 2003. *Mexico: Reaching the Poor with Basic Health Services. En Breve.* Washington, D.C.: World Bank.

Martinez, J., and T. Martineau. 1998. "Rethinking Human Resources: An Agenda for the Millennium." *Health Policy and Planning* 13 (4): 345–58.

Mathur, S., M. Greene, and A. Malhotra. 2003. *Too Young to Wed: The Lives, Rights, and Health of Young Married Girls.* Washington, D.C.: ICRW.

Matinga, P., and F. McConville. 2002. "A Review of Sexual Beliefs and Practices Influencing Sexual and Reproductive Health and Health Seeking Behaviour." DFID, Lilongwe, Malawi.

Mavalankar, D. 1997. "Auxiliary Nurse Midwife's (ANM) Changing Role in India: Policy Issues for Reproductive and Child Health." Indian Institute of Management, Ahmedabad.

———. 2003. "Study of the Technical Top Management Capacity for Safe Motherhood Program in India." Study commissioned by the World Bank. New Delhi.

Mayhew, Susannah. 2002. "Donor Dealings: The Impact of International Donor Aid on Sexual and Reproductive Health Services." *International Family Planning Perspectives* 28 (4): 220–24.

McCaw-Binns, A. 2003. "Jamaica, 1991–1995." In M. Koblinsky, ed., *Reducing Maternal Mortality: Learning from Bolivia, China, Egypt, Honduras, Indonesia, Jamaica and Zimbabwe.* Washington, D.C.: World Bank.

McCormick, M., H. Sanghvi, B. Kinzie, and N. McIntosh. 2002. "Preventing Postpartum Hemorrhage in Low-Resource Settings." *International Journal of Gynecology and Obstetrics* 77 (3): 267–75.

McCoy, D., H. Ashwood-Smith, Ester Ratsma, J. Kemp, and Mike Rowson. 2004. "Going from Bad to Worse: Malawi's Maternal Mortality. An Analysis of the Clinical, Health Systems and Underlying Reasons, with Recommendations for National and International Stakeholders." Background paper for the UN Millennium Project Task Force on Child Health and Maternal Health. New York.

McCoy, D., and S. Khosa. 1996. "Free Healthcare Policies." In D. Harrison, P. Barron, and J. Edwards, eds., *South African Health Review 1996.* Durban: Health Sytems Trust.

McCoy, D., and M. Rowson. 2004. "Improving Maternal Health in Low and Middle Income Countries Effectively and Equitably." Background paper for the UN Millennium Project Task Force on Child Health and Maternal Health. New York.

McGinn, Therese. 2000. "Reproductive Health of War-Affected Populations: What Do We Know?" *International Family Planning Perspectives* 26 (4): 174–80.

McIntyre, Di. 1997. "Alternative Healthcare Financing Mechanisms: A Review of the Literature." Working Paper 29. Health Economics Unit, School of Public Health and Family Medicine, University of Cape Town, Cape Town.

———. 2004. Personal communication. Cape Town, South Africa.

McIntyre, Di, Gerald Bloom, Jane Doherty, and Vish Brijlal. 1995. *Health Expenditure and Finance in South Africa.* Durban: The Health Systems Trust.

McIntyre, Di, and Barbara Klugman. 2003. "The Human Face of Decentralisation and Integration of Health Services: Experience from South Africa." *Reproductive Health Matters* 11 (21): 108–19.

McIntyre, James. 2003. "Mothers infected with HIV." *British Medical Bulletin* 67 (1): 127–35.

McPake, B., D. Asiimwe, F. Mwesigye, M. Ofumbi, P. Streefland, and A. Turinde. 2000. "Coping Strategies of Health Workers in Uganda." In Paulo Ferrinho and Wim Van Lerberghe, eds., *Providing Health Care under Adverse Conditions: Health Personnel Performance and Individual Coping Strategies.* Studies in Health Services Organisation and Policy 16. Antwerp: IRG Press.

Meessen, Bruno, Zhang Zhenzhong, Wim Van Damme, Narayanan Devadasan, Bart Criel, and Gerald Bloom. 2003. "Iatrogenic poverty." *Tropical Medicine and International Health* 8 (7): 581–84.

Mercer, H., Mario Dal Poz, Orvill Adams, Barbara Stilwell, James Buchan, N. Dreesch, Pascal Zurn, and R. Beaglehole. 2003. "Human Resources for Health: Developing Policy Options for Change." In P. Ferrinho and M. R. Dal Poz, eds., *Towards a Global Health Workforce Strategy.* Studies in Health Services Organisation and Policy 21. Antwerp: IRG Press.

Michaud, Catherine. 2003. "Development Assistance for Health (DAH): Recent Trends and Resource Allocation." Paper prepared for the Second Consultation of the Commission on Macroeconomics and Health, October 29, Geneva.

Miller, Alice. 2000. "Sexual but Not Reproductive: Exploring the Junction and Disjunction of Sexual and Reproductive Rights." *Health and Human Rights: An International Journal* 4 (2): 68–109.

Miller, Suellen, and others. 2003. *Improving the Health and Well-Being of Married, Pregnant and Parenting Adolescent Girls.* New York: Population Council.

Miller, Suellen, Argelia Tejada, and Patricio Murgueytio. 2002. "Strategic assessment of reproductive health in the Dominican Republic." Population Council, USAID, and Secretaria de Salud Pública y Asistencia Social (SESPAS), New York.

Minister of Health and Others v. Treatment Action Campaign and Others, 2002 (5) SA 721 (CC), 2002 10 BCLR 1033.

Ministerial Summit on Health Research. 2004. "The Mexico Statement on Health Research: Knowledge for Better Health: Strengthening Health Systems." November 16–20, Mexico City.

Miranda, J. J., and Alicia E. Yamin. 2004. "Reproductive Health without Rights in Peru." *The Lancet* 363 (9402): 68–69.

Mooney, Gavin. 2003. "PHC funding: recognising the problems as a route to finding the solutions. Some relevant experiences from Aboriginal Australia." Presented at Celebrating the Achievements of Alma Ata: Strengthening Primary Healthcare in South Africa. Gauteng, South Africa.

Moya, Miriyam, and David Acurio. 2003. "Cuidados obstétricos y participación de las mujeres: La acción en derechos hace sostenibles los servicios obstétricos de emergencia (Obstetric Care and Participation of Women: Action to Enforce Rights Renders Emergency Obstetric Care Sustainable)." Paper presented at AMDD Network Conference, October 21–23. Kuala Lumpur, Malaysia.

Mumtaz, Z., S. Salway, M. Waseem, and N. Umer. 2003. "Gender-Based Barriers to Primary Healthcare Provision in Pakistan: The Experience of Female Providers." *Health Policy and Planning* 18 (3): 261–69.

Murray, Susan F., and N. Nyambo. 2003. "Private for Profit Maternity Services: Tanzania Case Study." Options Consultancy Services Ltd., DFID, and Kings College, London.

Murray, Susan F., and Steve Pearson. 2004. "Maternity Referral Systems in Developing Countries: Challenges and Next Steps. A Scoping Review of Current Knowledge." Background paper commissioned by the UN Millennium Project Task Force on Child Health and Maternal Health and the World Health Organization. New York.

Murthy, Laxmi. 2003. "No Kidding: Apex Court Enforces Two-Child Norm." [www. infochangeindia.org/features123.jsp].

Murthy, Ranjani, Barbara Klugman, Silvana Weller, and Lila Aizenberg. Forthcoming. "Service Accountability and Community Participation in the Context of Health Sector Reforms." In T. K. S. Ravindran and H. de Pinho, eds., *Right Reforms? Health Sector Reforms and Sexual and Reproductive Health.* Johannesburg: Women's Health Project.

Mwabu, G. M. 1989. "Referral Systems and Healthcare Seeking Behavior of Patients: An Economic Analysis." *World Development* 17 (1): 85–91.

Nanda, Geeta. 2003. "Utilization of Professional Delivery Care by Rural Women with Intrapartum Complications in Karnataka, India." Paper presented at the AMDD Network Conference, October 20–22, Kuala Lumpur, Malaysia.

Narasimhan, Vasant, Hilary Brown, Ariel Pablos-Mendez, Orvill Adams, Gilles Dussault, Gijs Elzinga, Anders Nordstrom, Demissie Habte, Marian Jacobs, Giorgio Solimano, Nelson Sewankambo, Suwit Wibulpolprasert, Timothy Evans, and Lincoln Chen. 2004. "Responding to the Global Human Resources Crisis." *The Lancet* 363 (9419): 1469–72.

Narayan, Deepa. 2000. *Voices of the Poor: Can Anyone Hear Us?* New York: Oxford University Press.

National Research Council, Committee on Population Commission on Behavioral and Social Sciences and Education. 1989. *Contraception and Reproduction: Health Consequences for Women and Children in the Developing World.* Washington, D.C.: National Academy Press.

Ndeso-Atanga, Sylvester. 2004. "Healthcare Quality and the Choice of Care Providers: Cameroon II." In L. C. Chen, J. L. Leaning, and V. Narasimhan, eds., *Global Health Challenges for Human Security.* Cambridge, Mass.: Harvard University Press.

Neupane, S. 2004. *Evaluation of Community Based Safer Motherhood Emergency Funds.* Nepal.

Oliveira-Cruz, Valeria, Christoph Kurowski, and Anne Mills. 2003. "Delivery of Priority Health Services: Searching for Synergies Within the Vertical Versus Horizontal Debate." *Journal of International Development* 15 (1): 67–86.

Oxfam. 2003. "The IMF and the Millennium Development Goals: Failing to Deliver for Low Income Countries." Oxfam Briefing Paper 54. Oxford, U.K.

———. 2004. "From 'Donorship' to Ownership? Moving towards PRSP Round Two." Oxfam Briefing Paper 51. Oxford, U.K.

Oxford Policy Management. 2000. "Medium Term Expenditure Frameworks—Panacea or Dangerous Distraction?" OPM Review Paper 2. Oxford, U.K.

Padarath, A., C. Chamberlain, D. McCoy, A. Ntuli, M. Rowson, and R. Loewenson. 2003. "Health Personnel in Southern Africa: Confronting Maldistribution and Brain Drain." EQUINET Discussion Paper. EQUINET, Health Systems Trust and MEDACT, Harare.

PAHO (Pan American Health Organization). 2002. *Trade in Health Services: Global, Regional and Country Perspectives.* Washington, D.C.

Palmer, N., Dirk H. Mueller, Lucy Gilson, Anne Mills, and Andy Haines. 2004. "Health financing to promote access in low income settings—how much do we know?" *The Lancet* 364(9442): 1365–70.

Pangu, K. 2000. "Health Workers' Motivation in Decentralized Settings: Waiting for Better Times." *Studies in Health Services Organisation and Policy* 16:19–29.

Parker, Louise, Mark Pearce, Heather Dickinson, Murray Aitkin, and Alan Craft. 1999. "Stillbirths Among Offspring of Male Radiation Workers at Sellafield Nuclear Reprocessing Plant." *The Lancet* 354 (9188): 1407–14.

Pathmanathan, Indra, Jerker Liljestrand, Jo Martins, Lalini Rajapaksa, Craig Lissner, Amala de Silva, Swarna Selvaraju, and Prabha Joginder Singh. 2003. *Investing in Maternal Health in Malaysia and Sri Lanka.* Washington, D.C.: World Bank.

Paul, Vinod, and M. Singh. 2004. "Regionalized Perinatal Care in Developing Countries." *Seminars in Neonatology* 9 (April): 11–24.

Paxton, Anne, Patricia Bailey, Samantha Lobis, and Deborah Fry. 2004. "Measuring Progress towards the Millennium Development Goal for Maternal Health: Arguing for an Indicator of the Health System's Ability to Respond to Obstetric Complications." Background paper commissioned by the UN Millennium Project Task Force on Child Health and Maternal Health. New York.

Pelletier, D. L., E. D. Frongillo, and J. P. Habicht. 1993. "Epidemiologic Evidence for a Potentiating Effect of Malnutrition on Child Mortality." *American Journal of Public Health* 83 (8): 1130–33.

Penn-Kekana, L., D. Blaauw, and H. Schneider. 2004. "'It Makes Me Want to Run Away to Saudi Arabia:' Management and Implementation Challenges for Public Financing Reforms from a Maternity Ward Perspective." *Health Policy Plan* 19 (Suppl 1): i71–77.

Petchesky, Rosalind, and Karen Judd, eds. 1998. *Negotiating Reproductive Rights: Women's Perspectives Across Countries and Cultures.* New York: Zed Books.

Peter, David, and Shiyan Chao. 1998. "The Sector-Wide Approach in Health: What Is It? Where Is It Leading?" *International Journal of Health Planning and Management* 13 (2):1 77–90.

Petersen, S., J. Nsung-Sabiiti, W. Were, X. Nsabagasani, G. Magumba, J. Nambooze, and G. Mukasa. 2004. "Coping with Paediatric Referral—Ugandan Parents' Experience." *The Lancet* 363 (9425): 1955–56.

Pfeiffer, James. 2003. "International NGOs and Primary Healthcare in Mozambique: The Need for a New Model of Collaboration." *Social Science and Medicine* 56 (4): 725–38.

Physicians for Human Rights. 2004. *An Action Plan to Prevent Brain Drain: Building Equitable Health Systems in Africa.* Boston.

Pillsbury, B., G. Maynard-Tucker, and F. Nguyen. 2000. *Women's Empowerment and Reproductive Health: Links Throughout the Life Cycle.* New York: UNFPA (United Nations Population Fund).

Potter, Christopher, and Richard Brough. 2004. "Systematic Capacity Building: A Hierarchy of Needs." *Health Policy and Planning* 19 (5): 336–45.

Pratinidhi, A., U. Shah, A. Shrotri, and N. Bodhani. 1986. "Risk-Approach Strategy in Neonatal Care." *Bulletin of the World Health Organization* 64 (2): 291–97.

Pritchett, Lant H., and Michael Woolcock. 2004. "Solutions When the Solution Is the Problem: Arraying the Disarray in Development." *World Development* 32 (2): 191–212.

Purdin, Susan. 2002. "Bibliography of Material, Dated after June 2000, on Reproductive Health Issues Concerning Populations Affected by Armed Conflict." [www.rhrc.org/pdf/Sel_RHR_Bib_0902.pdf].

Ramakrishnan, U. 2004. "Nutrition and Low Birth Weight: From Research to Practice." *American Journal of Clinical Nutrition* 79 (1): 17–21.

Ramakrishnan, U., and R. Martorell. 1998. "The Role of Vitamin A in Reducing Child Mortality and Morbidity and Improving Growth." *Salud Pública de México* 40 (2): 189–98.

Rana, T. Geetha, Rashmi Rajopadhyaya, Binod Bajracharya, Manju Karmacharya, and David Osrin. 2003. "Comparison of Midwifery-Led and Consultant-Led Maternity Care for Low Risk Deliveries in Nepal." *Health Policy and Planning* 18 (3): 330–37.

Ranson, M. Kent, Robert Beaglehole, Carlos M. Correa, Zafar Mirza, Kent Buse, and Nick Drager. 2002. "The Public Health Implications of Multilateral Trade Agreements." In K. Lee, K. Buse, and S. Fustakian, eds., *Health Policy in a Globalising World*. Cambridge, U.K.: Cambridge University Press.

Ravindran, T. K. Sundari, Desire Kikomba, and Daniel Maceira. Forthcoming. "The Impact of Health Financing Reforms in Developing Countries on Reproductive and Sexual Health Services: A Review." In T. K. S. Ravindran and H. de Pinho, eds., *Right Reforms? Health Sector Reforms and Sexual and Reproductive Health*. Johannesburg: Women's Health Project.

Ravindran, T. K. Sundari, and Silvana Weller. Forthcoming. "Public-Private Interactions in Health: Implications for Sexual and Reproductive Health Services." In T. K. S. Ravindran and H. de Pinho, eds., *Right Reforms? Health Sector Reforms and Sexual and Reproductive Health*. Johannesburg: Women's Health Project.

Ravindran, T. K. Sundari, and U. S. Mishra. 2000. "Unmet Need for Reproductive Health in India." *Reproductive Health Matters* 9 (18): 105–13.

Razzak, J. A., and A. L. Kellermann. 2002. "Emergency Medical Care in Developing Countries: Is It Worthwhile?" *Bulletin of the World Health Organization* 80 (11): 900–05.

Reality of Aid. 2004. *Reality of Aid 2004: Focus on Governance and Human Rights*. Manila. [www.realityofaid.org].

Reed, H., Marge Koblinsky, and W. H. Mosley, eds. 2000. *The Consequences of Maternal Mortality and Maternal Morbidity: Report of a Workshop*. Washington, D.C: National Academy Press.

Roberts, Marc J., William Hsiao, Peter Berman, and Michael R. Reich. 2004. *Getting Health Reform Right: A Guide to Improving Performance and Equity*. New York: Oxford University Press.

Roll Back Malaria. 2004. "Malaria in Pregnancy." [Retrieved July 7, 2004, from http://rbm.who.int/cmc_upload/0/000/015/369/RBMInfosheet_4.htm].

Rosenfield, Allan, and Deborah Maine. 1985. "Maternal Mortality—A Neglected Tragedy: Where's the M in MCH?" *The Lancet* 2 (8446): 83–85.

Rush, D. 2000. "Nutrition and Maternal Mortality in the Developing World." *American Journal of Clinical Nutrition* 72 (1): 212–40.

Rwanda, Ministry of Health. 2003. "Of Determining the Conditions and Modalities for Healthcare Delivery to Persons Living with HIV/AIDS." Ministerial Instruction No. 1. Ministry of Health in charge of HIV/AIDS and related diseases. Kigali.

Safe Motherhood Initiative. Website. [www.safemotherhood.org/].

Samara, Renee, Bates Buckner, and Amy Ong Tsui. 1996. "Understanding How Family Planning Programs Work: Findings from Five Years of Evaluation Research." The EVALUATION Project, Carolina Population Center, University of North Carolina. Chapel Hill, N.C.

Save the Children. 2001. *State of the World's Newborns*. Washington, D.C. [www.savethechildren.org/publications/newborns_report.pdf].

Schaay, Nikki, Arthur Heywood, and Uta Lehmann. 1998. "A Review of Health Management Training in the Public Health Sector in South Africa." Health Systems Trust. Durban, South Africa.

Schellenberg, J. A., C. G. Victora, A. Mushi, D. de Savigny, D. Schellenberg, H. Mshinda, and B. Bryce. 2003. "Inequities Among the Very Poor: Healthcare for Children in Rural Southern Tanzania." *The Lancet* 361 (9357): 561–66.

Schellenberg, J. A., T. Adam, H. Mshinda, H. Masanja, G. Kabadi, O. Mukasa, T. John, S. Charles, R. Nathan, K. Wilczynska, L. Mgalula, C. Mbuya, R. Mswia, F. Manzi, D. deSavigny, D. Schellenberg, and C. G. Victora. 2004. "Effectiveness and Cost of

Facility-Based Integrated Management of Childhood Illness (IMCI) in Tanzania." *The Lancet* 364 (9445): 1583–94.

Schiffman, J. 2003. "Generating Political Will for Safe Motherhood in Indonesia." *Social Science and Medicine* 56 (6): 1197–1207.

Scholl, T. O., M. L. Hediger, and D. H. Belsky. 1994. "Prenatal Care and Maternal Health During Adolescent Pregnancy: A Review and Meta-Analysis." *Journal of Adolescent Health* 15 (6): 444–56.

Schuler, Sidney Ruth, Syed M. Hashemi, and Ann Hendrix Jenkins. 1995. "Bangladesh's Family Planning Success Story: A Gender Perspective." *International Family Planning Perspectives* 21 (4):132–37, 166.

Scott, James C. 1998. *Seeing Like a State: How Certain Schemes to Improve the Human Condition Have Failed.* New Haven, Conn.: Yale Unversity Press.

Scott, T., R. Mannion, M. Marshall, and H. Davies. 2003. "Does Organizational Culture Influence Health Care Peformance? A Review of the Evidence." *Journal of Health Services Research and Policy* 8(2): 105–17.

Segall, Malcolm. 2000a. "From Cooperation to Competition in National Health Systems—and Back?: Impact on Professional Ethics and Quality of Care." *International Journal of Health Planning and Management* 15 (1): 61–79.

———. 2000b. "Human Development Challenges in Healthcare Reform." Studies in *Health Services Organisation and Policy* 16: 7–16.

———. 2003. "District Health Systems in a Neoliberal World: A Review of Five Key Policy Areas." *International Journal of Health Planning and Management* 18 (Supp): S5–26.

Seltzer, Judith R. 2002. *The Origins and Evolution of Family Planning Programs in Developing Countries.* Santa Monica, Calif.: RAND Corporation.

Sen, Amartya. 2001. *Development as Freedom.* New York: Oxford University Press.

Sen, Gita, A. Iyer, and A. George. 2002. "Class, Gender and Health Equity: Lessons from Liberalizing India." In G. Sen, A. George, and P. Ostlin, eds., *Engendering International Health: The Challenge of Equity.* Cambridge, Mass.: Massachusetts Institute of Technology Press.

Seoane, G., R. Equiluz, M. Ugalde, and J. C. Arraya. 2003. "Bolivia, 1996–2000." In M. Koblinsky Ed., *Reducing Maternal Mortality: Learning from Bolivia, China, Egypt, Honduras, Indonesia, Jamaica and Zimbabwe.* Washington, D.C.: World Bank.

Sethuraman, Kavita, Meera Shekar, and Kathleen Burz. 2003. "Towards Achieving the Hunger and Malnutrition Millennium Development Goal: Tailoring Potential Country-Level Solutions to Needs—the 'Candidate Actions' Approach." Input for the UN Millennium Project Task Force on Hunger. ICRW, Washington, D.C.

Setty-Venugopal, V., and U. S. Upadhyay. 2002. "Birth Spacing: Three to Five Saves Lives." Population Reports, Issues in World Health Series L number 13. USAID.

Shah, I., and E. Aahmane. Forthcoming. "Age Patterns of Unsafe Abortion in Developing Countries." *Reproductive Health Matters* 12 (Supplement).

Shelton, James D. 2001. "The Provider Perspective: Human After All." *International Family Planning Perspectives* 27 (3): 152–53, 161.

Shepard, Bonnie. 2000. "The 'Double Discourse' on Sexual and Reproductive Rights in Latin America: The Chasm between Public Policy and Private Actions." *Health and Human Rights* 4 (2): 110–43.

Shisana, O., E. J. Hall, R. Maluleke, J. Chauveau, and C. Schwabe. 2004. "HIV/AIDS Prevalence among South African Health Workers." *South African Medical Journal* 94 (10): 846–50.

Shrimpton, R. 2003. "Preventing Low Birthweight and Reduction of Child Mortality." *Transactions of the Royal Society for Tropical Medicine and Hygiene* 97 (1): 39–42.

Sibley, L., T. A. T. Sipe, and Marge Koblinsky. 2004. "Does Traditional Birth Attendant Training Improve Referral of Women with Obstetric Complications: A Review of the Evidence." *Social Science and Medicine* 59 (8): 1757–68.

Simmons, R., R. Mita, and M. A. Koenig. 1992. "Employment in Family Planning and Women's Status in Bangladesh." *Studies in Family Planning* 23 (2): 97–109.

Simmons, Ruth, Laila Baqee, Michael A. Koenig, and James Phillips. 1988. "Beyond Supply: The Importance of Female Family Planning Workers in Rural Bangladesh." *Studies in Family Planning* 19 (1): 29–38.

Simms, C., M. Rowson, and S. Peattie. 2001. *The Bitterest Pill of All: The Collapse of Africa's Health Systems.* London: Save the Children Fund.

Singh, S., J. Darroch, M. Vlassoff, and J. Nadeau. 2003. *Adding It Up: The Benefits of Investing in Sexual and Reproductive Healthcare.* New York: The Alan Guttmacher Institute.

Smith, J. B., N. A. Coleman, J. A. Fortney, and others. 2000. "The Impact of Traditional Birth Attendant Training on Delivery Complications in Ghana." *Health Policy and Planning* 15 (3): 326–31.

Special Rapporteur on the Right to Health. 2004. "Report to the Secretary-General of the United Nations on the Right of Everyone to the Enjoyment of the Highest Attainable Standard of Physical and Mental Health." UN Document A/59/422. New York.

Ssengooba, F., Valeria Oliveira-Cruz, and George Pariyo. 2004. "Capacity of Ministries of Health and Opportunities to Scale up Health Interventions in Low Income Countries: A Case Study of Uganda." Background paper commissioned by the UN Millennium Project Task Force on Child Health and Maternal Health. New York.

Standing, Hilary. 2002a. "Gender—a Mission Dimension in Human Resources Policy and Planning for Health Reforms." *Human Resources for Health Development Journal* 4 (1): 27–42.

———. 2002b. "An Overview of Changing Agendas in Health Sector Reforms." *Reproductive Health Matters* 10 (20): 19–28.

———. 2004. "Understanding the 'Demand Side' in Service Delivery: Definitions, Frameworks and Tools from the Health Sector." University of Sussex. Sussex, U.K.

Standing, Hilary, and Gerry Bloom. 2002. "Beyond Public and Private? Unorganised Markets in Healthcare Delivery." Paper presented at the DFID workshop Making Services Work for Poor People in support of the 2003–04 *World Development Report,* November 4–5, Oxford University, Oxford, U.K.

Stewart, Frances, and Michael Wang. 2003. "Do PRSPs Empower Poor Countries and Disempower the World Bank or Is It the Other Way Round?" QEH (Queen Elizabeth House) Working Paper 108. Oxford University, Oxford, U.K.

Stewart, John F., Guy Stecklov, and Alfred Adewuyi. 1999. "Family Planning Program Structure and Performance in West Africa." *International Family Planning Perspectives* 25 (Supplement): S22–29.

Stoltzfus, Rebecca. 2003. "Iron Deficiency: Global Prevalence and Consequences." *Food and Nutrition Bulletin* 24 (4 Supp): S97–101.

Stoltzfus, Rebecca, Luke Mullany, and Robert Black. 2004. "Iron Deficiency Anaemia." In M. Ezzati, A. Lopez, A. Rodgers, and C. Murray, eds., *Comparative Quantification of Health Risks: Global and Regional Burden of Disease Attributable to Selected Major Risk Factors.* Geneva: WHO.

Streak, Judith. 2004. "Child Specific Spending on the Right to Health in MTEF 2004/05—An Identification Problem." Children's Budget Series: Budget Brief 146. IDASA. Cape Town.

Supratikto, Gunawan, Meg Wirth, Endang Achadi, S. Cohen, and Carine Ronsmans. 2002. "A District-Based Audit of Causes and Circumstances of Maternal Deaths in South Kalimantan, Indonesia." *Bulletin of the World Health Organization* 80 (3): 228–35.

Swinkels, R., and R. Turk. 2002. "Achieving the Vietnam Development Goals: An Overview of Progress and Challenges. Summary of the Eight Papers on Localising the MDGs for Poverty Reduction in Vietnam." World Bank, Washington, D.C.

Tajer, Debora. 2003. "Latin American Social Medicine: Roots, Development During the 1990s, and Current Challenges." *American Journal of Public Health* 93 (12): 2023–43.

Thaddeus, S., and Deborah Maine. 1994. "Too Far to Walk: Maternal Mortality in Context." *Social Science and Medicine* 38 (8): 1091–1110.

Thairu, A., and K. Schmidt. 2003. "Training and Authorizing Mid-Level Providers in Life-Saving Skills in Kenya." In Sandra Crump, ed., *Shaping Policy for Maternal and Newborn Health: A Compendium of Case Studies*. Baltimore, Md.: JHPIEGO.

Toole, Mike, Bev Snell, Wendy Holmes, Clement Malau, Rajitha Perera, Cathy Vaughan, Mick Creati, Chris Morgan, Bruce Parnell, and John Clements. 2003. "Harnessing the New Global Health Resources to Build Sustainable Health Systems." Background paper commissioned by the UN Millennium Project Task Force on Child Health and Maternal Health. Centre for International Health, Burnet Institute. Melbourne.

Travis, P., S. Bennett, A. Haines, T. Pang, Z. Bhutta, A. A. Hyder, N. R. Pielemeier, A. Mills, and T. Evans. 2004. "Overcoming Health-Systems Constraints to Achieve the Millennium Development Goals." *The Lancet* 364 (9437): 900–06.

UN (United Nations). 1979. *Convention on the Elimination of All Forms of Discrimination Against Women*. United Nations General Assembly resolution 34/180. New York.

———. 1994. "Report of the International Conference on Population and Development." Document A/CONF.171/13. New York.

———. 1995. *Report of the Fourth World Conference on Women*. A/CONF.177/20. New York.

———. 1999a. "Key Actions for the Further Implementation of the Programme of Action of the International Conference on Population and Development." General Assembly Resolution A/Res/S-21/2. New York.

———. 1999b. "Twenty-First Special Session of the General Assembly for an Overall Review and Appraisal of the Implementation of the Programme of Action of the International Conference on Population and Development: Report of the Secretary-General." General Assembly Document A/54/442. United Nations. New York.

———. 2002. "World Population Monitoring 2002: Reproductive Rights and Reproductive Health: Selected Aspects." Document ESA/P/WP.171. Presented at the Commission on Population and Development, Thirty-fifth Session, April 1–5, New York.

UNAIDS (Joint United Nations Programme on HIV/AIDS). 2003. *Where There's a Will, There's a Way: Nursing and Midwifery Champions in HIV/AIDS Care in Southern Africa. Best Practice Collection*. Geneva: UNAIDS.

UN CESCR (United Nations Committee on Economic, Social and Cultural Rights). 2000. "General Comment 14 on the Right to Health." E/C.12/2000/4. Geneva.

UN CRC (United Nations Committee on the Rights of the Child). 2003. "General Comment 4: Adolescent Health and Development in the Context of the Convention on the Rights of the Child." CRC/GC/2003/4. Geneva.

UNCTAD (United Nations Conference on Trade and Development). 1997. "International Trade in Health Services: Difference and Opportunities for Developing Countries." TD/B/COM.1/EM.1/2. Geneva.

UNDP (United Nations Development Programme). 2003. *Human Development Report: Millennium Development Goals: A Compact among Nations to End Human Poverty*. New York: Oxford University Press.

UNFPA (United Nations Population Fund). 2002a. "Coverage of Population and Development Themes in PRSPs: Challenges and Opportunities for UNFPA." Population and Development Branch Technical Support Division. New York.

———. 2002b. "Future Generations Ready for the World: UNFPA's Contribution to the Goals of the World Summit for Children." New York.

———. 2002c. "Promoting Reproductive Health as a Poverty Reduction Strategy." Information note distributed at the Consultation on Population, Reproductive Health, Gender, and Poverty Reduction, September 30–October 2, Princeton, N.J.

———. 2003a. *State of World Population 2003: Making 1 Billion Count: Investing in Adolescents' Health and Rights*. New York.

———. 2003b. *Population and Poverty: Achieving Equity, Equality, and Sustainability*. Population and Development Strategies Series 8. New York.

———. 2003c. "Preventing Fistulae and Other Disability." Website. [www.unfpa.org/mothers/disability.htm].

Unger, J. P., P. De Paepe, and Andrew Green. 2003. "A Code of Best Practice for Disease Control Programmes to Avoid Damaging Healthcare Services in Developing Countries." *International Journal of Health Planning and Management* 18 (Supp): S27–39.

UN Global Coalition on Women and AIDS. 2004. *Facing the Future Together: Report of the Secretary-General's Task Force on Women, Girls and HIV/AIDS in Southern Africa*. Geneva.

UNHCR (Office of the United Nations High Commissioner for Refugees). 1999. "Inter Agency Manual on Reproductive Health in Refugee Situations." Geneva.

UNHCR (Office of the United Nations High Commissioner for Refugees) and Save the Children, UK. 2002. "Sexual Violence and Exploitation: The Experience of Refugee Children in Guinea, Liberia and Sierra Leone." Note for Implementing and Operational Partners based on initial findings and recommendations from the UNHCR Assessment Mission, October 22–November 30.

UNICEF (United Nations Children's Fund). 2003a. *Africa's Orphaned Generations*. New York.

———. 2003b. "A Rights-Based Approach to Saving Women's Lives in the Eastern Region of Nepal." Paper prepared for the Averting Maternal Death and Disability Network Conference, October 21–23, Kuala Lumpur, Malaysia.

———. 2003c. *State of the World's Children 2003*. Geneva.

———. 2004. *Progress for Children: A Child Survival Report Card*. Vol. I 2004. New York.

UNICEF and UNAIDS. 2002. *Children on the Brink: A Joint Report on Orphan Estimates and Program Strategies*. Washington, D.C.: USAID.

UNICEF, WHO, and UNFPA. 1997. *Guidelines for Monitoring the Availability and Use of Obstetric Services*. New York: UNICEF.

UNICEF, WHO, and UNU (United Nations University). 2001. *Iron Deficiency Anaemia: Assessment, Prevention, and Control: A Guide for Programme Managers*. Geneva: WHO.

UN Millennium Project. 2005a. *Investing in Development: A Practical Plan to Achieve the Millennium Development Goals*. London: Earthscan.

———. 2005b. *Taking Action: Achieving Gender Equality and Empowering Women*. Report of the Task Force on Education and Gender Equality. London: Earthscan.

USAID (U.S. Agency for International Development). 2003. "The Health Sector Human Resource Crisis in Africa." Issues paper. Bureau for Africa, Office of Sustainable Development. Washington, D.C.

———. 2004. "Child Survival Partnership." USAID Child Survival Agenda press release. [www.usaid.gov/press/releases/2004/pr_040602.html].

Uvin, Peter. 2004. *Human Rights and Development*. Bloomfield, Conn.: Kumarian Press.

van Damme, Wim, Wim van Lerberghe, and Marleen Boelaert. 2002. "Primary Healthcare vs. Emergency Medical Assistance: A Conceptual Framework." *Health Policy and Planning* 17 (1): 49–60.

Van Lerberghe, Wim, Claudia Conceicao, Wim Van Damme, and Paulo Ferrinho. 2002. "When Staff is Underpaid: Dealing with the Individual Coping Strategies of Health Personnel." *Bulletin of the World Health Organization* 80 (7): 581–84.

Van Lerberghe, Wim, X. de Bethune, and Vincent De Brouwere. 1997. "Hospitals in Sub-Saharan Africa: Why We Need More of What Does Not Work as It Should." *Tropical Medicine and International Health* 2 (8): 799–808.

Van Look, P. F. A., and J. Cottingham. 2002. "Unsafe Abortion: An Avoidable Tragedy." *Best Practice and Research Clinical Obstetrics and Gynecology* 16(2): 205–20.

Vaz, F., S. Bergstrom, M. Vaz, J. Langa, and A. Bugalho. 1999. "Training medical assistants for surgery. Policy and practice." *Bulletin of the World Health Organization* 77 (8): 688–91.

Vega, J., and A. Irwin. 2004. "Tackling Health Inequalities: New Approaches in Public Policy." *Bulletin of the World Health Organization* 82 (7): 482.

Victora, C. G., A. Wagstaff, J. A. Schellenberg, D. R. Gwatkin, M. Claeson, and J. P. Habicht. 2003. "Applying an Equity Lens to Child Health and Mortality: More of the Same Is Not Enough." *The Lancet* 362 (9387): 233–41.

Visaria, Leela, Shireen Jejeebhoy, and Tom Merrick. 1999. "From Family Planning to Reproductive Health: Challenges Facing India." *International Family Planning Perspectives* 25 (Supplement): S44–49.

Wagstaff, Adam. 2002. "Intersectoral Synergies and the Health MDGs: Preliminary Cross-Country Findings, Corroboration and Policy Simulations." Background paper for the Development Committee Accelerating Progress Towards the Health Nutrition and Population Millennium Development Goals. World Bank, Washington, D.C.

Wagstaff, A., J. Bryce, F. Bustreo, and others. 2003. "Inequalities in Child Health—Are We Narrowing the Gap?" Health, Nutrition, and Population Discussion Paper. World Bank, Washington, D.C.

Wagstaff, A., and M. Claeson. 2004. *The Millennium Development Goals for Health: Rising to the Challenges*. Washington, D.C.: World Bank.

Wahba, J. 2004. "Health Labor Markets: Incentives or Institutions?" Working Group 7, Joint Learning Initiative on Human Resources for Health and Development. Global Health Trust, Harvard University.

Walboomers, J. M., M. V. Jacobs, M. M. Manos, F. X. Bosch, J. A. Kummer, K. V. Shah, P. J. Snijders, J. Peto, C. J. Meijer, and N. Munoz. 1999. "Human papillomavirus is a necessary cause of invasive cervical cancer worldwide." *Journal of Pathology* 189 (1): 12–19.

Waldman, Ronald, Alfred Bartlett, Carlos C. Campbell, and Richard Steketee. 1996. "Overcoming the Remaining Barriers: The Pathway to Survival." Current Issues in Child Survival. BASICS (Basic Support for Institutionalizing Child Survival), Arlington, Va.

Walford, Veronica. 2002. "Health in Poverty Reduction Strategy Papers (PRSPs): An Introduction and Early Experience." DFID Health Systems Resource Centre Issues Paper. London.

Walker, C. F., and R. E. Black. 2004. "Zinc and the Risk for Infectious Disease." *Annual Review of Nutrition* 24: 255–75.

Walker, Liz, and Lucy Gilson. 2004. "'We Are Bitter but We Are Satisfied': Nurses as Street-Level Bureaucrats in South Africa." *Social Science and Medicine* 59 (6): 1251–61.

Walsh, J. A., and K. S. Warren. 1979. "Selective Primary Healthcare: An Interim Strategy for Disease Control in Developing Countries." *New England Journal of Medicine* 301 (18): 967–74.

Walt, Gill, Enrico Pavignani, Lucy Gilson, and Kent Buse. 1999. "Health Sector Development: From Aid Coordination to Resource Management." *Health Policy and Planning* 14 (3): 207–18.

Watson-Jones, Deborah, John Changalucha, Balthazar Gumodoka, Helen Weiss, Mary Rusizoka, Leonard Ndeki, Anne Whitehouse, Rebecca Balira, James Todd, Donatila Ngeleja, David Ross, Anne Buve, Richard Hayes, and David Mabey. 2002. "Syphilis in Pregnancy in Tanzania. I. Impact of Maternal Syphilis on Outcome of Pregnancy." *The Journal of Infectious Diseases* 186 (7): 940–47.

Watts, Geoff. 2004. "Bangladesh Group Has Trained 30,000 Community Health Workers." *British Medical Journal* 329 (7475): 1126.

Wen, W., X. O. Shu, J. D. Potter, R. K. Severson, J. D. Buckley, G. H. Reaman, and L. L. Robison. 2002. "Parental Medication Use and Risk of Childhood Acute Lymphoblastic Leukemia." *Cancer* 95 (8): 1786–94.

WHO (World Health Organization). 1992. *International Classification of Diseases.* 10th revision. Geneva.

———. 1998. "Workload Indicators of Staffing Need (WISN): A Manual for Implementation." WHO/HRB/98.2. Geneva.

———. 1999. "Interpreting Reproductive Health." Paper prepared for the ICPD+5 Forum, February 8–12, The Hague.

———. 2000a. "Managing complications in pregnancy and childbirth: a guide for midwives and doctors." Integrated Management of Pregnancy and Childbirth report. Department of Reproductive Health and Research, Geneva.

———. 2000b. *World Health Report: Health Systems Improving Performance.* Geneva.

———. 2002a. *Strategic Directions for Strengthening Nursing and Midwifery Services.* Geneva.

———. 2002b. *The WHO Reproductive Health Library.* Vol. 5. Geneva: World Health Organization, Department of Reproductive Health and Research.

———. 2002c. *Global Action for Skilled Attendants for Pregnant Women.* Geneva.

———. 2003a. *Adolescent Pregnancy: Unmet Needs and Undone Deeds: A Review of the Literature and Programmes.* Geneva.

———. 2003b. "Primary Healthcare: A Framework for Future Strategic Directions." Document WHO/MNC/OSD/03.01. Geneva.

———. 2003c. "Reproductive Health: Draft Strategy to Accelerate Progress towards the Attainment of International Development Goals and Targets." EB113/15 Add.1. Geneva.

———. 2003d. "RTIs and STIs Including HIV/AIDS." Website. [www.who.int/reproductive-health/rtis/index.htm].

———. 2003e. *Safe Abortion: Technical and Policy Guidance for Health Systems.* Geneva.

———. 2003f. *World Health Report: Shaping the Future.* Geneva.

———. 2003g. Issues Papers. Meeting of Interested Parties. MIP/2003/3. November 3–7, Geneva. [www.who.int/mip/2003/official/en/issues-en.pdf].

———. 2004a. *Beyond the Numbers: Reviewing Maternal Deaths and Complications to Make Pregnancy Safer.* Geneva.

———. 2004b. "Estimates of DALYs by Sex, Cause and WHO Mortality Sub-region, Estimates for 2001, 2002." [www3.who.int/whosis/menu.cfm?path=evidence,burden,burden_estimates,burden_estimates_2001,burden_estimates_2001_subregion&language=english].

———. 2004c. "Health System Metrics: Monitoring the Health System in Developing Countries." PowerPoint presentation at the Health System Metrics: Monitoring the Health System in Developing Countries Conference, October 6–7, Glion, Switzerland.

———. 2004d. "Making Pregnancy Safer: The Critical Role of the Skilled Attendant." A joint statement by WHO, the International Confederation of Midwives, and the International Federation of Gynaecologists and Obstetricians. Geneva.

———. 2004e. *PRSPs: Their Significance for Health: Second Synthesis Report.* Geneva.

———. 2004f. "Reproductive Health: Draft Strategy to Accelerate Progress towards the Attainment of International Development Goals and Targets." Annex EB113/15/Add.1. Geneva.

———. Forthcoming. *Perinatal and Neonatal Mortality in the Year 2000.* Geneva.

WHO Division of Family Health. 1993. "The Prevention and Management of Unsafe Abortion: Report of a Technical Working Group." Document (WHO/MSM/92.5). Geneva.

WHO and UNICEF. 2004a. *Antenatal Care in Developing Countries: Promises, Achievements and Missed Opportunities. An Analysis of Trends, Levels and Differentials, 1990–2001.* Geneva: WHO.

———. 2004b. "Joint statement: Management of pneumonia in community settings." WHO/FCH/CAH/04.06. [Retrieved October, 2004, from www.who.int/child-adolescent-health/New_Publications/CHILD_HEALTH/Pneumonia.pdf].

WHO, UNICEF, and UNFPA. 2001. *Maternal Mortality in 1995: Estimates Developed by WHO, UNICEF, UNFPA.* Geneva.

———. 2004. *Maternal Mortality in 2000: Estimates Developed by WHO, UNICEF, and UNFPA.* Geneva.

Williamson, John. 1993. "Democracy and the 'Washington Consensus'." *World Development* 21 (8): 1329–36.

Wirth, Meg, D. Balk, A. Storeygard, Emma Sacks, E. Delamonica, and A. Minujin. 2004. "Setting the Stage for Equity-Sensitive Monitoring of the Health MDGs." Background paper commissioned by the UN Millennium Project Task Force on Child Health and Maternal Health. New York.

World Bank. 1993. *World Development Report 1993: Investing in Health.* New York: Oxford University Press.

———. 2000. *World Development Report 2000/2001: Attacking Poverty.* New York: Oxford University Press.

———. 2003a. *A User's Guide to Poverty and Social Impact Analysis.* Washington, D.C.

———. 2003b. *World Development Report 2004: Making Services Work for Poor People.* New York: Oxford University Press.

———. 2004a. Overview of Poverty Reduction Strategies. Website. [www.worldbank.org/poverty/strategies/overview.htm].

———. 2004b. *A Review of Population, Reproductive Health and Adolescent Health & Development in Poverty Reduction Strategies.* Washington, D.C.

———. 2004c. *World Development Report 2005: A Better Investment Climate for Everyone.* New York: Oxford University Press.

World Bank Operations Evaluation Department. 2004. *The Poverty Reduction Strategy Initiative: An Independent Evaluation of the World Bank's Support through 2003.* Washington, D.C.

Wyss, Kaspar. 2004. "An Approach to Classifying Human Resources Constraints to Attaining Health-Related Millennium Development Goals." *Human Resources for Health* 2 (11): [www.human-resources-health.com/content/2/1/11].

Xu, K., D. B. Evans, and others. 2003. "Household Catastrophic Health Expenditure: A Multicountry Analysis." *The Lancet* 362 (9378): 111–17.

Yamin, Alicia. 2000. "Protecting and Promoting the Right to Health in Latin America." *Health and Human Rights* 5 (1): 116–48.

Yamin, Alicia E., and Deborah Maine. 1999. "Maternal Mortality as a Human Rights Issue: Measuring Compliance with International Treaty Obligations." *Human Rights Quarterly* 21 (3): 563–607.

Yumkella, F., and F. Githiori. 2000. "Expanding Opportunities for Postabortion Care at the Community Level through Private Nurse-Midwives in Kenya." University of North Carolina, Program for International Training in Health (INTRAH). Chapel Hill, N.C.

Zurn, Pascal, Mario Dal Poz, Barbara Stilwell, and Orvill Adams. 2002. "Imbalances in the Health Workforce." Briefing paper for Evidence and Information for Policy, Health Service Provision. WHO, Geneva.